SWINGBACK

SWINGBACK

Getting Along in the World with Harper and Trudeau

MIKE BLANCHFIELD

McGill-Queen's University Press
Montreal & Kingston • London • Chicago

ISBN 978-0-7735-4875-6 (cloth)
ISBN 978-0-7735-4897-8 (ePDF)
ISBN 978-0-7735-4898-5 (ePUB)

Legal deposit first quarter 2017
Bibliothèque nationale du Québec

Printed in Canada on acid-free paper that is 100% ancient forest free (100% post-consumer recycled), processed chlorine free

McGill-Queen's University Press acknowledges the support of the Canada Council for the Arts for our publishing program. We also acknowledge the financial support of the Government of Canada through the Canada Book Fund for our publishing activities.

Library and Archives Canada Cataloguing in Publication

Blanchfield, Mike, 1964–, author
  Swingback : getting along in the world with Harper and Trudeau
/ Mike Blanchfield.

Includes bibliographical references and index.
Issued in print and electronic formats.
ISBN 978-0-7735-4875-6 (cloth). – ISBN 978-0-7735-4897-8 (ePDF). –
ISBN 978-0-7735-4898-5 (ePUB)

FC649.B63 2016   327.71009'051   C2016-906046-2
                                                C2016-906047-0

This book was set by True to Type in 11/14 Sabon

For Clara, Edie, and Kathy

Contents

Preface

The inspiration for this book goes back to a Paris hotel room in the summer of 2006. I had been travelling with Stephen Harper on his first major multi-country trip for about a week. I've spent most of my career covering Canadian politics, sometimes abroad in the company of various prime ministers. He was my first Conservative prime minister, though I had covered the two previous Liberals and was to go on to cover Justin Trudeau.

I had been based on Parliament Hill for eight years for the *Ottawa Citizen*, but had deep interest in what was happening beyond Canada's borders. I started reporting outside Canada on my own dime at first, going to Eastern Europe in the spring of 1990. I visited the Prague headquarters of Vaclav Havel's Civic Forum and reported on the first Czechoslovak election following the Velvet Revolution. I took myself to East Africa and Southeast Asia later in the decade before I was assigned to cover the 1999 NATO-led war against the former Yugoslavia, travelling to Kosovo in its aftermath. In 2001 and 2002, I spent many months on the road in Afghanistan, Pakistan, and throughout Central Asia covering the war that started after the September 11 attack on the United States. I returned to Pakistan, Afghanistan, and the region several times over the years. In 2003, I was part of a large team of journalists from the *Citizen* and *Southam News* that covered the U.S.-led war on Iraq and its aftermath. These, and other travels, as well as my time in Ottawa, gave me a unique perspective on where Canada had a part to play and where it didn't really matter at all.

This book is the result of the world coming to me and of me getting out into the world whenever I could. It was made possible by my past employer, the *Ottawa Citizen*, and my current one, the Canadian Press, who have always supported my attempt to understand Canada's role in the world. It is also the product of two years starting in 2013, when I returned to Carleton University in Ottawa, mid-career, to pursue a graduate degree at the School of Journalism and Communication. That period of academic analysis allowed me to step back and try to make some sense of what I witnessed and reported.

I have lived the story of this book. I reported it first-hand from Ottawa, from international war zones, from world capitals, legislatures, parliaments, and from many carefully staged photo-ops. Other talented journalists contributed to this narrative through their daily reportage and other writings, and I've acknowledged them throughout this text. Returning to university plunged me into reading many more books, articles, and scholarly essays. I've sourced that great writing in this book, and I encourage curious Canadians to read further, and deeper.

I asked Stephen Harper for an interview in early 2016 after his defeat, but I did not get a positive response. One day, I look forward to reading his memoirs. In the meantime, this is my view of how his unprecedented time in power played out on the global stage. In trying to assess it, I had a rewarding time researching our country's history from the end of the Second World War to Harper's arrival in power in 2006. I watched him closely as he navigated the world on Canada's behalf. Since his departure from politics, I've also benefitted from a front-row view of where the country is headed internationally under his successor, Justin Trudeau.

Who we are as a people is a combination of how we project ourselves to the world and how the world sees us. Our prime ministers play a big part in this. These two particular prime ministers, Stephen Harper and Justin Trudeau, defined Canadians in new, unusual ways. That set them apart from their predecessors.

Acknowledgments

The road to writing this book began when I returned to Carleton University in 2013 to pursue a master's in journalism twenty-six years after receiving my undergraduate degree. My goal was to put myself in a position where I would be forced to write something like this. I was inspired and helped along the way by numerous professors and fellow students. These include Paul Adams, Susan Harada, and Klaus Pohle.

Since coming to Parliament Hill in 1998 to cover defence and foreign affairs, I have worked in some powerhouse organizations, including the Parliamentary bureaus of the *Ottawa Citizen-Southam News*, and my current employer, the Canadian Press. I learned much from many, many talented colleagues over the years, and that continues every day. I will always hold a special place in my heart for those – they know who they are – whose reassuring voices on the telephone helped me do my job in dangerous places far away.

I owe thanks to the R. James Travers Foreign Corresponding Fellowship, which I won in 2013. It enabled me to travel to Europe, South Asia, and the United States to conduct research on cluster bombs, the seventh chapter of this book. This story would not have been told had it not been for the support of this fellowship.

I was very lucky to find myself working with Susan Glickman, a talented copy editor, who saved me from myself on several occasions. I also owe a special debt to Jacqueline Mason, my editor at McGill-Queen's University Press, who championed this project and offered encouragement and valuable feedback as I pushed it towards the finish line. And I'm forever grateful to Professor Randy Boswell, my Carleton University thesis adviser, who is a talented writer, storyteller, and a true student of history. His hard work, painstaking attention to detail, rigorous intellect, and passion for history and journalism infused this work.

Finally, there is my immediate and extended family, including my hardworking parents, Peter and Joann. I tried to get this done as quickly, efficiently, and unobtrusively as possible. But I didn't, so my sincere apologies.

With much love, this book is for my wife, Kathy, and our two daughters.

General Tommy Franks, the commander of the U.S. war on terrorism, arrives at Kandahar Air Field for an unannounced visit in the spring of 2002. Franks had no illusions that Western forces had vanquished the Taliban and al-Qaida. Photo by Mike Blanchfield.

Two of the Siad sisters, 16-year-old Lubna (left) and 23-year-old Arwa (right), with their mother, Enam (middle), in their suburban Baghdad home in April 2003. Enam is displaying photos of her daughters' training to fight American forces in their country. Photo by Mike Blanchfield.

Prime Minister Stephen Harper poses with students and staff moments after his arrival at the Aschiana co-ed school in Kabul in 2007. Harper visited the school in an attempt to spin the message about the Canadian Forces combat mission. Photo by Mike Blanchfield.

The author in central Baghdad in April 2003, in the square where two days earlier, U.S. Marines pulled down the statue of Saddam Hussein, sending the dictator into hiding. The Liberal government kept Canada out of the U.S.-led invasion but opposition leader Stephen Harper wanted Canadian troops on the front lines of this conflict. Photo courtesy of Mike Blanchfield.

Hilay Siddiquizi, 20, a graduate of the Lycée Malalay, an elementary school for girls in Kabul, celebrates the first day of school at her alma mater in March 2008. The promise of peace still remains unrealized after Canada and most of its Western allies have pulled out of Afghanistan. Photo by Mike Blanchfield.

Prime Minister Stephen Harper visits the tomb of the Unknown Soldier in Warsaw, Poland, in June 2015. Photo by Mike Blanchfield.

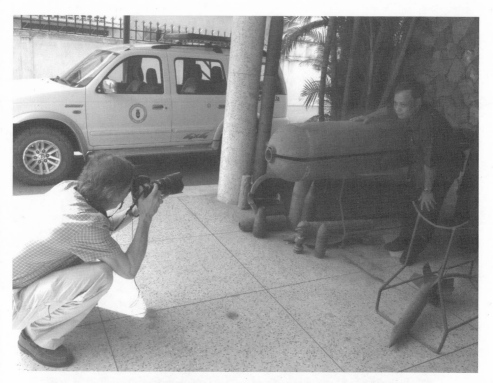

Wanthong Khamdala, the deputy director of the Laotian national cluster bomb clearance agency, poses for a photo by Canadian Press photographer Paul Chiasson in front of a decommissioned cluster bomb, a legacy of the U.S. military's covert saturation-bombing of his country during the Vietnam War. Photo by Mike Blanchfield.

Prime Minister Stephen Harper comes face to face with the horrors of the Holocaust at the Nazi death camp in Auschwitz in April 2008. The director of the Auschwitz-Birkenau State Museum, Piotr Cywinksi, accompanies him. Photo by Mike Blanchfield.

Prime Minister Justin Trudeau conducts a press conference on board his plane while it is airborne between Turkey and the Philippines in November 2015. This marks the start of a new era in prime ministerial–media relations. Photo by Mike Blanchfield.

Prime Minister Justin Trudeau works the room at a reception celebrating forty years of Canadian relations with the European Union in February 2016. Trudeau inherited the Canada-EU free trade deal from Harper, and was determined to ratify it. Photo by Mike Blanchfield.

SWINGBACK

Prologue

20 OCTOBER 2015
It is the day after. The previous evening, nine and a half years of Conservative rule under Stephen Harper came crashing to an end. Justin Trudeau and the Liberals stopped the Conservatives in their tracks with their decisive majority in the federal election. Now Trudeau is in Ottawa for a victory rally at the Westin Hotel. The hotel sits next door to the conference centre where, in the summer of 2011, Harper boldly told his supporters that Canada would not simply "go along to get along" in the world. Trudeau has already had a busy day after waking up as the prime minister designate of Canada. It started in Montreal, where he posed for a round of selfies at a subway stop. Now he is in the capital, in front of a boisterous room full of supporters. His voice remains hoarse, as it has been in recent frenzied days, but it delivers a firm message aimed outside these hotel walls, this city, and this province, and outside Canada.

"To this country's friends, all around the world," Trudeau says. "Many of you have worried that Canada has lost its compassionate and constructive voice in the world over the past ten years.

"Well, I have a simple message for you. On behalf of thirty-five million Canadians, we're back."

A new search for Canada's international role had begun – the second one in less than a decade. Their respective foreign policies differed sharply, but Harper and Trudeau arrived at them the same way, by adhering to their opposing beliefs as they drove full tilt towards the same point on the horizon: domestic political power.

* * *

12 JULY 2006

Stephen Harper's government jetliner is almost wheels-up, bound for Europe carrying the prime minister on his first extensive international trip since winning power a few months earlier. First he will meet in London with his seasoned counterpart, Tony Blair, before going on to his first international summit, the G8 in St Petersburg, Russia, before a final stop in France. As Harper's plane prepares to taxi down a runway in Ottawa, the first reports emerge that Israeli warplanes are ripping up the tarmac of Beirut international airport. The attack is retaliation for Hezbollah killing three Israeli soldiers and kidnapping two more: a brazen cross-border incursion into Israeli territory by the militant group marking the start of what will be a short, nasty, summer war. France and Russia – and later in the day, the European Union – denounce Israel's massive bombardment of the Lebanon-based Hezbollah as a "disproportionate" response to the killings and kidnappings.

I speak separately with three of Harper's communications staff as they circulate the rear aisles of the prime minister's plane. I urge them to bring him to the back of the cabin to address the journalists travelling with him about these developments. Employed by the *Ottawa Citizen*, I'm seated near the back of the Airbus jetliner with more than a dozen journalists. In addition to us, photographers and television specialists, and a larger than usual contingent of columnists from the *Globe and Mail*, *Le Devoir*, and the *Toronto Star* are also in tow. The extra turnout is understandable: there is plenty of curiosity about Harper's first major overseas trip. He doesn't have a lot of international experience, and there wasn't much foreign policy talk during the election campaign that brought him to power.

Eventually Harper emerges from the front of the plane and finds his way to us, pausing in an aisle as we crane over the seats to get closer to him. He has removed his contact lenses in favour of wire-rimmed glasses. He looks me in the eye, and I ask him if he thinks Israel has acted in a disproportionate manner as the leaders of France and Russia, for instance, were saying just hours earlier. He speaks for three minutes in all, gives his answers, and departs. We all drop back into our seats, don our headphones, and start transcribing. Harper's words will be widely reported hours later when his plane touches down in London.

These comments will represent his first line in the sand to distinguish Canada under his leadership. Harper calls the Israeli bombardment a "measured response."

Harper's characterization of the start of this war marked the beginning of what was to be a nearly decade-long discussion about how he saw the world – and what it meant for Canada's place in it. From that moment on, something had changed in Canadian foreign policy. It wasn't that previous Liberal and Progressive Conservative governments weren't pro-Israeli. It was just that Harper's characterization struck many as taking sides in the intractable Middle East conflict. It also marked the beginning of a discussion about whether Harper had pushed foreign policy too far in one direction, and what it meant for Canada's reputation.

Fast forward to June 2011. Harper is delivering a speech to the Conservative party faithful at downtown Ottawa's gleaming new convention centre. It is one month after he has finally vanquished the Liberals – reducing the party to third-place status behind the NDP – and won his first majority government. Five years after becoming prime minister, his foreign policy outlook is becoming more sharply focused. On this day, Harper draws a second, definitive line in the sand. He declares that under his watch, Canada will not play the co-operative nice guy; it will "no longer just go along and get along with everyone else's agenda. It is no longer to please every dictator with a vote at the United Nations. And I confess that I don't know why past attempts to do so were ever thought to be in Canada's national interest." That declaration will be faithfully adopted by his new foreign affairs minister John Baird, Canada's top diplomat from May 2011 until his abrupt resignation in February 2015.

Harper's post-election moment of celebration comes after a less auspicious occasion. In October 2010, the prime minister presided over one of the country's most embarrassing moments in the international arena: Canada's loss of a temporary seat on the United Nations Security Council. But at the Conservative event in Ottawa, Harper is moving on, separating the past from the present. Deciding not to "go along" became the overriding rule of Canadian foreign policy under Harper. It represented a repudiation of Canada's time-honoured practice of multilateral engagement, most notably with the UN. This was significant because "Our policy towards the UN cannot be separated from our foreign policy as a whole. The perception that member states have of us and the influence we can have over UN decisions depend as much on what we do outside the organization as what we do in it," according to Louise Frechette, a former Canadian ambassador to the UN, and the first deputy secretary-general of the UN.[1]

One of the main ways in which a country interacts with the world is how it gets along in the big international pool of organizations, umbrella groups for various configurations of countries. And the biggest such organization, love it or hate it, is the United Nations. Measuring how Canada got along in the largest multilateral club tells us a lot about where we went under the Harper government, and why. Harper moved Canada away from the approach to global affairs that emphasized cooperation within the many clubs Canada had joined since the end of the Second World War.

Shortly after Harper won power, Ian Brodie, his first chief of staff, asked a retired ambassador to tell him what he thought Canada's core international interests were. The ex-diplomat told Brodie that as far as he was concerned, Canada had "no interests, except for fish and softwood lumber."[2] Going back to 1945, Canada's foreign policy boiled down to a few essentials in Brodie's view: Canada does what it needs to do to defend North America, usually in the joint Canada-U.S. North American Aerospace Defence Command (NORAD), and it does what it can "to preserve the western alliance, from external threats (in Europe and, recently, elsewhere) and internal divisions (during the Suez Crisis and in Cyprus)." And of course, Brodie added, "we always defend Canadian fisheries and softwood lumber interests."[3] Otherwise, Canadian governments are "free to pick" when and where to engage internationally.

Harper wasn't the first prime minister to be skeptical of the UN but he took a much harder line towards the organization than any other leader. David Black, the director of the Centre for Foreign Policy Studies at Dalhousie University, and Greg Donaghy, the head of the Historical Section at the Foreign Affairs Department, said Harper never intended "to abandon completely Canada's strong postwar attachment to working multilaterally." But they said his government approached its commitments more "sparingly and selectively."[4]

When Harper won power in 2006, he had to deal with the ripples of the 1979 invasion of Afghanistan by the Soviet Union and the decades of turmoil that flowed to 11 September 2001. Five years later, Harper found himself the inheritor of the bloody Afghanistan combat mission from Paul Martin's Liberals. This defined Harper's foreign policy in the early years of his minority government rule, from 2006 to 2011. At first, Harper embraced the inherent militarism of the mission. But after pledging to never "cut and run" from Afghanistan in 2006, he ultimately did just that, setting in motion a chain of events as early as 2008 to extract Canada from the NATO-led, UN-sanctioned combat mission in Kandahar as its death toll skyrocketed. Canada ultimately joined its allies and rushed for the exit in Afghanistan as Harper lost all interest in frontline military intervention. But not before his government tried to craft a more benevolent narrative that might be more palatable to the Canadian public: that its soldiers were equal partners with its diplomats and aid-workers in helping embattled Afghans rebuild their country. Later, he would find a way to quickly insert the Canadian Forces into what seemed like a compact war with a convenient beginning and end – the UN-sanctioned, NATO-led bombing of Libya. But that ended badly too. The mission was prematurely declared accomplished, and Libya eventually descended into anarchy, becoming a strategically important base for the newly risen Islamic State of Iraq and the Levant.

Harper did not turn his back on multilateralism entirely. He embraced international financial institutions with great enthusiasm, working hard within them to fight another battle that defined his term in office: the Great Recession of 2008–09. In 2010 Harper hosted the first permanent G20, as it was becoming the lead organization for dealing with the global economy. He pushed hard to strengthen the world's fractured financial architecture, and advocated passionately for governments to pay their debts and spend within their means.

During Harper's watch, Canada remained in the top ten of the UN's financial donors. That probably seems counterintuitive given what he and his government had to say about the UN. The Harper government's unwavering support of Israel, often displayed at the UN General Assembly, was a prime example of his disinclination to co-operate. This upset many, who saw it as a betrayal of a perceived tradition of Canadian fair-mindedness on the international stage. However, when it suited his political needs at home, Harper could embrace the UN. For example, he relied on its seal of approval for the Canadian Forces ground war in Afghanistan, and its air combat mission in Libya. And he sought out the UN as a partner on his main foreign aid initiative: improving the health of women and children in poor countries.

Back when he was Prime Minister Mackenzie King's external affairs minister, Louis St Laurent, later a Liberal prime minister, gave the first major speech trying to define Canada's place in the world. In the 1947 Gray Lecture, delivered in Toronto, he declared that Canada's future prosperity was tied to getting along in the UN. If there was one lesson Canadians had learned, St Laurent said, "It is that security for this country lies in the development of a firm structure of international organization." That was the same message Progressive Conservative prime minister Brian Mulroney would deliver to the UN General Assembly thirty-eight years later: "History shows the solitary pursuit of self-interest outside the framework of broader international cooperation is never enough to increase our freedom, safeguard our security, or improve our standard of living."[5]

These historical declarations held little sway with the Harper government, which decided the time had come for a re-evaluation of Canada's global engagement, especially with an increasingly ineffective UN. So why did Stephen Harper deviate from the longstanding cross-party consensus of how Canada should govern itself outside its borders? In part, he was driven by an ideology forged in the long years leading to the creation of the new conservative movement. The other driver of Harper's worldview was much more straightforward: to perpetuate his party's power. These two factors resulted in a much more conservative stamp on Canada's foreign policy.

Ideology and the perpetuation of his party's power also lay behind Harper's unwavering criticism of Russia's aggression in Crimea and eastern Ukraine, and his tough talk against the rise of ISIL in Syria and Iraq. Harper may have had little international experience and shown scant interest in the world beyond his country's borders before coming to power, but his philosophy was shaped early on, through his relationship with his father, and his intellectual explorations as a young man. Harper often viewed the world as black-and-white, good-versus-evil; there were few, if any, shades of gray. This worldview was inextricably fused with his new brand of conservative politics. This meant that Russian president Vladimir Putin and the faceless evil of ISIL militants were reduced to a collective "them" from which only Harper and his brand of tough-talking government could keep "us" – the Canadian citizenry – truly safe. Under Harper, Canada turned away from nuanced diplomacy. He left that work to Canada's major allies. His fellow G7 leaders talked to Putin, but Harper did not. That didn't seem to trouble Harper because he was more concerned about reaching out to others – namely, the 1.3 million Canadians of Ukrainian descent who also detested the Cold War authoritarianism that Putin represented.

As Harper moved Canada away from multilateral cooperation, he pushed the country towards smaller, ad-hoc alliances: coalitions of the willing, like the one Canada rejected in 2003 when the United States led its invasion of Iraq. That was how the Canadian Forces found themselves in Iraq and Syria in 2015 as part of an American-led coalition along with Britain, France, and Germany. Harper deployed half a dozen warplanes to bomb Islamist targets in Iraq, and eventually Syria. He also deployed special forces trainers to Iraq to train local security forces, but they took a more active role in the fight against ISIL when they became embroiled in firefights with militants on the ground in northern Iraq.

Harper also never lost sight of the reality that Canada's number one foreign-policy priority was the United States. That complex and intertwined trade, economic, and security relationship quite literally runs itself every day. But when Harper came to power in 2006, the relationship was strained at the executive level between the George W. Bush Republicans and the Paul Martin Liberals. Relations were in tatters in 2015 when the Harper Conservatives said goodbye to the Obama Democrats.

In the end, Harper staked new ground for Canada on the international stage. Under Harper's watch, Canada was no longer an honest broker or helpful fixer, roles which many had suggested were best suited to the country. The notion of Canada being some sort of well-intentioned, all-around-reliable good guy may be rooted as much in myth as in fact. Were we ever really that guy? Brodie,

Harper's former chief of staff, did not think so. He believed Harper
was right to reject the label. "There is nothing morally praiseworthy
in trying to reconcile with evil intentions," he wrote. "This irks some
observers. But it is possible the world would be closer to an Israeli-
Palestinian entente if others had opposed Hamas and Hezbollah instead of pretending to be honest brokers over the last few years."[6]

At one time, Canada certainly tried to cooperate broadly. In 1945,
when St Laurent laid down the marker that it was better to get along
than not, the country was motivated by the loss of 42,000 young citizens on the battlefields of Europe. Seven decades later, Justin
Trudeau promised to return Canada's foreign policy to the sentiment of that era. When he told the world, "We're back," it marked a
repudiation of Harper's mantra that Canada would no longer go
along "to get along." But, as he would discover, foreign policy in dangerous times has a steep learning curve. The fight against ISIL was-
n't going to be the same kind of battle that was waged in the Second
World War; this wasn't the same kind of threat those of St Laurent's
generation were called to answer. Yes, the values they were fighting
for were the same, so the postwar institutions that were created to
uphold them might still have some validity. But the way these wars
would be fought differed profoundly.

In defeat, the Conservatives clung to their policies on Iran, Israel,
Ukraine, and the UN, and continued to fight against the Liberal
government's embrace of multilateralism and soft diplomacy. As
Trudeau began to change the country's direction, Canadians were
left to ponder how they had arrived at this point in their history.
What had just happened to their country in the intervening decade?

Canada, under Harper, had become a different sort of global citizen, one that occupied a new, unfamiliar position: the odd man out.
Trudeau wanted to bring the country back to the international fold.
His first steps onto the world stage were also unprecedented for a
Canadian prime minister – for the first time in history, Canada's political leader was an international celebrity. But as he began to reengage Canada with the world, Trudeau's actions raised another
important question for Canadians. Where, exactly, was he planning
to take us in an increasingly uncertain and volatile world?

CHAPTER ONE

Canada before Harper:
Finding Its Way in the World

13 JANUARY 1947

More than two thousand people are overflowing Toronto's Convocation Hall to hear a speech from their new secretary of state for external affairs, Louis St Laurent. The hall is packed with university dignitaries, including Sidney Smith. In a decade, Smith will become external affairs minister in the Progressive Conservative government of John Diefenbaker that unseats the Liberals after twenty-two uninterrupted years in power. But the end of St Laurent's decade as prime minister is still ten years away on this night. The chords of an organ fill the air, leading the crowd into "O Canada," sung in both French and English. Large-reeled tape recorders are rolling so that the evening's address may eventually be heard in Great Britain. This is the first of what will become an annual lecture established by George Leishman Gray to honour the memories of his two sons, Duncan and John, who died during the war.[1]

"The first general principle upon which I think we are agreed is that our external policies shall not destroy our unity," St Laurent tells the assembled gathering. "This consideration applies not only to the two main cultural groups in our country. It applies equally to sectionalism of any kind. We dare not fashion a policy which is based on the particular interests of any economic group, of any class or of any section in this country." Canada, says St Laurent, "will prosper only as we maintain this principle, for a disunited Canada will be a powerless one." St Laurent also makes clear that Canada's future prosperity is contingent on the emerging international order, which he calls "the rule of law among states." Canadians, he says, unanimously support the work of international tribunals and courts of arbitration:

> The growth in this country of a sense of political responsibility
> on an international scale has perhaps been less rapid than some
> of us would like. It has nevertheless been a perceptible growth:
> and again and again on the major questions of participation in
> international organization, both in peace and war, we have
> taken our decision to be present. If there is one conclusion that
> our common experience has led us to accept, it is that security
> for this country lies in the development of a firm structure of
> international organization.

The 1947 Gray Lecture laid the foundation of Canada's commitment to a multilateral worldview for decades to come. As Royal Military College professor Adam Chapnick concludes, St Laurent had one important message: "Foreign policy was unique; it was not the place for electioneering or partisan disputes."[2] St Laurent realized that Canadians might disagree on aspects of foreign policy but they must resolve those differences of opinion internally. "International relations were too important to become politicized, and Canadians had duties that extended beyond their immediate self-interest," Chapnick wrote.[3] As political scientists David Dewitt and John Kirton have also observed, St Laurent was making the point that "foreign policy must be discussed inside and outside Parliament without becoming a matter of partisan controversy among political parties."[4] St Laurent saw value in getting along with global partners as he "vigorously defended the need to develop new international institutions," including the UN.[5]

St Laurent was adopting a notion of foreign policy that was taking root at that time. In the early postwar years, the U.S. Republican senator Arthur H. Vandenberg, chair of the Foreign Relations Committee, gave Democratic president Harry S. Truman bipartisan support as the U.S. was helping to create the NATO alliance to counter the rising Soviet Union and rebuild a shattered Europe through the Marshall Plan. "We must stop partisan politics at the water's edge," Vandenberg declared, establishing the so-called "water's edge principle" that internal domestic politics should be kept at home, and out of international affairs.[6]

In fact, Tom Keating, one of Canada's leading historians on multilateralism, said that as early as 1943 the Department of External Affairs, as it was then known, was determined to "secure the peace and win a place for Canada in the council of nations."[7] John Holmes, one of Canada's most influential diplomats during this era, offered a convincing explanation of why multilateralism mattered. It was a simple notion that holds to this day: Canada is a small country that can't defend itself, so it needs allies. Holmes said there was "nothing particularly high-minded" about a country adopting a strongly internationalist policy when that country "obviously cannot protect its people and its interest except in collaboration with others."[8]

In the spring of 1945, Canada arrived at the international conference in San Francisco that ultimately created the UN with two competing but not mutually exclusive goals: to avoid being subsumed by the interests of the four great superpowers of the time (the United States, the United Kingdom, Russia, and China, minus the eventual fifth member of the permanent Security Council, France) while finding a way to make this new organization a success.[9] Canada joined with Australia to oppose the veto powers that these permanent members were seeking, but they ultimately failed and had to settle for some additional powers on economic and social issues.[10] "The smaller states, including Canada, accepted these conditions and were fully aware of their implications. They understood that the future peace of the world depended on keeping the Great Powers engaged and interacting," Chapnick wrote. "The Canadian government took the correct approach in 1945 by publicly accepting the hopelessness of the Security Council debate and eventually diverting some of its best negotiators to issues that presented better opportunities to make a genuine difference."[11]

Canada wanted its voice to be heard in this new world body, especially when it came to how its soldiers might be used in future UN military operations. Canada and its fellow "middle powers" managed to infuse the UN Charter with some provisions that tried to balance the clout of the superpowers.[12] They worked for the inclusion of Article 23, which stated that due regard should be given to a state's contribution to peace and security when competing for a non-

permanent seat on the Security Council.[13] Without referring specifically to that section, Harper invoked the sentiment of that article
some sixty-five years later when he stressed Canada's military contribution and losses in Afghanistan in a final unsuccessful effort to help
Canada win a temporary two-year term on the Security Council. In
1945, UN peacekeeping as the world would come to know it was still
more than a decade away, but Canada successfully pushed for another
key section, Article 44, which allowed non-members access to the Security Council to deliberate on how their troops might be used in UN
enforcement missions.[14] However, Canada failed to ensure that non-
superpower countries would get the "near permanent" representa-
tion to the Security Council that they wanted.[15]

Despite that disappointment, the government remained committed to making the UN succeed. Escott Reid, a second secretary in external affairs, played a major role in Canada's early UN engagement
along with fellow diplomat Hume Wrong, and Lester Pearson, then
ambassador to the United States. Reid was disappointed by how
Canada fared, but he insisted that it was better to have a seat at the
table than not. "One way in which Canada can help to remedy the
weaknesses in the Security Council is by acting in the Security Council not in defence of the special interest of Canada but in defence of
the interests of the United Nations as a whole," he wrote in a 1947 letter.[16] Five years earlier, as the Second World War still raged, Reid had
written about the importance of multilateralism to Canada's future
interests, saying "a small state like Canada would have an opportunity
to exert a reasonable amount of influence in international politics
at the cost of putting various aspects of its sovereignty into an international pool."[17] He felt that getting along in this emerging international organization was essential to Canada's interests.

Canadians played an integral role in setting up the machinery
that would allow the United Nations to operate. After the United
Nations Charter was signed on 26 June 1945, a body called the Executive Committee of the Preparatory Commission went to work
setting up the UN's rules of procedure and the administration of the
UN Secretariat and the General Assembly, among other things. Reid,
Holmes, and Pearson spent almost three months in London from
August to November 1945 representing Canada, one of fourteen
countries on the committee.[18]

It was a reflection of Canada's elevated status: the country emerged as the third-strongest Western power in the aftermath of the Second World War. But Canada would have little time to enjoy this high rank.[19] The decade and a half that followed the UN's creation was a turbulent period. Despite the formidable disappointments generated by the veto-wielding Soviet Union, the federal government avoided direct criticism of the UN itself, and it never seriously questioned the value of working within the institution. Coming out of the Second World War, Canada's relative strength was due in large part to the decimation of Germany and Japan. The recovery and growth of other countries would soon knock Canada down a few notches. Canada contributed to this course correction because it backed the drive to expand the UN's membership in the 1950s. It lobbied for the admission of sixteen new members in the face of strong U.S. opposition.[20]

The U.S. threatened to stop buying Canadian oil but the health minister, Paul Martin Sr, brokered a deal that would see the number of UN members double by 1965, a breakthrough that kept the Soviet Union engaged with the UN and made it more reflective of the broader international community.[21] "In helping to break the UN membership impasse in 1955, Canada had fostered a dramatic change in the agenda of the UN," wrote Keating.[22] Such efforts reflected the core belief of Canada's political leaders and diplomats: that their country was better off with the UN than without it. As Holmes said, it may be comprised "of all the brawling nations who cause all the troubles" but "I cannot see any hope in a world without the UN."[23]

On 10 January 1946, the UN General Assembly opened for business in London. The foreign minister of Belgium, Paul-Henri Spaak, was elected its president, and two days later the election for the first temporary, non-permanent seats on the Security Council took place. Canada, despite its efforts to help create the new organization, wasn't able to win one, losing the seat on a technicality. And this loss simply cannot be seen as equal to the thumping Canada received in 2010. The 1946 loss was a dramatic, nail-biting disappointment.

"Electioneering is going strong," Wrong wrote in a 9 January 1946 cable to Ottawa, which reported that Canada was optimistic it had the support to win a seat as part of a joint slate of countries that had the backing of the Latin American and Arab groups.[24] Everything seemed to be fine until Australia came along. "There were two unpleasant meetings last week of the Commonwealth countries," Wrong reported. The Australian delegation had been given orders to run for the Security Council. This would pit two Commonwealth countries against each other. Wrong said the Australians didn't want to keep Canada off the Council, they just thought both countries could win. Canada thought otherwise. Wrong believed that Australia "may cut into our vote, but we should get through." There was also "serious talk, especially from the United States delegation" that Canada might supply the first UN secretary-general, "probably Pearson."[25]

Canada was jolted back to reality when the voting finally began three days later. Brazil, Egypt, Mexico, Poland, and the Netherlands all received more than the required thirty-four votes to win in what was then a fifty-one-member General Assembly. Canada fell just short of the two-thirds support needed with thirty-three votes, ahead of Australia at twenty-eight.[26] "In fact we secured the required two-thirds vote of the thirty-four on the first ballot, but the Nicaraguan delegate spoiled his ballot by signing his name and it was properly rejected under the rules," Wrong explained in a cable to Ottawa, the day after the defeat.[27]

The spoiled Nicaraguan ballot forced Australia and Canada to face off on a second ballot to decide the winner of the remaining seat. The Australians turned the tables and won by a twenty-seven to twenty-three margin (there was one more spoiled ballot). They faced off again for third vote, but nothing really changed. Australia won the ballot twenty-eight to twenty-three, still short of the thirty-four needed to win. That's when St Laurent announced that Canada would stand down. "The members of the Canadian delegation fully realize how embarrassing it must be to their fellow delegates to go on balloting between two of the Dominions of the Commonwealth, with each of which they have always had such cordial and mutually satisfactory relations," he said.[28]

St Laurent called on the chamber to unanimously support Australia on a final vote. Two countries spoiled their ballots, and three voted for Canada anyway. But the remaining forty-six members voted for the Australians in the secret ballot cementing their victory.

"The results of the elections of the Security Council were, I know, a shock to you all in Ottawa," Wrong wrote in his post-mortem cable. The "Big Five" permanent members had all agreed in a pre-vote deal which six countries they wanted to see win. "Their slate was elected easily except for the substitution of Australia for Canada." Wrong believed the Big Five all voted for Canada initially, and he had been told the U.S., Britain, and the Soviet Union supported Canada in the run-offs with Australia. "I am fairly certain that the French also did so but I do not know what the Chinese did." So who turned on Canada? Perhaps Mexico and some other Western Hemisphere countries that had won on first ballot and didn't want to share the Council with another North American country. "I still thought that we would be chosen and the British and the Americans both said they were sure of the outcome," Wrong said, adding that the "unofficial whip of the Latin American group told me that we could count on the support of his group but he was clearly wrong in this."[29]

Canada agonized over making its next run for the Security Council. Lester Pearson laid the groundwork in the final years of his diplomatic life, before entering politics in the fall of 1948 as external affairs minister. Pearson strongly believed that an Arab-Jewish conflict was likely to break out after the British mandate over Palestine expired.[30] He thought that the territory should be divided into two states, one Arab and one Jewish, but justice minister J.L. Ilsley, head of the Canadian delegation at the General Assembly, disagreed. Pearson pushed for a working group on Palestine and supported the termination of the mandate on 1 August 1948, and partition under UN supervision.[31] None of this brought peace to the region but it was a key moment in the development of Canadian diplomacy at the UN.[32] This happened outside the Security Council because of the deadlock involving the Soviet Union and its veto, a development that was creating division at External Affairs over the "wisdom of seeking election to a two-year term as one of the non-permanent members."[33]

Back in Ottawa, Wrong, likely still sore from the defeat he'd watched a year earlier, lobbied against running for the Council. In London, Holmes argued a run for the Council would be good for morale. He thought it could strain the resources of the department, "though he did point out that a refusal to stand would further weaken the United Nations."[34] Pearson was caught in the middle. He was not overly enthusiastic, "but he feared that a decision not to seek election might be misinterpreted in Canada as a loss of faith in the organization and might prejudice chances for election in future years."[35]

In the end, Pearson recommended to St Laurent that Canada should run. Cabinet approved the proposal in August. On 30 September 1947, Canada was elected for 1948–49 along with Argentina, with each country winning forty-one of a possible fifty-seven votes, easily defeating their rivals.[36] Afterwards, justice minister Ilsley, who cast the country's vote with Pearson at his side, said Canada was "deeply conscious of the new responsibilities" it now had. He said Canada believed the UN was the best way to secure peace and prosperity in the world. "If we are to enjoy the benefits of such an organization, we must accept its responsibilities. That we are prepared to do."[37]

This foundation of Canada's stance towards the UN, and the history of constructive participation that ensued, are significant on many levels. The one-month campaign in 1947 between deciding to run and actually winning a temporary seat on the Security Council was whiplash fast compared to the years-long, expensive campaigns that would be a feature of Security Council bids in the decades to come. Most of all, it spoke to Canada's standing in the international community in the immediate postwar era, a counterpoint to its decisive loss at the UN in October 2010.

During its first stint on the Security Council in 1948–49, Canada played a lead role in major conflicts far from its border. This term marked Canada's debut as a tangible contributor to global peace and stability. The country's first permanent ambassador to the UN, retired general Andrew McNaughton, led the country's efforts and extended its influence into security matters in Central and South Asia. McNaughton played a role in the India-Pakistan dispute over Kashmir, and helped broker the birth of Indonesia, which would become the world's most populous Muslim country. The issues facing both areas may have been "remote from Canada geographically and from Canada's direct interests."[38] But this area would not remain remote to Canada's interests in the century to follow, especially after the 11 September 2001 terrorist attacks on the United States brought the geopolitics of the Islamic world home to Canadians. Canada's first stint on the Security Council represented a significant early connection the region long before its thirteen-year military engagement in Afghanistan.

McNaughton was chair of the Security Council in February 1948, just the second month of Canada's term. Throughout early 1948, McNaughton continued informal consultations with India and Pakistan, helping to co-author a resolution on the crisis that was passed on 21 April by the Council. It provided for the withdrawal of the Pakistani tribesmen and the reduction of Indian forces in Kashmir to the minimum required for "the maintenance of law and order."[39] After much delay and difficulty, including opposition in India, a deal was reached on 1 January 1949. McNaughton called it "a most important and encouraging event in the history of the United Nations," and said its effects would extend far beyond India and Pakistan.[40] His words were prophetic in a way he didn't intend. By the early twenty-first century, the still unstable Pakistan would see its tribal lands along its Afghan border harbour al-Qaida terrorists attacking Western coalition allies in Afghanistan.

Meanwhile, the armed conflict between the Netherlands and the Indonesian Republic that started in 1945 had to be addressed. On 11 March 1949, McNaughton proposed a conference, which the Security Council approved less than two weeks later, to settle the dispute. Talks began in April and continued into November and December. On 27 December 1949, the Dutch formally transferred sovereignty, and Canada immediately recognized the new Indonesian Republic.[41] This marked the beginning of the end of Dutch colonial rule in the Southeast Asian archipelago.

McNaughton's grandson, retired lieutenant general Andrew Leslie, recalled the contributions of his grandfather and his contemporaries. "He established very strong relationships with a whole host of people from the Americans, the Indonesians, the Chinese, to even the Russians," Leslie told me in an interview, several months before he ran successfully for the Liberals in the 2015 federal election. "You had a confluence of remarkable men and women who saw themselves as the natural sort of interlocutor between some of the Americas and Russia and China."

The principles laid out in St Laurent's Gray Lecture set the stage for Canada's most influential moment in international diplomacy. The struggle over the Suez Canal was a showcase example of Canada not always getting along with other countries, including some of its closest UN allies, yet staying the course, and working within the system to make a difference. Canada butted heads with Britain, which along with France was secretly backing an Israeli attack on Egypt, after Gamal Abdul Nasser, its Soviet-leaning president, nationalized the Suez Canal.[42] Publicly, St Laurent expressed "regret" that the British and French were planning the attack, but in private he was clearly angry at the Brits.[43] Canada used the UN to push back against its old colonial rulers, Britain.

Enter Pearson.

With the backing of U.S. president Dwight Eisenhower, Pearson proposed that the French and British troops be transformed into a United Nations force.[44] Pearson accomplished this with the backing of Prime Minister St Laurent, whom he considered "a very close friend" and who told him: "Do the right thing, and I'll back you."[45] A decade earlier, when he was still a diplomat, Pearson had sent a handwritten note to Gerry Riddell, the foreign service officer who had actually drafted and revised St Laurent's Gray Lecture. Somewhat prophetically, Pearson scrawled: "This, I think, very good stuff indeed – if the minister doesn't use it, I would like to put in a bid for it."[46]

Crucially, Pearson and St Laurent had the support of their political opponents. Official opposition leader John Diefenbaker wrote in his memoirs how, in 1956, he himself had proposed some kind of "an organization under the United Nations, a watching force, a presence between the Israeli and Arab forces" to help defuse the Suez Crisis.[47] It was Pearson, though, who would lay the groundwork for the creation of that very first UN peacekeeping force, which would earn him the Nobel Peace Prize in 1957. In the House of Commons debates on the peacekeeping deployment, Diefenbaker criticized St Laurent for what he saw as a "bitter speech."[48] Diefenbaker was staunchly pro-British, and was uncomfortable with Pearson antagonizing the Empire. But in the end, the Progressive Conservative leader supported the Liberal government: "I endeavored then, as I always have on international affairs, to bring about non-partisan unity."[49]

Diefenbaker's Tories defeated the Liberals in 1957, in part by using their conduct of the Suez Crisis to domestic advantage. During his initial campaign, he accused the St Laurent government of not supporting "the mother country" because it was offside with Britain, a tactic that Keating observed was "one of the rare instances in which bipartisanship broke down in Canada's internationalist foreign policy and it may have had some influence on the Liberals' fall from power in the 1957 federal election."[50] But while the Liberals lost at home, they were big winners on the international stage with Pearson winning the Nobel Peace Prize that same year.

Once in power, Diefenbaker didn't rock the boat internationally. Though there was much speculation that Diefenbaker's new minority government might move Canada away from the UN, "Mr. Diefenbaker was clearly attracted by the United Nations and the opportunities it offered for taking up a position as a world statesman. In his speech to the General Assembly on 23 September, he declared that the United Nations was the cornerstone of Canada's foreign policy."[51] In doing so, Diefenbaker was able to establish the principle of a non-partisan foreign policy in modern, postwar Canada. External affairs minister Howard Green, who replaced Sidney Smith after his sudden death on 17 March 1959, displayed great enthusiasm for Canada's accomplishments at the UN in a November 1959 television interview with the CBC. In his folksy manner, Green conveyed a sincere desire for Canada to make a significant contribution and find consensus during its time on the Council. He took pride in winning unanimous approval for a study of the harmful effects of radiation. Asked by his interviewer, Charles Lynch of *Southam News*, whether this was a move to force an end to nuclear bomb tests, Green replied: "Well of course the bomb tests are one feature of the situation but there's radiation from many other causes and we want them tested."[52]

In 1962, Diefenbaker used the United Nations as a foil against the United States to guide Canada's reaction to the Cuban missile crisis. Diefenbaker didn't get along with U.S. president John F. Kennedy, and he was skeptical of the threat of Soviet missiles in Cuba.[53] He wanted "irrefutable evidence" of Russian military installations in Cuba, and he urged Kennedy to call for UN inspectors to be sent to Cuba to verify their existence.[54] Some argue that Diefenbaker's personal loathing of the younger, more attractive American president may have clouded his judgment.[55] Regardless, it was an example of Diefenbaker defaulting to the UN. It had much in common with the stance taken by the Liberal government of Jean Chrétien in 2003 when it decided not to join the U.S.-led invasion of Iraq, which Stephen Harper supported in opposition. This is significant because Harper would later cite Diefenbaker as a foreign policy influence, in what seemed to be an attempt to downplay the dominance of the Liberals in that area. Yet the daylight between Harper and Diefenbaker on foreign policy is almost blinding.

Lester Pearson, who succeeded St Laurent as the next Liberal prime minister, presided over two minority governments from 1963 to 1968. But the glow of the Nobel Peace Prize, as well as the country's so-called golden era of diplomacy, had been considerably dulled. Internationally, Pearson had some nasty battles with U.S. president Lyndon Johnson over the Vietnam War. At home, he waged a hard battle to give Canada its new Maple Leaf flag, while Canada's enthusiasm for the UN waned and the country grew tired of its middle-power status.[56]

Pierre Trudeau arrived in power in 1968 with a relatively jaundiced view of Canada's relations with the UN and multilateralism in general. Out of that flowed his notion of "interest-based" foreign policy. Trudeau immediately commissioned a foreign policy review that emphasized "national interests as the basis for policy calculation and the initiation of policies and programs" in foreign affairs.[57] Trudeau wanted to jettison the "helpful fixer" image that Pearson had established – that of Canada as an altruistic, self-sacrificing nation always working for a greater good.[58] In 1970, Trudeau delivered his review, *Foreign Policy for Canadians*, which emphasized a new, more self-interested direction. It said: "In essence, foreign policy is the product of the Government's progressive definition and pursuit of national aims and interests in the international environment. It is the extension abroad of national interests."[59] Trudeau's Canada-first approach to foreign policy was also tempered by a more altruistic foreign aid policy that recognized the need for Canada to accept its fair share of the responsibility to alleviate poverty in poor countries. Still, political scientist James Eayrs dismissed Trudeau's new approach to international affairs as dollar diplomacy and "foreign policy for beavers."[60]

In many respects, Trudeau shared Harper's indifference to the UN. Harper was harshly criticized in 2009 for snubbing the General Assembly for a photo-op at a Tim Hortons outlet. Back in 1970, on the twenty-fifth anniversary of the UN's founding, Trudeau actually declined an invitation to address the General Assembly and lead off the debate marking the milestone, breaking with every other postwar prime minister.[61] Trudeau would wait until 1978 before addressing the UN at its Special Session on Disarmament. Keating viewed Trudeau's absence in 1970 as a reflection of the "new thinking that was guiding Canadian foreign policy with its greater emphasis on national interest and its denigration of the country's mediatory middle power roles."[62]

Paul Heinbecker, a speechwriter for Trudeau prior to becoming one of Canada's most distinguished diplomats, said his boss never disliked the UN. "Trudeau's attitude was not that he hated the UN, but that if he didn't have something worth saying, he wasn't going to go," Heinbecker explained in an interview. "He, like Harper, didn't like people very much. And one of the reasons you go to New York is because all those other leaders are there."

Still, Trudeau couldn't resist the pull of the UN, or give up entirely on multilateral diplomacy. "In practice, even a skeptic like Trudeau could not resist the pressures that were often placed on Canada to play intermediary roles in international disputes," wrote Keating. "Canadian diplomats and politicians had acquired a reputation that was not easily abandoned."[63]

For all of Trudeau's initial reticence towards the United Nations, he eventually found a reason to raise his voice there. On 26 May 1978, Trudeau finally addressed the UN about the nuclear arms at the heart of the Cold War between the Soviet Union and the United States. Drawing on the expertise of diplomat Klaus Glodschlag, he called for a nuclear "suffocation" strategy, "a coherent set of measures, including the comprehensive test-ban treaty, an agreement to stop the flight testing of all new strategic delivery vehicles, an agreement to prohibit all production of fissionable material for weapons purposes, and an agreement to limit and reduce military spending on new strategic nuclear weapons systems."[64] Though some critics initially dismissed the speech, it mirrored the views of U.S. president Jimmy Carter and the sprit of détente that was growing in the 1970s.[65] Lloyd Axworthy wrote in his memoirs that "Trudeau added a further element to the foreign affairs legacy established by Pearson."[66]

Axworthy saw Trudeau's nuclear activism – which included his swan song 1984 world-peace mission – to be a "classic middle power stance" that showed Canada as independent and unafraid to stand up to more powerful countries.[67] "This was defining a leading role for Canada in establishing norms of global behaviour and rules of law," wrote Axworthy. "It was a position that suited the growing maturity of Canada, and a lesson that needs to be built upon from generation to generation."[68]

But Trudeau's late-career peace initiatives had many detractors, none more hostile than Britain's Margaret Thatcher. Trudeau formally launched his campaign to rid the world of nuclear weapons in 1983, and planned to jet around the world meeting the heads of the nuclear states. Trudeau thoroughly annoyed Thatcher during their London meeting, angered India's Indira Gandhi in theirs, and had a bizarre encounter in Beijing with Chairman Deng Xiaoping in which he declared China could survive a nuclear war even if it killed two billion people.[69] U.S. president Ronald Reagan was cordial, but leaks to the media at the time of Trudeau's visit to Washington made it clear that that the Republican administration didn't want the prime minister meddling in U.S.-Soviet affairs.[70] At Trudeau's final international event, the 1984 G7 summit in London, Thatcher humiliated him by not recognizing him when he tried to speak, and by making no attempt to acknowledge his upcoming retirement or wish him well.[71]

It took a Progressive Conservative, Brian Mulroney, to revive Pearson-style multilateralism when he brought his party back to power in 1984 after the better part of two decades in opposition. Even though he moved Canada closer to the United States than any previous prime minister, Mulroney showed how Canada could balance two apparently competing foreign policy priorities – multilateralism and getting along with our massive southern neighbour. His government stressed the importance of multilateralism in his first Speech from the Throne in 1984, as he also emphasized how strengthening relations with the U.S. must be a priority. The Canada-U.S. free trade deal stands as Mulroney's most influential achievement in bilateral relations.

Mulroney also firmly endorsed the UN in his first foreign-policy review, which said that recent developments had "created a serious challenge to a principal vehicle of Canadian foreign policy, the world's multilateral agencies."[72] In his address to the UN General Assembly in 1985, Mulroney made it clear that the "solitary pursuit of self-interest outside the framework of broader international cooperation is never enough to increase our freedom, safeguard our security, or improve our standard of living."[73] That affirmation aligned Mulroney's Progressive Conservatives with past Liberal governments. And like the St Laurent-Pearson Liberals during the Suez Crisis of 1956, the Mulroney Progressive Conservatives used the UN to fight South African apartheid in the 1980s. Mulroney, too, surrounded himself with good help. He appointed former prime minister Joe Clark as his external affairs minister, and in a landmark demonstration of non-partisanship, he tapped New Democrat Stephen Lewis to be his UN ambassador. Together they led Canada's push for tough sanctions against the apartheid regime. They did this in the face of opposition from Canada's two closest allies, the U.S. and Britain.

In the end, they helped turn the tide against the racist regime. Lewis became friends with Nelson Mandela, who survived twenty-seven years as a political prisoner before becoming South Africa's first post-apartheid president. Lewis visited Mandela several times in retirement in South Africa between 2001 and 2009. As Lewis told me on the day Mandela died in December 2013, Brian Mulroney was one of Mandela's favourite topics of discussion. "He had a tremendous affection and regard for our former prime minister, who did do a really major job in the work to overthrow apartheid and have Mandela released," Lewis said over the phone from Toronto's Pearson airport, about an hour before he was to begin his latest journey to South Africa.

In a separate interview fifteen months later, Lewis described how – as a socialist – he was able to find common ground with and serve a conservative prime minister. The relationship worked because he and Mulroney left partisan politics at the water's edge. "He made it clear to me I could have a strong voice and that there were times I could disagree with the government policy and he wouldn't have a cardiac arrest," Lewis recalled. "We worked well together and we had two things in common: one was the determination to overthrow apartheid; the other was to give as much as aid as possible to struggling African countries."

Mulroney may have been famous for holding a grudge, for blacklisting people who had crossed him. But as Lewis recalled, that didn't extend to a robust and respectful political disagreement. "You could disagree fundamentally with Brian Mulroney and have a very good intellectual or verbal battle, and he wouldn't ostracize you," Lewis said. The Progressive Conservatives, like the Liberals before them, demonstrated how Canada could use the UN to make their country's voice heard in the world for a greater good, beyond our borders.

With the rise of the Chrétien Liberals, the "soft power" of the human security agenda became one of the signature foreign policy pursuits of the 1993 to 2005 era. It formed the backbone of Canada's agenda during its sixth stint on the UN Security Council in 1999–2000. The era was also marked by Prime Minister Jean Chrétien's decision – challenged by the Conservative opposition led by Stephen Harper – to align Canada with the UN in 2003, at a critical juncture in international affairs. Chrétien ultimately decided that Canada would not support the U.S.-led invasion of Iraq without the Security Council's approval. The UN proved instrumental in giving the Liberals the moral authority to oppose its top ally, the United States, under Republican president George W. Bush. Indeed, the UN empowered two of America's major allies on the Security Council – Germany and France – to just say no to joining the small invading coalition, which included Britain.

Canada was heavily engaged with the UN during the most recent era of Liberal rule. After a high-level campaign of lobbying that lasted half a decade, the Security Council stint of 1999–2000 gave Canada a forum to pursue its human security agenda, as espoused by foreign affairs minister Lloyd Axworthy. Canada assumed a leading role in the creation of three new international instruments: the passage of the Ottawa Convention of 1997 that banned anti-personnel landmines, the treaty that paved the way for the creation of the International Criminal Court in 1998, and the UN's later endorsement of the Responsibility to Protect doctrine (R2P) in 2005. Axworthy brought together the international coalition of non-governmental agencies and civil society groups that pushed for the landmines treaty, a movement destined to be recognized with a Nobel Peace Prize. In October 1996, Ottawa's conference centre, converted from

an old downtown train station, was the scene of a large meeting –
fifty international governments, several UN agencies, the International Committee of the Red Cross, and many other NGOs – kicking
off what became known as "the Ottawa Process." As the meeting
closed, Axworthy threw down the gauntlet to those assembled: come
back to Ottawa by the end of 1997 to sign a treaty. On 3 December
1997 they did, just weeks after the Nobel Prize had been awarded to
U.S. activist and Axworthy collaborator Jody Williams and her International Campaign to Ban Landmines.[74]

They were never able to persuade the United States to join, and
still haven't. But the treaty won the support of U.S. president Bill
Clinton.[75] Some seventeen years later, Axworthy remained optimistic that the Americans would eventually join because of U.S. secretary of state John Kerry's comment in an op-ed for *USA Today* that
his country would work to "find ways" to accede to it.

Canada also played a leading role in the events that led to the creation of the International Criminal Court: the signing of the Rome
Treaty on 17 July 1998. Though it's closely associated with Axworthy, the ICC had its roots in the last days of Mulroney's Progressive
Conservative government when the external affairs minister, Barbara McDougall, was moved by the conditions she saw in Bosnian
refugee camps. That alone speaks to the non-partisan nature of the
initiative.[76] Several other Canadians such as Philippe Kirsch, who
chaired the Rome conference that led to the treaty, played key roles
in the creation of the ICC.[77] Canada provided financial support to
the UN Trust Fund so that poor countries could take part in the negotiations, and to non-governmental organizations in developing
countries "to mobilize public support for the ICC."[78]

Canada also led the drive for the UN to adopt the Responsibility
to Protect doctrine, which provided rules for intervention within
the borders of a sovereign state to prevent its leaders from harming
their own people. Axworthy helped get the R2P ball rolling in his
final year in politics. In 1999, NATO decided to lead the international mission to bomb the former Yugoslavia to protect ethnic Albanians in Kosovo province, without UN approval. The UN Security
Council was blocked by the veto of Russia and China, so after some
agonizing debate within Foreign Affairs, Canada joined the NATO-
led mission.[79] In the end, after a robust military intervention, a civilian

population was protected, laying the foundation for the Responsibility to Protect.

Axworthy exploded at the Security Council in 1999, saying that as
an "emasculated" and "obsolescent" institution, it was powerless to
halt the carnage of Kosovo, but he later backed off from the criticism. Yes, the Liberals could – and occasionally did – lose patience
with the UN. But unlike the Harper government, they continued to
work within it, funding the International Commission on Intervention and State Sovereignty, helping select its members and or-
ganizing meetings, all in an attempt to find a solution – a new set
of rules – that would prevent a repeat of the 1990s genocides in
Rwanda and Bosnia and the UN's failure to act in Kosovo. R2P went
through various rewrites before it was adopted at the 2005 UN World
Summit. Sadly, the lofty ideals of R2P have never truly been realized;
the world's inaction in response to the long Syrian civil war that has
left hundreds of thousands dead and forced millions from their
homes stands as a tragic failure of the original concept.

The Axworthy soft power agenda was not universally revered, including at home in Canada. Fen Hampson, the head of the global
security program at the Centre of International Governance Innovation in Waterloo, Ontario, has said that while human security had its
virtues, it "could be had on the cheap" compared to the high price
of peacekeeping. "Pulpit diplomacy, as critics dubbed it, did not ask
Canadians to open their wallets when the collection plate got passed
around."[80] Hampson noted that under Mulroney, Canada also
pushed hard for human rights abroad, particularly for the sanctions
that helped topple South Africa's apartheid regime. And he pointed out that Axworthy's human security agenda was "largely deriva-
tive," drawing on Harvard academic Joseph Nye's concept of "soft
power" and the 1994 Human Development Report by the United
Nations Development Programme.[81] Hampson conceded that "Axworthy's chief legacy, however, is that he raised Canada's profile internationally – and it is indeed Canada's name that is associated with
landmines and various other human security initiatives, and not so
much Mr Axworthy himself."[82]

Prime Minister Paul Martin succeeded Chrétien in 2003 and tried
to focus Canada more on international affairs. Despite his short
term in office, Martin undertook a lengthy foreign-policy review

that some critics complained was unnecessary and self-indulgent. "By avoiding visionary pronouncements about our foreign policy and ceasing to moralize and talk about our superior values, we could finally bring to an end our long spasms of bipolar behaviour, promote our national interest and gain both self-esteem and the respect of nations," Allan Gotlieb, Canada's ambassador to the U.S. from 1981–89, wrote at the time.[83] Martin laid the groundwork for some of the policies that Harper would either follow or take credit for. Martin restored billions of dollars to the Canadian Forces in his final 2005 budget, and he also brought Canada closer to Israel by deciding Canada would end its practice of abstaining from votes at the UN that criticized the country.

While that was all well and good, it was the decade of Liberal soft power before that, under Chrétien, that left an indelible Liberal stamp on Canadian foreign policy. It was that policy footprint that Stephen Harper was determined to erase, like a high tide crashing on a beach. When he came to power, Harper wanted nothing to do with the Liberal foreign policy legacy and set out to make something more to his liking.

CHAPTER TWO

Stephen Harper:
Finding His Way in the World

OCTOBER 1987

A young, disillusioned Stephen Harper is in Winnipeg. He's just quit his job as a staffer with the Progressive Conservatives. He is addressing a seminal meeting of the Reform party. It is early days in the grassroots movement, and among the manifestos and policy documents, there's little vision of the world outside Canada's borders. Harper has aligned himself with a heady young group of Western Canadians determined to remake the country politically. The group's ideological and practical considerations are inseparable, and revolve around one thing: winning power. At this point, Western Canadian alienation – summed up in the rallying cry "The West Wants In" – is all about how to redefine the country from within.

As Harper himself ascended the ranks of the newly emerging "Canadian Right" – a formulation of conservatism borrowed from U.S. politics – he would win a seat in Parliament in 1993. But he resigned in 1997, doubting Reform's chances, only to return in 2002 to lead a reconstituted conservative movement dedicated to toppling the Chrétien-Martin Liberals. It culminated in a tumultuous fight for power between 2001 and 23 January 2006, when Harper finally won power.

There were many preliminary battles. He had to win the leadership of both the official opposition, the Canadian Alliance, in 2002 and the newly merged Conservative party in March 2004; then he failed to unseat the Liberals in the general election of 28 June 2004 that resulted in the minority Paul Martin government; he also failed to bring that minority government down in May 2005.[1] All along that hard road, Harper continued to ruminate, write, and make speeches, occasionally dropping hints as to where his foreign policy might take Canada one day.

Prior to 2006, Harper showed little interest in international affairs. When he touched on the topic, his views were driven by one sacrosanct principle: creating a unified right wing that would unseat the Liberals as the natural governing party of Canada. Three major influences shaped Harper's thinking on international affairs in the two decades before he won power.

First, there was the domestic political landscape, which in Harper's view would allow the Liberals to govern in perpetuity because of a divided Right.[2] In writings that spanned the late 1980s to the early 2000s, from the creation and demise of Reform and the Canadian Alliance to the birth of the new Conservative Party of Canada, Harper hashed out what was essentially a manifesto-in-progress with the purpose of defining a conservative alternative to the Liberals for Canadian voters. Occasionally this vision would touch on foreign policy, which was mostly about how the Liberals were getting it wrong.

Secondly, recent history had helped form his Manichean view of the world: a black-and-white, right-or-wrong perspective. He was influenced by readings about Soviet communism and Nazi fascism during the 1930s. He drew lessons from the successes of British and American conservatives under Margaret Thatcher and Ronald Reagan in the 1980s, as well as Australia's John Howard in the 1990s and early 2000s.

Thirdly, the political debates that led to Canada's refusal to participate in the U.S.-led invasion of Iraq in 2003 forced Harper to articulate his most definitive foreign policy to that point: a stridently anti-Liberal, anti-UN worldview.

In a 1996 Next City Magazine article co-written with University of Calgary political scientist Tom Flanagan, Harper laid out the stark reality facing conservatives: the Liberals had won fourteen of twenty-two elections since 1921. Harper bemoaned the fractured opposition that he believed would keep conservatives from power; his assessment was dire, and his desire for power was palpable. "In the last 50 years, the only Progressive Conservative majority governments were John Diefenbaker's in 1958 and Brian Mulroney's in 1984 and 1988."[3]

Harper's political timeline is illuminating for another reason: it shows that the Liberals were able to dominate Canadian foreign policy in the postwar era. Rarely out of power, they became Canada's default political interlocutor with the world. Mulroney and Diefenbaker, for the most part, rejected a partisan approach and followed the flow of this tide, accepting it as Canadian rather than representative of a particular party. In contrast, Harper appeared intent on breaking with multilateralist, Pearsonian, small-L liberal internationalism. Demolishing sacred cows meant rewriting the foreign policy playbook.

Prior to winning power, Harper didn't spend a lot of time on foreign policy discussions. But when he did, it was clear that he thought the Liberals had made a big mess of things. "The Liberal party should be understood not as a centre-left party, like the American Democrats or British Labour, alternating in office with a centre-right alternative," he wrote with Flanagan in *Next City*. "Rather it is a true centre party, comparable to the Christian Democrats in Italy, the Liberal Democrats in Japan, and Congress in India, standing for nothing very definitive but prevailing against a splintered opposition."[4]

As Harper delved into the machinations of the ruling coalitions of Germany, France, and Australia, it all came back to a question of domestic political tactics – how lessons learned from abroad might be used to help conservatives win power in Canada. "Each of these countries uses something other than first-past-the-post voting," Harper lamented, hinting at a momentary interest in electoral reform that was later expunged from his political agenda. "Both the Reform party and the Bloc Québécois, or even the PCs, could go on for decades without ever becoming national parties."[5]

In a 29 January 1997 interview on CBC's *The National*, Harper was asked about the 1989 promise made to the United Nations to end child poverty in Canada by 2000. His answer did not acknowledge the UN or engage any kind of meaningful discussion. He called the resolution adopted by Parliament "the high-water mark of political stupidity in this country."[6] He ridiculed the notion that "the Parliament of Canada could just declare that child poverty was going to be outlawed and that it was going to throw enough money at it, to do it."[7] He equated international aid with domestic welfare programs. "I think taxpayers feel we are throwing lots of money at social programs. The question is whether they're effective," he continued. "And I think to do that, you have to start to examine the incentive structure of those social programs."[8]

It was one of Harper's earliest known pronouncements on international aid, a key aspect of foreign policy. It came thirteen years before he would in fact start throwing some big money – billions of dollars – at his signature initiative to help pregnant women and their children in the developing world. At the same time, Harper would first freeze then cut overall foreign-aid spending, leaving it well below UN targets. To Harper, the interest of the Canadian taxpayer was paramount. He was determined to show how targeted aid dollars could have an immediate measurable outcome versus funding a broad array of development projects, many of them through UN institutions.

In a 28 May 2002 speech in the House of Commons, his first after becoming opposition leader, Harper articulated his top foreign-policy priority: having a strong relationship with the United States. He did this through an attack on Jean Chrétien's handling of relations with the United States. He criticized Chrétien for lack of progress on resolving the softwood lumber dispute, getting restrictions lifted on agricultural imports, and neglecting the military.[9]

"For nine years the government has systematically neglected the Canadian Forces and undermined our ability to contribute to peace enforcement and even peacekeeping operations, including recently our premature withdrawal from Afghanistan," he added.[10] (Chrétien ended Canada's initial six-month commitment of combat troops to Kandahar in 2002 exactly on schedule.) Meanwhile, Harper praised Brian Mulroney because "he understands a fundamental truth. He understood that mature and intelligent Canadian leaders must share the following perspective: the United States is our closest neighbour, our best ally, our biggest customer, and our most consistent friend."[11] However, Harper conveniently ignored the other prong of Mulroney's foreign policy: support of the UN.

In a 14 December 2004 speech to the Canadian Club in Ottawa, Harper attempted to burnish his foreign affairs *bona fides*. He quoted Reform founder Preston Manning intermittently and Mulroney extensively "to bring a historical imprint to the party's foreign affairs stance," wrote one of Harper's early biographers, Lloyd Mackey.[12]

He presented some fundamental principles. "For Conservatives, the defining element of our approach to foreign policy is to better advance the national interest, including the security of Canadian territory; the economic prosperity of the Canadian people; and the values of democracy, freedom and compassion that define the Canadian nation."

It was an approach that echoed Trudeau's initial coolness towards the UN but showed no trace of the Liberal leader's later embrace of the UN in pursuit of his anti-nuclear agenda. He referenced Manning on the need to "think big" in terms of relations with the United States.[13] This pro-U.S. stance was common throughout Harper's pre-election years. He extolled the need to move closer to the U.S. and lambasted the frequent American-bashing of the Liberals. In the speech, Harper also suggested that he had "inherited" a proud conservative tradition of "constructive internationalism."[14] Harper touted Mulroney's record on development assistance and international security and how he led the fight against apartheid in South Africa, "disagreeing with the United States without being disagreeable, without in any way jeopardizing our bilateral relationship." In evoking Mulroney and Diefenbaker, Harper was attempting to "provide some gravitas and historical context to party policy on foreign affairs, since 'a government-in-waiting' gets asked some of its most serious questions in that field," wrote Mackey.[15]

But that didn't translate into substance by the time the party crafted its forty-six-page platform for the 2006 federal election: foreign policy consisted of three sentences and less than two hundred words. Despite the brevity, it still managed to take shots at the Liberals: "Too often, Liberal foreign policy has compromised democratic principles to appease dictators, sometimes for the sake of narrow business interests. Foreign aid has been used for political purposes, not to ensure genuine development."[16] It was a vague policy plank, providing no specifics about how the Liberals had tried to achieve their political goals through foreign aid, and little detail about how the Conservatives would do this better.

The behaviour of dictators as well as some of the fiercer democratic partisans of the twentieth century profoundly influenced Harper. William Johnson, in a biography of the Conservative leader published before he won power, described how as a thoughtful, introspective young man in his twenties, Harper was drawn to Ian Hunter's biography of Malcolm Muggeridge, the *Manchester Guardian* reporter who covered the Ukrainian famine imposed by Josef Stalin in the 1930s.[17] Millions starved as Stalin exported the region's grain to speed the industrialization of the Soviet Union. Muggeridge undertook an unauthorized trip, smuggling his reports out in a diplomatic pouch.[18]

The book clearly helped shape Harper's anti-communist worldview. Two years after he became prime minister, Harper made Canada one of the first countries to declare the 1932–33 Ukrainian famine, known as the Holodomor, to be an act of genocide. Harper was also drawn to Austrian economist Friedrich Hayek's *The Road to Serfdom*, a post-Depression account of the perils of a state-driven economy. Johnson suggests that his work exposed Harper to the notion of a "clash of ideologies between communism, fascism, and liberal democracy, which led to world wars and military occupation."[19] Hayek rejected the planned economy, seeing it as a "threat to freedom" that would put society on a path to "totalitarianism."[20] In 1974, Hayek won the Nobel Prize in economics, and his principles would influence a new generation, including Harper.[21]

Years later, Harper would explain exactly how the perceived evils of communism fit his political ideology, writing in *Citizens Centre Report*: "The fall of the Berlin Wall signaled the collapse of Soviet Communism as a driving world force, depriving conservatives of all shades of a common external enemy."[22] In Harper's view, the conservatives needed the "common enemy" of communism. And losing that had domestic policy implications – it meant the conservatives needed a new opponent. "What this means for conservatives today is that we must rediscover the common cause and orient our coalition to the nature of the post-Cold-War world," Harper wrote.[23]

After winning power, Harper waged a spirited political battle to build a large monument to victims of communism on Ottawa's main ceremonial street. The project was pursued over the vocal objections of the chief justice of the Supreme Court of Canada, Ottawa's mayor, local Liberal and New Democrat MPs, the Royal Architectural Institute of Canada, the Ontario Association of Architects, and no fewer than seventeen past presidents of the Canadian Bar Association, all of whom criticized the plan for the massive memorial on a site next to the Supreme Court building. The Liberals ended that project in 2015, opting for a more scaled-down version at another, less prominent location.

As a young man, Harper's fascination with communism was also stoked by Peter Brimelow's *The Patriot Game: National Dreams & Political Realities.* That book, wrote Johnson, was "a call to arms" at a "time of disillusionment" for people like Harper.[24] The book was fuel for the anti-Liberal fire that would burn in Harper in the coming years. "For Brimelow, the Liberal Party is the villain of Canadian history. It imposed a way of thinking about the country, a vision, that was detrimental," wrote Johnson. "In effect, the Liberal Party became the surrogate of French Quebec, ruling the country because our parliamentary electoral system allowed a minority to rule the majority: French Canada voted as a bloc, while English Canada was split."[25] Brimelow saw this as leading to the creation of a "New Class" of politicians, civil servants, employees of multiple Crown corporations such as the CBC, welfare workers, teachers, and journalists.[26] It is not too big a stretch to see how Harper would incorporate the international multilateral framework, most notably the United Nations, into Brimelow's view of an elitist, establishment club. Brimelow gave Harper a theoretical foundation for his deep-seated antipathy towards the Liberals and his eventual desire to crush the party's brand. Brimelow also encouraged Harper's suspicion of the institutions he saw as supporting the status quo he so vehemently opposed.

Harper viewed the success of Reagan and Thatcher in the 1980s in an ideological light. As he explained in his 2003 article for *Citizens Centre Report*, he admired their ability to vanquish their domestic political opponents. "The Reagan-Thatcher revolution was so successful that it permanently undermined the traditional social-democratic/left-liberal consensus in a number of democratic countries," he wrote. "It worked domestically to undermine the left-liberal or social-democratic consensus, causing those parties to simply stop fighting and adopt much of the winning conservative agenda."[27]

Here again, Harper saw suppport for the idea that he needed to cripple or destroy the Liberals to make the Conservatives the natural governing party of Canada. In the 1980s, Harper was drawn to Thatcher and Reagan because he had grown disillusioned with Mulroney's brand of conservatism. He agreed with Thatcher's party manifestos from the 1979 and 1983 elections and embraced "the turn towards free markets," wrote Johnson, which made him question what he saw as Mulroney's lack of commitment to those principles.[28]

More than a decade later, the example of Australia's John Howard offered more than ideological inspiration: it gave Harper's team some concrete examples of how to appeal to voters. Howard introduced Harper to the importance of political branding. As Tom Flanagan, Harper's former top adviser and occasional co-author, wrote: "People are looking for a sharper definition of what the alternative government stands for." Flanagan recalled a memo from one of Harper's senior advisers in April 2004 that said: "We must define ourselves in our own ads from the outset before the Liberals define us." That eventually led to the creation of the Conservatives' "Stand Up for Canada" motto. "Around the world, Conservative parties rarely win elections unless they become identified as the party of patriotism; certainly that has been true of the Republicans in the United States and the Conservatives of Great Britain," wrote Flanagan. "But we would have to work to reclaim the ground of Canadian patriotism that the Liberals had managed to appropriate for themselves."[29]

The 2002–03 political debates over Canada's possible participation in the U.S.-led coalition to topple Saddam Hussein in Iraq brought Harper's worldview into sharp focus. The debates laid bare Harper's antipathy towards the Liberals and his disdain for multilateralism as embodied by the United Nations. The Chrétien government, in what was an eleventh-hour decision just before the first U.S. bombs fell on Baghdad, decided Canada could not join the attack because it was not sanctioned by a new UN Security Council resolution authorizing force. Harper vehemently opposed the government's decision on several grounds: he believed existing UN resolutions on Iraq, which were routinely ignored, provided the authority for an attack. "Our position is that current United Nations resolutions provide sufficient international justification for action." In addition, Harper saw Canada's bilateral relationship with the U.S. as paramount – it trumped the UN. Moreover, Harper saw it as offensive for Canadian foreign policy interests to be essentially dictated by the UN.

In the first Iraq debate in the House of Commons on 1 October
2002, Harper said Canada's response would be "a test of its values, vision, reliability as an ally, and its sense of international responsibility." He expressed willingness to work outside the UN if necessary to
stop Saddam, thereby distinguishing himself from the Liberals, who
generally insisted on working within the UN. "Whether or not the
Security Council passes a new resolution, a clear and unmistakable
message must be sent to Saddam Hussein that his failure to comply
completely with not only UN weapons inspection, but also with the
removal of any and all weapons of mass destruction and their components, constitutes legitimate ground for direct action to remove
the threat of those weapons."

Harper attacked the Liberals for their "neutralist" position, criticizing the UN as ineffective and Chrétien for being bound by what
he saw as the waffling of the Security Council. "The government
undermines Canada's reputation with its allies and does nothing
to uphold the credibility of the United Nations by not joining in
sending a clear message to Hussein that failure to comply will
bring consequences."

In the second Iraq debate in the Commons on 29 January 2003,
Harper again stressed that Canada could not be bound by the will
of the United Nations. "Let us talk about the importance of the United Nations. Since the Gulf War in 1991, it has passed some fifteen
resolutions. It is important for the UN's credibility to have these resolutions respected. If Saddam Hussein can ignore some fifteen resolutions on this matter, what value will the United Nations have in
the future?" Harper argued. "In my opinion, if the United Nations
cannot act in the future, it is up to each sovereign nation to take its
own decisions." Fellow MPs Chuck Strahl, Jason Kenney, and Stockwell Day echoed the leader's position: If an ineffective UN could not
deal with Iraq, Canada must not be bound by it.

Harper's speech in the House of Commons on 20 March 2003,
after Chrétien announced Canada was opting out of the U.S.-led
coalition, was significant for another reason – it was quite literally
transformed into a tool of partisan politics. The speech, shot through
with denunciation of the Liberals, was reprinted and distributed to
party faithful, apparently as a fundraising initiative. Flanagan, his
former senior advisor, recalled how "thousands of copies" of the

speech were printed in pamphlet form and mailed out. "As far as I could judge, there was strong support from the grassroots of the party," Flanagan wrote.[30] This is perhaps one of the strongest examples of Harper's team using international affairs for domestic political gain. In the pamphlet, Harper offered his supporters one more scathing indictment of the Liberals:

> We will not be neutral. We will be with our allies and our friends, not militarily but in spirit we will be with them in America and in Britain for a short and successful conflict and for the liberation of the people of Iraq ... We will not be with our government, for this government, in taking the position it has taken, has betrayed Canada's history and its values. Reading only the polls and indulging in juvenile and insecure anti-Americanism, the government has, for the first time in our history, left us outside our British and American allies in their time of need. However, it has done worse. It has left us standing for nothing, no realistic alternative, no point of principle and no vision of the future. It has left us standing with no one ...[31]

Harper unleashed one more political rocket at the Liberals over Iraq. He wrote an op-ed article that appeared in the *National Post* almost a month after George W. Bush's infamous "Mission Accomplished" 1 May 2003 photo-op on a U.S. aircraft carrier, in which the U.S. president prematurely declared victory in Iraq. Harper wrote that the time had come to "rethink the fundamentals of Canada's foreign policy" because a "series of events since 9-11 has laid bare the failure of the Liberals to uphold Canada's values and interests in the world." He derided Canada's past adherence to UN multilateralism and – ignoring the commitments to it by Diefenbaker and Mulroney – labelled it an entirely Liberal phenomenon. He accused the Liberals of a "weak nation strategy" that used "multilateral participation to conceal and deny dependency on its key ally" and called for unequivocal support for the United States to overcome the "unreliable" rules of the multilateral system. "The time has come to recognize that the United States will continue to exercise unprecedented power in a world where international rules are unreliable and where the security and advancing of the free, democratic order still depends significantly on the possession and use of military might."³²

In a separate op-ed, this one published less than two weeks after the invasion, Harper had taken his argument to a wider audience: the American public. Harper co-wrote a much shorter but no less forceful op-ed article with his foreign affairs critic, Stockwell Day, which ran in the *Wall Street Journal* under the headline "Canadians Stand with You." They accused Chrétien of making a "serious mistake" by keeping Canada out of the Iraq coalition. Harper and Day brought a domestic disagreement to the American public: "Make no mistake, as our allies work to end the reign of Saddam and the brutality and aggression that are the foundations of his regime, Canada's largest opposition party, the Canadian Alliance will not be neutral. In our hearts and minds, we will be with our allies and friends. And Canadians will be overwhelmingly with us," they wrote. "But we will not be with the Canadian government."³³

There could be no clearer rejection of "water's edge" politics.

In the fullness of time, those grand gestures would bring Harper and his political allies crashing down on the wrong side of history. I got a first-hand preview of the anti-American uprising that would eventually tear through Iraq and leave the country awash in blood in the years to come. It came in mid-April 2003, when I visited the Siad family in the relatively comfortable Baghdad suburb of Al-Adhamiyah about a half-hour drive from the Palestine Hotel where I was staying. It was the week after U.S. Marines pulled down the Saddam statue in central Baghdad across from the hotel, cementing the fall of Iraq to the American-led invading coalition. Saddam was driven from power, and into hiding. Baghdad was in chaos. It was being looted and burned as traumatized Iraqis came to terms with the loss of their dictator and the sudden appearance of foreign troops on their streets.

The Siad household appeared to be an oasis of civility in this chaos. The only sign of war in their neighbourhood was the bombed-out telephone exchange a few streets from their house – a mangled pile of concrete and steel. Inside their home, a veritable feast awaited us: pitchers of chilled pomegranate juice and a buffet of fish, lamb, rice, vegetables, salad, and hummus. Refrigeration requires electricity and there wasn't much of that in Baghdad at this moment.

The sitting room was bustling with activity. Children were running around, and older men were stopping by to see the visitors – myself and two other foreign journalists. We had asked the driver we were sharing to take us to meet an Iraqi family that had survived the recent twenty-one-day invasion. He thought the Siad family would fit the bill.

As we settled in, we couldn't help but notice the large framed picture of a youthful, smiling Saddam Hussein on top of an upright piano. We were soon joined by the three Siad sisters – twenty-three-year-old Arwa, nineteen-year-old Raghda, and sixteen-year-old Lubna – who told us more about their family and why that picture was so prominently displayed in their main sitting room. "We love Saddam Hussein very much," Arwa told us. "He has the power from God. He is not a normal man."

Raghda, wearing a green T-shirt and flared jeans embroidered with beads, bowed her head and looked away. "Look at my sister. She is crying because Saddam is gone," said Arwa, who spoke English better than her sisters, in a soft, melodic tone. She was dressed more conservatively in a floor-length gown and scarf.

Lubna leaned over to whisper something to Arwa.

"My sister says to you, 'We are Fedayeen,'" Arwa said. "In the school, we were taught to use arms."

In the presence of their older relatives, the Siad sisters went on to explain that they had trained as guerrilla fighters for two months the previous summer near Baghdad with the Jerusalem Brigade, also known as Al Quds, a group of irregular Iraqi fighters who were extremely loyal to Saddam and had links to groups that claimed responsibility for suicide bombings against Israeli targets.

Once the ice had been broken on that subject, the sisters pulled out two dozen or so photographs from their summer training course. They were wearing military fatigues in all of them. In one, they were standing by a bus in a group of about a dozen with a gray-haired male instructor. In others, they were preening in groups of three or four. Always they were in a desert setting, always clad in fatigues, and occasionally with an AK-47. In one, Raghda was in profile, bent at the knees, with both her arms straight out in front holding a handgun.

"We don't want Americans walking in our streets," Arwa said in her singsong voice. "We must take them out of here, over our dead bodies."

Lubna, dressed in black head to toe in a tapered blouse, slacks, and shoes, pulled a heart-shaped locket out of her blouse. Inside was a picture of Saddam's face. "Saddam Hussein wants us to liberate the Palestinians from the Zionists," she explained. "But now we must liberate ourselves." Lubna said the time had come to make a plan to deal with the Americans. "We must be strong. We must get rid of them, kick them out."

We bade our polite farewells, after taking a few photographs of our own. I don't know what became of the Siad sisters after that, and as far as I know neither do the two other journalists who travelled with me. I suppose it's possible they were pulling our legs, and having one on at our expense to ease the boredom of the bombing lockdown they'd just endured. But the sentiment they represented was real. In the decade to come, about half a million Iraqis would die in the ensuing uprising and continuing violence, along with about 4,500 U.S. soldiers.

Saddam Hussein's suspected arsenal of weapons of mass destruction – the rationale for the U.S.-led invasion – was eventually proven to have been fiction. U.S. president George W. Bush and British prime minister Tony Blair would leave their respective offices with their legacies tarnished by Iraq. Chrétien left Canadian politics with his very much burnished by his decision to just say no to the Americans.

More than a decade later, Chrétien said he got along fine with Bush during the period. His real problem was with Blair. "To be honest, the president was very nice to me about it. He was never tough or unpleasant. He never put a lot of pressure on me. It was Tony Blair who had that job. Tony was to look after the colony, you know," Chrétien told the December 2015 meeting of the Canadian American Business Council in Ottawa. Chrétien recalled a conversation with Blair in South Africa, where he made a strong pitch for Canada to join the anti-Iraq coalition.

"He said to me, 'Jean, we have to get rid of Saddam. He's a terrible dictator.' I said, 'Of course, but if we are in business of taking care of the people we don't like, why don't we do that in Zimbabwe here, next door?'

"He said, 'Jean, Saddam and Mugabe, it's not the same.'

"I said, 'No, it's not the same. Mugabe has no oil.'"

Then Chrétien delivered his punch line: "He didn't talk to me for a year."

Harper eventually admitted he had made a mistake about Iraq. During the 2008 federal election campaign, Bloc Québécois leader Gilles Duceppe pressed him on the issue. Their exchange happened on a televised leaders' debate, five years after the Iraq invasion, and after the hugely unpopular war was raging. "It was absolutely an error," Harper said of his earlier support of the Iraq war. "The evaluation of weapons of mass destruction proved not to be correct – that's absolutely true."[34] That admission did not hurt Harper. Under his leadership, the Conservatives went on win their second minority government in 2008. Iraq had simply ceased to be an issue in Canadian politics.

Harper had successfully adjusted his foreign policy outlook, dictated by the heat of domestic political warfare. It would not be the last time he did so.

CHAPTER THREE

Elusive Endgames in Afghanistan and Libya

MARCH 2006

I'm bouncing along the gravel roads of Kandahar Air Field in a bus carrying an entourage of journalists, just after Stephen Harper's military transport plane has landed in Afghanistan. Harper has been the prime minister of Canada for a little over a month and he's making his first foreign trip. After two days of travel, he emerges from the belly of a Hercules C-130. "It's pretty desolate scenery," the prime minister declares as he takes his first steps on Afghan soil under a dull gray sky, the remnant of a fierce dust storm. "It's exciting. What can I say?" Harper immediately acknowledges that the country he has left behind may be ambivalent towards this military mission. "Just remember I was lower in the polls and I won."

Our military escorts take the group of journalists accompanying Harper, seventeen of us, to a separate bus for a preliminary tour of the base. All of this is unfolding under a cone of silence, agreed to by the Parliamentary Press Gallery for security reasons. Soon, the new prime minister's mission here will no longer be a secret to the Canadian public, or to the insurgents here. And before we leave Kandahar, the Prime Minister's Office will do their best to keep a few more secrets.

As our bus bumps along, our military escorts crack jokes about "Emerald Lake," the giant green sewage lagoon that we pass. Depending on which way the desert wind blows, its rancid stench periodically wafts across this base, a long maze of prefabricated buildings and metal shipping containers. There's even a wooden boardwalk with a small food court boasting well-known pizza and burger joints. Relatively speaking, this is a suburban heaven on earth compared to the otherwise medieval geography outside the base. We are fifteen kilometres due east of Kandahar City, on the footprint of what was once an international airport built by the United States government in the 1960s. Afghanistan's second city is a maze of orangey-brown, mud-walled compounds, the tallest no more than two storeys, encircled by jagged gray mountain peaks.

This area was the birthplace of the Taliban, the region from which the September 11 attacks on the United States were masterminded. In the months to come it will be site of the rebirth of a reconstituted Taliban/al-Qaida insurgency that will leave Western military forces, including Canada's, fighting at a level Canadians have not experienced in more than fifty years. This is also the place where Stephen Harper will commit his first major act of foreign policy. Part of it will be a propaganda campaign to persuade Canadians that a fierce war is not what is really going on here.

Our bus winds its way to a macabre parking lot. Warehoused in this engineering compound are the mangled metal hulks of several large Canadian military vehicles, among them a Bison armoured vehicle, a G-Wagon, and a LAV-3. They are graphic and vivid representations of the deadly power of the various improvised explosive devices, rocket-propelled grenades, and suicide bombers that Canadian military personnel are currently facing in Afghanistan. Two months earlier, Canadian diplomat Glynn Berry was killed in his G-Wagon when a suicide bomber rammed it. Is this his battered vehicle before us? We'll never find out.

The Prime Minister's Office ensured that plenty of images of Harper were generated during this trip. He was seen sitting in the cockpit of the Hercules, chowing down with troops in the mess hall, clad in a flak jacket for a helicopter ride. But an image of the prime minister standing with the gutted remains of a bombed out G-Wagon wasn't the sort of picture his office wanted Canadians to see. Yet this compound was one of the first destinations the military wanted to show us after we touched down here. The troops themselves wanted Canadians to see the carnage wrought by the terrorist insurgency intent on driving Canadian soldiers and their allies from this land. Military officials said a visit here was on the prime minister's itinerary for the next day. And then, it was not. According to the PMO, it was never part of the plan.

Harper's office did its best to prevent the journalists on this trip from any assessment of the real risks to Canadian soldiers here.

When the Harper government assumed power in February 2006, the vanquished Liberals of Paul Martin handed the Conservatives a responsibility with life-and-death political ramifications: a combat mission in southern Afghanistan that was less than a year old. This region was the most violent in Afghanistan. As the traditional home of the Taliban, Kandahar city and province were the closest thing to a front line in the asymmetrical war against al-Qaida that would break out with a vengeance in the summer of 2006, just a few months after Harper first set foot here.

Before the uprising, eight members of the Canadian military had died in Afghanistan. But on Harper's watch, the death toll would rise to 158. Harper was now overseeing the bloodiest military operation since the Korean War of 1950–53. Canada was embroiled in a full-scale war, and like all wartime governments, the Harper Conservatives were determined to manage communications around it. Their communications offensive was launched with one goal in mind: minimize any and all political damage from the inevitable carnage that would unfold on Afghanistan's desert battlefields. "It was spin. There was an unending stream of bad news, 2007–08, and I think the Harper government was trying to find a bit of sunshine in an otherwise extraordinarily gray time," retired lieutenant general Andrew Leslie, the commander of the Canadian Army between 2006 and 2010, told me in the months before his successful run as a Liberal in 2015.

From Kandahar, we flew by helicopter to Canada's Provincial Reconstruction Team, a large walled compound named Camp Nathan Phillips in the heart of Kandahar City. This trip was organized by the Harper team to help us paint a portrait of a benevolent development operation in action. But it didn't unfold as smoothly as they would have liked.

We avoided Kandahar City altogether, flying in a small armada of helicopters borrowed from the American air force. The governor of Kandahar province, Assadullah Khalid, greeted us when we arrived. Clad in a dapper blue blazer and crisp, white open-collared dress shirt, Khalid was eager to explain the threats facing his country. I was part of a small group that stopped to talk with him. "I will tell the Canadian people we have to defend (against) terrorism in Afghanistan," he told us. "If we don't do this, now, today in Afghanistan, tomorrow we will need to do this in Europe and in Canada."

History proved him correct.

One of Harper's handlers decided it was time to move along, and bellowed: "The prime minister's schedule is continuing." We didn't move. Neither did the Canadian soldiers watching Khalid and us. So the governor carried on, telling us how Afghans had had enough of the last thirty years of war. Khalid was particularly concerned about the new phenomenon of suicide bombings; Afghanistan had experienced many forms of violence in the preceding decades but this was something new. Afghans, he said, want peace, stability, and "they want reconstruction." But now, he said, "We just have suicides, which is very new in Afghanistan. And when we arrest a couple of weeks ago ... a network of terrorists ... They are coming from abroad."

And with that, we were all whisked away, straggling to catch up to the prime minister. Harper was posing with some local mechanics working on a pair of banged-up cars that had seen better days, but were relatively unscathed. They would soon be requisitioned by the new Afghan police force that Canada was helping to train.

On the second day, Harper addressed about a thousand coalition troops, the vast majority from Canada's contingent of 2,200 military personnel. He boldly pledged that Canada would never "cut and run" from Afghanistan while he was prime minister. In fact, five years later the last Canadian troops were withdrawn from southern Afghanistan. The military would remain for three more years as trainers of Afghan security forces. In 2014, during Harper's eighth year in power, all military personnel were pulled out of Afghanistan once and for all.

The war in Afghanistan dominated Stephen Harper's era in power, even though it was well under way by the time he arrived in office. Nor was it the only conflict he had to contend with in the first half of his rule, a time when he was governing with minority mandates. The situation in Libya was deteriorating in the months leading up to the 2011 federal election that would bring him his first majority government. In February 2011, the popular uprising that would ultimately lead to the downfall of Moammar Gadhafi began, after four decades of totalitarian rule. In March 2011, the

United Nations passed resolutions to protect Libyan civilians and enforce a no-fly zone.

Harper sent Canada to war under the authority of the United Nations and the operational command of NATO, commiting significant military resources including fighter jets, a warship, and eventually the commander of the force, Lt-Gen. Charles Bouchard. As seasoned Canadian diplomats such as Louise Frechette had previously noted, Harper usually displayed "a distinct reticence" towards the UN. Frechette, a former UN deputy secretary-general, wrote that the prime minister has "shown no particular interest in the life of the organization," with one major exception – invoking it as providing the mandate for having Canadian combat troops in Afghanistan.[1] This would serve his purpose in Libya as well.

Some analysts posited that Harper was trying to craft a new narrative that celebrated Canada as a so-called "warrior culture." They said Harper's approach to Afghanistan was part of his broader plan to "redefine the Canadian identity with a Conservative twist, linking pride in the nation and a celebration of Canada with the military."[2] Others took a more nuanced view, especially in light of Harper's decision to join the fight in Libya. They said he was driven by a "call of duty," which they defined as his "strong belief that Canada cannot shirk from its duty or duck when bullets are flying, bombs are falling and global order is threatened."[3] Harper believed Canada had an obligation to support like-minded allies who were coming to the assistance of those in distress.[4] As an essay in the 2015 *Canada among Nations* compilation argued: "Harper's code, which emphasizes a duty to NATO allies, making foreign policy decision on the basis of values and deep-held notions of right and wrong, and that downplays – at the margins – the role of formal international institutions and hard-and-fast legal obligations, has emerged at a time when legitimate doubts about the ability of the postwar institutions to manage conflict and avert catastrophe are common."[5]

Harper expressed that view in his 2006 speech to Canadian troops in Kandahar. "You can't lead from the bleachers," Harper told them, against a backdrop of dent-free military vehicles. "I want Canada to be a leader ... A country that really leads, not a country that just follows ... Serving in a UN-mandated, Canadian-led security operation that is in the very best of the Canadian tradition." This assertion didn't make Harper a follower of the "liberal internationalist consensus" which many of his critics would accuse him of abandoning. Harper might have harboured skepticism about the methods of the institutions that were created after 1945, but that didn't mean he rejected "the legitimacy or usefulness of the UN-centred, law-based system that the United States built in the wake of World War II, but his moral code questions whether strict adherence to the letter of the law should be an end unto itself."[6]

Harper may have been driven by a deeply held sense of moral duty, but he was also governed by domestic politics. The fact of the matter was that Canada's engagement in Kandahar became increasingly unpopular once Berry was killed in the suicide bomb attack, and as the death toll of Canadian soldiers rose.

Somehow Canadians had failed to recognize that Kandahar province was an incredibly dangerous place. It is the spiritual birthplace of the Taliban, which governed Afghanistan from 1996 until late 2001, when they were routed by U.S. airstrikes and Afghan rebel ground forces following the September 11 attacks. The Taliban gave Osama bin Laden the sanctuary he needed to plan and execute 9-11. It wasn't as if Canadians were somehow hermetically sealed from that reality – journalists covered the early days of the post 9-11 war more thoroughly than any recent conflict leading up to it, and certainly any since.

I got my first good look at Kandahar City in May 2002 just months after the Taliban had been defeated there. Foreboding hung over Kandahar in those first relatively quiet post-9-11 months. It was as thick and oppressive as the fifty-degree dust-encrusted humidity. Travelling discreetly by car with a local fixer and driver, we explored the sprawling city in an effort to talk to locals and international organizations. We scurried in and out of our car and into buildings, because we had no security of our own. We were unarmed and at least one member of our entourage – me – was wearing a very large target on his back. Rumours were rife that the Taliban's one-eyed leader, Mullah Omar, was alive and well and plotting revenge. One rumour making the rounds was that Taliban and al-Qaida leadership had put out the word that killing a Westerner – a reporter would do, but an American commando would be much better – would earn a ticket to heaven.

At one stop, we scurried up a ladder to the roof of a mosque where I found sixteen-year-old Baqt Jan. The teenager was armed with an AK-47 machine gun and at least three rocket-propelled grenades. "The Taliban is around here," he told me through my translator, from behind a tower that rendered him invisible from the ground but offered a good view of the prehistoric-looking gray hills beyond this low-lying city. "They might attack us. That is why we keep these weapons."

A few days later, I was back on the landing strip of Kandahar Air Field as the U.S. general appointed by President George W. Bush to command the war on terrorism was walking towards the terminal. Having just landed, General Tommy Franks was quick to offer a few thoughts to the journalists and military personnel accompanying him over the dusty ground. "The mission that we were given by our own president," Franks explained, "is to destroy the terrorist networks in Afghanistan, destroy the Taliban. I don't know about you, but I'm not yet convinced that that work is totally done. And as long as I'm not convinced, you and more of my friends are going to be here, working with Afghans to give Afghanistan a chance, something they haven't had in a long, long time."

Five years later, I was back in Afghanistan for the second time in as many years with Harper and his heavily guarded entourage. On his first trip in 2006 Harper didn't shy away from talk of combat, of "taking on the dangers and advancing the kind of things that go to the heart of what Canada is all about as a country." But by 2007, Canadian deaths had risen to fifty-four. While Harper was making his return voyage to Central Asia – a trip that took two full days – twenty-four people died in two separate attacks in Afghanistan. The violence was spreading beyond southern Afghanistan to the relatively peaceful northern town of Kunduz and the eastern city of Gardez. On his May 2007 trip, the prime minister chose his words carefully: he was laying the groundwork for a narrative that attempted to play down the bloody Taliban insurgency.

Harper started out in the capital, Kabul, where he visited the Aschiana co-ed school near a busy downtown boulevard dotted with shops and a steady flow of pedestrians. This part of Kabul had the appearance of a peaceful, bustling Asian city. The European Commission and the Swedish government provided most of the school's annual budget but it also received about $40,000 from the Foreign

Affairs Department. This was not the first time its students were exposed to Conservative politicians trying to sell a softer view of the Afghan mission to the Canadian public. Earlier the same year, before he was shuffled to the defence portfolio, foreign affairs minister Peter MacKay had visited, and in November 2006, a group of students spent some time with international co-operation minister Josée Verner. She didn't actually make it to their school; instead they were bused over to the Canadian Embassy compound to meet her.

The travelling media arrived in the school's inner courtyard shortly before Harper, an arrangement facilitated by the prime minister's handlers so we would be able to set up our cameras to record his arrival. Harper's shiny black armoured SUV pulled into the courtyard and the prime minister emerged. Three boys and three girls waited for him, holding flowers. "Why don't we get a photo with the group of kids here?" Harper said, barely skipping a beat after getting out of the vehicle.

After a short pause for pictures, Harper moved through the bustling building. Like any elementary school, it was a hive of activity – more than usual on this day. As the prime minister moved from one classroom to the next, where he saw music, art, and trades such as carpentry being taught, heavily armed Canadian commandoes followed him, never more than a few steps away. Before we got inside, I saw one climb up a makeshift ladder straddling the side of the building and quickly take up his position on the roof.

Inside, a young girl sat among a group of painters and offered the prime minister a brush, but he politely declined. "I don't want to spoil it. I think she's doing much better than I could," said Harper. "I have no talent for painting at all. Zero." The tour of the school ended after forty-five minutes, but not before the prime minister and his staff distributed pencil cases, exercise books, and candies to the students.

A short time later, Harper was at the leafy green palace of President Hamid Karzai, whom he had visited briefly during his first trip to Afghanistan in March 2006. "We are not daunted by shadows because we carry the light that defines them – the light of freedom and democracy, of human rights and the rule of law. The light of this country's tangible progress to date, and its determination and hope for the future," Harper told Karzai.

Karzai said he hoped Canadian troops would remain in Afghanistan to help fight the scourge of terrorism in his country, one that
would become a threat to Canada as well if it was not contained.
But before their joint press conference ended, Harper managed to
soften the tone, disregarding consideration of the military situation.
After handing out the candies and pencil cases at the school, the
prime minister pulled out one more special gift for one more special
little boy. It was a tiny Ottawa Senators hockey jersey, a gift for
Karzai's four-month-old son. Harper held it up for the assembled
cameras – local Afghan media, international correspondents based
here, and us, the entourage that accompanied him from Canada. A
beaming Karzai proudly accepted the gift. He said that he hoped his
son would be able to play hockey "as soon as he can walk on his feet."

In March 2008 I was back in Kabul, at another school brimming
with hope – this one outside the bubble of the Harper PMO.
The grounds of the Lycée Malalay were idyllic on the first day of
school, two days after Afghanistan celebrated its New Year. Two
young boys swung from the top bars of a tall play-structure, while
girls in bright dresses paraded through the sun-dappled playground.
A large blue sign stood at school's entrance bearing its name and the
message: "Made possible by the support of the French people."

Shortly before my arrival, Canada's aid strategy was criticized in
a report from a government-appointed panel headed by former Liberal cabinet minister John Manley. The Manley Commission offered
Harper some political cover by recommending an extension of the
combat mission for two years beyond the 2009 deadline for withdrawal. One of its major findings was to do something about the
fact that the $120 million in annual development spending that
Canada was sending to Afghanistan was all but invisible. The commission said that the Canadian International Development Agency
ought to be branding its spending by finding a "signature project"
– maybe a hospital or dam – that could carry the Canadian logo, to
show the people of Kandahar that our country was doing some
good for them. This would be better, the report argued, than the
current practice of disbursing Canadian aid funds through UN agencies, the World Bank, and other international groups, which then
filtered them into broad spending envelopes for worthy, yet faceless,
international initiatives. Bev Oda, who had since succeeded Verner

in the development portfolio, had previously expressed much skepticism about signature projects. So too did many aid agencies, who saw this as an impure version of true development work.

France's decision to reopen this historic young women's academy in 2002 was certainly appreciated by the students here on this 2008 spring morning. Afghan education minister Hanif Atmar read out a letter of thanks to the two hundred students and guests in the school's assembly hall. This school and one other academy for boys were the centrepiece of France's development strategy for Afghanistan. The French government had easily sunk tens of millions of dollars into this place. "France, like Afghanistan," French ambassador Regis Koetschet told me, "attaches great importance to the education of young girls."

Clad in blue jeans under her blue waistcoat and scarf, twenty-year-old Hilay Siddiquizi was a good example of modern Afghanistan. She graduated from the school after returning here in late 2001 after the fall of the Taliban, and after her family had spent eight years as refugees in Pakistan. "I never thought one day we'd sit in our country and watch people speak on the stage," she told me, sitting next to her mother, Asifa, who had been a teacher in the pre-Taliban era. Hilay was two years away from finishing her teacher training and graduating university with an English literature degree. Now she sat watching a new generation of girls starting down the same road she had travelled at her old school. Stories such as Hilay Siddiquizi's were examples of the tangible difference Western countries were making in Afghanistan. It was an authentic slice of something positive.

The Harper government was starving for such feel-good narratives about the war. They did everything they could to invent them, but their results paled in comparison to scenarios such as this. The Conservatives adopted and honed what was a relatively unheard of and insidious communications control tool: the Message Event Proposal. The MEP, as it came to be known in the federal public service, was a template that would become the standard, mandatory form that every federal public servant and political communications staffer would be forced to use. It had one goal: to plan, in advance, every conceivable public utterance by a politician on a given topic. If an MP was going to announce some money in a constituency, an MEP was needed. Planning a ribbon cutting? An MEP would choreo-

graph the event. This tool even extended to speeches and public appearances by senior diplomats, including ambassadors in foreign
countries. Every possible public event would have to be mapped out
in advance. The report, sometimes several pages long, was then to
be submitted to the Prime Minister's Office, or its public service
arm, the Privy Council Office.

In late 2009, I obtained more than one thousand pages of MEP
documents from several government departments, including the
Department of National Defence, Foreign Affairs, and the now defunct Canadian International Development Agency using the Access to Information Act. The content of this tall stack of documents
was striking in its uniformity. They all had the same headings:
Event; Event type; Desired headline; Key messages; Media lines;
Strategic objectives; Desired sound bite; Ideal speaking backdrop;
Ideal event photograph; Tone; Attire; Rollout materials; Background; Strategic considerations.

As I wrote with my colleague Jim Bronskill from the Canadian
Press at the time, the MEP was part of a systematic effort by the Conservatives to "persuade Canadians their country was primarily engaged in development work to rebuild a shattered nation rather than
hunting down and killing an emboldened insurgency." The government used MEPs to spell out the exact words that it wanted to hear
coming out of the mouths of its senior diplomats, aid workers, and
cabinet ministers in 2007–2008. The Conservatives attempted to pre-
plan and spoonfeed the actual components of a story – quotes,
sound bites, key messages, as well as manipulating the visual ele-
ments of a narrative through the use of staged backdrops and carefully considered photo-ops.

As the July 2007 deployment date for the first group of Quebec-
based troops was drawing closer, the Conservative communications-
spinners directed their attention to selling the war in what is
arguably Canada's most anti-war province. As the Royal 22nd Regi-
ment – the Van Doos – was preparing to be deployed, demonstrators
marched through the streets of Quebec City and a June 2006 poll
showed that 70 per cent of Quebeckers were opposed to the war.[7]
The MEP for that event suggested giving the Van Doos a "compassionate" send-off that was designed to "showcase the achievements

in development." Verner, the French-speaking minister for CIDA, was tapped to be the spokesperson for the event.

In May 2008, the Canadian death toll in Afghanistan stood at eighty-three, more than half the eventual total. The weight of the multiplying casualties was pressing down on Harper personally. To his immense credit, he telephoned the families of every fallen soldier, but he found himself "making far more calls than he would have anticipated."[8] So Canada's ambassador to Afghanistan, Arif Lalani, was brought home to help change the narrative of the war from combat to development. And their MEPs made it clear they were leaving nothing to chance; one document prepared for the Privy Council Office said: "Desired sound bite: 'Canada's mission in Afghanistan is refocusing its mission towards development, reconstruction and diplomatic efforts.'"

The MEP for Lalani's trip listed ten possible interviews that he might give to major print, television, and radio stations between 26 and 30 May. *Question Period*, the Sunday morning political talk show on CTV, was the government's favourite. "The appearance would serve to move the national narrative forward beyond the parliamentary arena and refocus Canadian interest in Canada's civilian efforts in Afghanistan, emphasizing development, reconstruction and diplomacy efforts," the MEP said. The PMO also recommended an interview with CBC's Peter Mansbridge because his program was seen as "a window into the lives of Canadian decision makers and influencers." The PMO figured a Lalani appearance on CBC could be leveraged "to stress Canada's increased civilian focus, emphasizing development, reconstruction and diplomacy efforts."

Years later, I read some of this to Leslie, the former army commander turned politician. After a brief pause, he said: "It was an attempt to spin the message away from essentially a militarily dominated information flow to one which was more focused on diplomacy, development."

The government also decided to mobilize some carefully chosen members of the Canadian International Development Agency to speak to the media. An MEP laid out the rationale for this: "First-hand accounts by Canadians who have lived and worked in Afghanistan add credibility to Canada's role." The MEPs also told aid workers exactly what to say. This was the desired headline that the government wanted to see from planned interviews with members of the Canadian International Development Agency: "Perspective from the ground: Canada makes progress in terms of development and reconstruction in Afghanistan."

The MEPs described exactly how two particular CIDA employees, Helene Kadi and Kevin Rex, were going to help convey that perspective. For a scheduled 5 February 2008 interview, Kadi's MEP outlined the "key message" that she was expected to deliver to a CBC radio station in Thunder Bay: "As a returned CIDA field staff, I have seen and experienced first-hand the accomplishments and results achieved in Afghanistan, thanks to Canada's role in that country." The "key message" for Rex's 12 February 2008 interview with the Alberta weekly newspaper, the *Airdire Echo,* was to be this: "As a returned CIDA field staff, I have seen and experienced first-hand the accomplishments and results achieved in Afghanistan, thanks to Canada's role in that country." In their separate MEPs, the plan was for Kadi and Rex to utter this identical statement in their separate interviews: "While the pace of progress may appear to be slow to those on the outside, I can personally attest to the reality of progress and the results of positive advancement in Afghanistan." Beyond an insidious level of message control that approached the Orwellian, the MEPs also focused on unfiltered broadcast interviews rather than interviews with print journalists, which greatly reduced the prospect of any critical questioning.

Within the federal bureaucracy, this new level of spin was hard for some to swallow. At the peak of the combat, there were close to three thousand troops in theatre while there were maybe fifty civilians. "They had a problem with the narrative. It didn't jibe with reality," I was told by one senior government official who worked in the Privy Council Office, and who spoke on the condition of anonymity because they didn't want to lose their job or be reprimanded for speaking to a journalist without authorization. "There was an awful lot of emperor-has-no-clothes moments," the source added. "That was clearly what the message was – Afghanistan is about development, CIDA, building schools, building roads, helping Afghans, which is all good stuff ... but not necessarily to the exclusion of reality."[9]

In 2008, the Canadian government settled in on its signature aid project for Afghanistan: it wasn't a school or a hospital. It was the Dahla Dam rehabilitation. The $50 million project was designed to irrigate the arid Afghan south to help farmers prosper. In 2011, when the Harper government withdrew combat troops from Kandahar, Canada's involvement with the project came to an end. The last of Canada's military personnel left Afghanistan once and for all when their three-year, non-combat training mission came to an end in 2014. In January 2016, the new governor of Kandahar called upon the country's Ministry of Water and Energy to investigate what had happened to the dam. Governor Humayun Azizi said an unknown quantity of the $71 million spent on a recently completed upgrade had been embezzled, while 40 per cent of the dam was still filled with silt.[10]

The Dahla Dam corruption probe was one just one small piece of misery to befall Afghanistan in 2015. The United Nations reported that 2015 was the worst year for civilian casualties in Afghanistan, with 3,500 killed and almost 7,500 wounded. That included a 37 per cent rise in the number of women killed, and a 14 per cent increase in the number of children. By then not only Canada, but most of its Western allies had withdrawn all their forces from Afghanistan, leaving 9,800 American troops behind.

Afghanistan's decline was epitomized by the Taliban's April 2016 attack in the heart of downtown Kabul, when a suicide truck-bomb detonated near a government building killed more than sixty and injured three hundred, including many women and children. Scanning the news photos of that spring day, one struck me as particularly moving. An Associated Press photo showed two boys no more than ten years old, each with a full backpack, trudging down a rain-slicked boulevard past several armed men surveying the aftermath of the bombing. As they went purposely on their way, these boys didn't look any less determined than the students I had seen on my visits to Kabul in 2007 and 2008, when there was at least the appearance of a country moving towards a brighter future. The two boys were doing something that Afghans have become very good at: getting on with their day, in defiance of their country's dark, violent legacy.

*   *   *

11 OCTOBER 2011. TRIPOLI
A black motorcade rumbles down a boulevard strewn with graffiti, garbage, discarded water bottles, and burned-out cars as it enters
the sprawling tree-lined compound of Bab al-Azizia. Until recently,
this resplendent palace was the home of Libyan president Moammar Gadhafi. It has been six weeks since rebels drove Gadhafi out of
Tripoli and it is just nine days before his life will come to a barbaric end, about 400 kilometres east of here. Gunfire crackles in the distance as foreign affairs minister John Baird steps out of his vehicle
and walks towards the large gutted building that Gadhafi once
called home. Under dark clouds, Baird enters the wasteland of graffiti and garbage where a macabre and festive scene is unfolding. The
building he approaches is riddled with bullet holes, covered with
more graffiti and strewn with yet more garbage.

There's a makeshift market in what was once a vast entryway. A series of tables and stalls are set up where a few families mingle. Most
of the people congregating around the stalls or skulking through
the unlit upper floors are teenagers and young adults. Three tables
sell souvenirs of the civil war taking place in this country, an array
of goods bearing the red, green, and black tricolour of the country's
freedom-fighters: ball caps, necklaces, earrings, flags, pins, and wrist-
bands. Doctored photos depicting Gadhafi in various humiliations
are on offer at another table: in one he's dressed as a baby while in
others he's pushing a wheelbarrow or emerging from a sewer. A for-
lorn popcorn machine sits silently in one corner.

Baird hands out a few souvenirs of his own, Canada flag pins, and
he poses for photos with the youths, many of whom have cellphone
cameras. The language barrier doesn't prevent what is a friendly exchange between these young shopkeepers and their Canadian guest.
There's even a smattering of English from one or two of them. Baird
is ushered away from the building to an open, treeless area where
there is a hole in the ground. It's the entrance to an underground
tunnel, part of what was Gadhafi's secret subterranean network.
"They go on for kilometres," Baird says. "It's just unbelievable."

Half an hour later, Baird's convoy departs. It passes evidence of
the nearly seven months of bombing that has taken place here, a UN-

sanctioned mission to protect civilians, commanded by a Canadian general working for NATO. It has also clearly hit Gadhafi where he once lived, leaving massive piles of crushed cement and twisted metal rods on the grounds of his former palace.

It was the most memorable of the many photo-ops on Baird's whirlwind, five-and-a-half-hour visit to Libya, the minister's second in less than four of the five months he had been on the job. This time he had come with $10 million to help the country secure weapons, including some capable of mass destruction. It was part of a Canadian show of support to get the country up and running, both politically and economically – especially its oilfields, where Canada's Suncor had been pumping 50,000 barrels of oil a day before the anti-Gadhafi uprising shut production down. Baird also reopened Canada's embassy, which had been closed for months because of the violence. Before he raised the Maple Leaf outside, he inspected the new bullet holes inside.

Baird said he was hoping that Canadian support might help disarm militias and lock down other vulnerable arsenals. Government officials who briefed me on the trip said they hoped the new funds would help the Libyan government reclaim the 23,000 shoulder-fired, anti-aircraft missile launchers still in circulation, and do something to curb the reality of guns everywhere. There were other more serious worries.

"We know there are seven warehouses of weapons of mass destruction, chemical weapons, that Gadhafi showed the world," Baird told me in a brief interview on the tarmac of the Tripoli airport as he was wrapping up his trip. "So we want to ensure that the people of Libya are kept safe and the people of the world are kept safe so they don't fall into the wrong hands." Baird hauled out the talking point that he'd been repeating about how he saw Libya's future: that the country wouldn't be able to go "from Gadhafi to Thomas Jefferson" overnight.

There were serious questions about the ability of Libya's rebels to govern the country if they were able to seize control of it. Some of Canada's allies didn't think the country's National Transitional Council had the military backing or the political acumen to govern. "We don't see them as a government in waiting; they're not capable enough of stepping into the regime's shoes once the regime collapses," one Western diplomat told me months earlier. But in June 2011, meeting some of the rebels on his first trip to Benghazi, Baird was impressed. "They couldn't be any worse than Colonel Gadhafi," he declared.

He could not have been more wrong.

Five years later, the world found itself dealing with something far worse than Moammar Gadhafi. It was called the Islamic State of Iraq and the Levant. It had established a foothold in Libya that was forcing the world to consider making it the target of another Western-led bombing campaign. After Gadhafi, Libya failed. It splintered into rival factions and heavily armed militias.

Remember all those unsecured weapons that Canada once had hopes of corralling? They had spread across Libya and North Africa like an explosion of magic fairy dust, bestowing a deadly bounty on the arsenals of ISIL and other militias.

*   *   *

On 24 November 2011, the Harper government declared its mission accomplished in Libya with an unprecedented display of military might on Parliament Hill. They put on a ceremony that cost taxpayers $850,000. Gadhafi had been killed a month earlier: the dictator had been pulled from a hole, beaten by a gang of rebels, and sodomized with a knife blade. "In terms of the particulars of the death of the former leader, I obviously don't take any great pleasure in that," Harper said shortly afterwards. "And obviously when you see things happen outside the rule of law, they concern you. But I also think we're all realistic enough to know that, given the way he had ruled the country, that the chances of him meeting an end like that were probably pretty high."

It was also a little more than three weeks since the NATO combat mission had been declared over. Canadian aircraft flew 1,500 sorties, about 10 per cent of the missions of the NATO coalition. On this day on Parliament Hill, the government staged an expensive tribute to them. There was an honour guard, marching bands, twenty-one-gun salute, and flybys by CF-18 fighter jets, a Polaris refuelling plane, and a gigantic C-17 Globemaster transport. But just like George W. Bush's ill-fated visit to the deck of an aircraft carrier in the spring of

2003, this Canadian declaration of mission accomplished was extremely premature.

After the expensive Parliament Hill flyover was finished and the hundred or so spectators had dispersed, Harper stood before the Senate and celebrated what was an artificial but convenient end to the military mission in Libya. "Heaven forbid that we should fail to do that of which we are capable, when the path of duty is clear," Harper said. "Canada is not that kind of nation. And Canadians are not that kind of people."

Libya would teeter for two more years before it finally plummeted into the abyss in February 2014, with the outbreak of a new civil war. In July 2014, Canada closed its embassy – the one I watched Baird reopen during his October 2011 trip – and moved it to Tunisia. Several hundred thousand Libyans also fled their country for Tunisia. Libya's government was forced to decamp to the eastern city of Tobruk while the capital, Tripoli, to the western edge, was taken over by a new Islamist movement called Libya Dawn. By late 2014, ISIL capitalized on the divide and reared its head in the eastern port of Derna.

"Violence and instability has escalated over the last four years, as competing extremist and militia groups vie for control and territory to avail themselves of Libya's abundant weapons," read the briefing note for Prime Minister Justin Trudeau that was prepared in the fall of 2015 by the Privy Council Office.

The memo outlined in stark detail the mess that the incoming Trudeau government would have to contend with in Libya, if it developed an appetite for involvement in that country again. It was also a testament to an epic global failure to lock down Libya's abundant supply of weapons. It noted that several terrorist groups, including ISIL and al-Qaida in the Islamic Maghreb, had taken advantage of the instability "to establish safe havens, train and conduct attacks across the region," making Libya a destination of choice for foreign fighters seeking to join ISIL or other groups. "The collapse of central authority along with insecure borders has permitted Libya to become an under-governed space, which serves as the centre for the illicit movement of people, weapons and drugs throughout the region, and a haven for militants from neighbouring countries. The security vacuum has been filled by numerous local militias which engage in wide-scale smuggling of arms and other goods," it said.

"Although the UN imposed an arms embargo on Libya at the start of the 2011 uprising, Libya has become one of the world's leading sources of illicit weapons. These are being sold to terrorist groups such as those in Mali, Tunisia, Chad, and Lebanon. According to a 2014 report from the UN Security Council's Libya sanctions committee, Libya is the primary source of the illegal weapons trade that is fuelling conflicts in at least 14 countries around the world."

Libya also became a haven for human traffickers who, who along with its militias, used it as a staging ground to fleece and then launch boatloads of desperate migrants across the Mediterranean Sea towards Europe. In the first five months of 2016, the United Nations High Commissioner for Refugees said more than 2,500 people died trying to cross the Mediterranean, a 35 per cent increase from January to May period the previous year.[11] Canada's Privy Council Office predicted the situation would get worse before it got better: "Should the conflict continue, and Libya's financial crisis worsen, the importance of these trafficking networks will grow. When Libyan financial institutions are no longer able to pay the salaries of militia members, the militias will turn increasingly to raising funds through human trafficking and other criminal activities."

By early 2016, ISIL gained control of land that stretched across Libya's Mediterranean coastline west of Tripoli to the central city of Sirte and to parts of Benghazi in the east, which led the U.S., France, and Britain to begin making plans for their second intervention in Libya in three years.[12] But Canada's new Liberal government wasn't interested in making any military commitments to Libya. In February 2016 Stephane Dion, the foreign affairs minister, said Canada wouldn't get involved unless there was a single Libyan government in place to speak for the country.[13]

A UN-backed unity government arrived in Libya by boat in April 2016 to set up shop in a fortified military base. But it more than had its work cut out for it. In May 2016, Canada's top general said this new government's performance would be a key determinant in whether the West would have to mount another military mission in Libya. General Jonathan Vance, the chief of the defence staff, said he was not convinced that "an inevitable Western intervention" in

Libya was on the horizon. Vance said Libya was "coming to grips with the new government," one that he said had a long way to go before it could form government institutions, "not to mention an armed forces that represents the country at large."

U.S. secretary of state John Kerry said in February 2016 that he was increasingly worried about the possibility of ISIL "metastasizing out to other countries, particularly Libya." More than five years after Baird declared that things couldn't get any worse in Libya, Kerry was pretty emphatic that they had. "The last thing in the world you want is a false caliphate with access to billions of dollars of oil revenue."[14] U.S. president Barack Obama later said that the "worst mistake" of his presidency was failing to prepare for the aftermath in Libya after the fall of Gadhafi.

Canada and its allies had no desire to stick around and help Libya rebuild after 2011, so collective international handwashing gave rise to chaos that threatened regional, and perhaps global, stability. The seemingly neat and tidy Libya mission also damaged the UN system itself because of what became known as "the big lie" behind it: that the Security Council resolution authorizing NATO to protect civilians had been exploited to justify regime change by overthrowing Gadhafi.[15] Remember that twisted pile of metal and cement Baird's convoy drove past in Bab al-Azizia? One explanation for it could have been the Tomahawk cruise missile that a British submarine in the Mediterranean Sea fired at Gadhafi's compound on 20 March 2011, three days after the UN Security Council resolution was passed. Then there's the May 2011 incident on the Mediterranean, when the Canadian frigate HMCS *Charlottetown* intercepted a tugboat loaded with weapons flying the flag of the Libyan rebels. It placed Canada in the heart of the debate over whether Canada was taking part in another part of NATO regime-change strategy: ignoring the arms embargo on Libya to help arm rebel forces to overthrow Gadhafi.[16]

A slickly produced YouTube video posted by NATO shows the Canadian warship intercepting the small tugboat in international waters off the coast of Libya. "There are lots of weapons and munitions on board from small ammunition to 105 Howitzer rounds and lots of explosives," radioes a Canadian officer. The rebels tell the Canadians they're on their way to Misrata to defend it from Gadhafi's forces. This is significant because the UN resolution also forbade arms transfers to either side of the Libyan conflict. The *Charlotte-town*'s commanding officer calls NATO headquarters and awaits instructions. NATO command allows the tugboat to carry on, fully loaded. Lt. Michael McWhinnie, a Canadian navy public-affairs officer, explains on camera that the tugboat "was transiting between two Libyan harbours" while the *Charlottetown*'s captain and crew "consulted NATO, received a legal opinion" and were told "release the vessel" and let it go on its way. The caption accompanying the video explains further, saying, "the arms had not come from outside Libya and were intended to defend civilians in Misrata."[17]

Bouchard, the Canadian general who commanded the NATO mission, made it clear that he had done everything possible to faithfully abide the rules of engagement. Bouchard said NATO's job was to stop the violence "against civilians, especially defenceless civilians – men, women and children who were being bombed indiscriminately." After the November 2011 ceremony on Parliament Hill, the general said, "I can tell you, hand on my heart, that our efforts were legal, ethical and moral."[18]

There is simply no reason to question Bouchard's sincerity. Even when considering that NATO forces regularly provided air support to Libyan rebels by targeting Gadhafi's forces – including in the fateful ground attack that eventually led to Gadhafi's death – a credible argument can be made, as one analyst put it, that while the Security Council resolution "did not specifically authorize this result, neither did it prohibit it."[19] But that misses a much larger point, one that has had tragic consequences for another country: Syria. In 2011 Russia and China, two permanent members of the Security Council, abstained when the Libya intervention was approved. But because they felt betrayed by how NATO had interpreted its UN mandate, they later used their vetoes to block any Security Council action on Syria. Russian president Vladimir Putin said NATO "violated the UN Security Council resolution" by undertaking active bombing instead of enforcing a no-fly zone. As a result, foreign minister Sergey Lavrov said Russia would refuse to allow any action in Syria because it "would never allow the Security Council to authorize anything similar to what happened in Libya."[20]

This meant the Security Council did not take any action to stop the bloodshed in Syria for the five years following the Libya mission. So 2011 was a pivotal year in Canadian military history. It marked the end of the fiercest fighting Canada had experienced since the Korean War: the combat in Afghanistan; and in Libya, the air and sea war that was over and done with in seven months. The bad guy lost his job and was killed.

In both cases, the Harper government answered the call of duty. Harper had no choice but to continue the Afghanistan war the previous Liberal government had begun, so he tried to argue that it was not, in fact, a war. Not being able to bend reality, he failed. When trouble reared its head in Libya, he decided to join Canada's allies in a mission that seemed to have a convenient and foreseeable endpoint. But it did not.

Afghanistan and Libya remain violently unstable. This became Canada's war legacy in the early twenty-first century – one that it shared with more powerful allies.

CHAPTER FOUR

Stormy Relations
with the United Nations

10 OCTOBER 2010
More than sixty African and Arab leaders are mingling in the Libyan coastal city of Sirte, the birthplace of their host, Moammar Gadhafi. It's the second such Arab-African summit and the mood is upbeat, without a hint of the violent turn of events that will unfold here 373 days from now. That's when rebel forces will slaughter Gadhafi, ending his four decades of dictatorial rule and plunging his oil-rich country into anarchy. Ferry de Kerckhove, Canada's ambassador to Egypt, is here, working the room and picking up strong hints about something foreboding about his own country's place in the world: the major international embarrassment that Canada will suffer in the next forty-eight hours.

That's when Canada will be competing against Germany and Portugal for two temporary seats on the United Nations Security Council in a vote at the General Assembly. Prior to arriving in Egypt in 2008, de Kerckhove spent four years at Foreign Affairs headquarters in Ottawa as the head of its international organizations unit – the branch that liaises with UN organizations. De Kerckhove expended much effort on wining and dining foreign diplomats to curry support for Canada's Security Council bid. Now out in the field, he has been dispatched with a number of other government officials – though no cabinet ministers – to Libya for this summit of one of the UN's most powerful voting blocs: fifty-four Arab-African members of the UN General Assembly, representing more than one-quarter of the UN's 190-plus nations.

"You have everybody that you needed to buttonhole. The Portuguese, who were fighting for their lives, sent a minister and therefore had greater access to all the leaders," de Kerckhove recalled in an interview. "I remember knocking on the elbow of the king of Saudi Arabia, who didn't think it was very funny, but he sent me to his foreign minister and we had the discussion."

As de Kerckhove continued to work the room, he started to get that sinking feeling. "I'm not going to start naming countries, but there were countries who were pretty clear about saying that our position on the Middle East was not helpful, and that Canada was no longer seen to be the balanced country that had helped in the past," he said. "So there was no question we were going to lose some of the Middle Eastern vote."

Two days later, the UN General Assembly delivered Canada an unprecedented rebuke. It elected Portugal on the third ballot, easily thumping Canada, which had to drop out because of a lack of support in the first two rounds of voting. Canada was denied a two-year, non-permanent stint for 2011–12. It ended Canada's run of six successful elections to the council since the late 1940s. After its initial loss in 1946, Canada was able to win two-thirds approval of the full General Assembly to serve in 1948–49, 1958–59, 1967–68, 1977–78, 1989–90, and 1999–2000. But in 2010, Canada threw in the towel after its dismal second-round showing: it got just 78 votes to Portugal's 113. Portugal actually needed 128 votes, but rather than face a further humiliation, Canada pulled the plug. Portugal got the support it needed on the third ballot. Adding insult to injury was the fact that Canada claimed to have had the written support of 135 UN countries – promises, it would seem, that were not worth the paper they were printed on.[1] Australia suffered the same fate in 1996, prompting its ambassador, Richard Butler, to coin the term "rotten lying bastards" to explain his country's loss.

Canada's defeat was widely seen as a repudiation of Harper's foreign policy. There was agreement among scholars and former diplomats that the loss could be pinned on a Conservative government that did a bad job of campaigning for the seat, leaving the push to win far too late in the game, and alienating potential supporters with some of its policies, including Canada's tilt towards Israel in the

Middle East conflict and its 2010 decision to freeze international aid to Africa.

Denis Stairs, professor emeritus of political science at Dalhousie University, blamed an inexperienced team of young aides in the PMO for blowing it at the UN, their eyes fixed on getting the Conservatives reelected in the next federal election. "Foreign policy is being made largely in the Prime Minister's Office by people who are preoccupied with domestic electoral politics, who are focused on the very short term, who are ignorant of the subtle nuances of international diplomacy and who are inclined to operate from ideological first premises rather than on the basis of a seasoned understanding of what is likely to be constructive and helpful in the international context," he wrote.[2] As a result, the government simply hadn't put in the diplomatic effort required to mount an effective campaign, as well as being impaired by its contentious foreign policy.

Bruce Carson, who served as an advisor to Harper from 2004 to 2009, said that when Harper first learned about the potential to run in 2010, he wasn't sure it was worth the effort. "I'm not sure what changed his mind, but it seemed a half-hearted attempt at best. Given the results, he should have stuck with his initial instincts on the matter," Carson wrote.[3] Stephen Lewis, the New Democrat who served as Brian Mulroney's ambassador to the UN in the 1980s, says the UN Security Council loss showcased the "ideological dogmatism of Stephen Harper" and had seriously hurt Canada in the eyes of the world. The pro-Israeli stance and numerous examples of indifference on climate change all undermined Canada's chances in the vote, Lewis told me.

Well into his seventies, Lewis was still active in the UN, working on sexual violence and peacekeeping operations, which took him to the offices of the under-secretary-general of legal affairs and the under-secretary-general of peacekeeping. He interacted with a lot of military leaders, a number of them from Africa, and rubbed elbows with Kofi Annan, the former secretary-general, and Nelson Mandela's widow Graça Machel, who has won international awards for her work easing the suffering of children in conflict. "When we have finished the business that we're dealing with specifically, like peacekeeping, we talk broadly about Canada's reputation and involvement and for everybody – everybody – there has been a significant diminution of Canada's reputation. They often ask me what's gone wrong, what's gone haywire, why is Harper behaving as he is behaving?"

De Kerckhove saw the first signs of trouble during his 2004–08 posting to Ottawa, his second to last job post before retiring in 2011. Three times a week he would host a luncheon at department headquarters for groups of foreign ambassadors to talk up Canada's candidacy for the Security Council. De Kerckhove recalled discussions with his friend the Brazilian ambassador. "I knew perfectly well he was going to be supporting Portugal and Germany, and not us." The problem was, the newly elected Harper government wasn't saying anything publicly about pursuing a seat. Outgoing Liberal prime minister Paul Martin green-lighted the campaign in 2004 as a matter of course – Canada's previous stint had finished four years earlier and it was taken for granted the country would run again, roughly a decade later, de Kerckhove recalled. "And that's perfectly legitimate for a government that comes to power to look around and say, 'Do I really want to continue that?'" he said. "What I'm blaming the government for is having hesitated for quite a while, and once they decided to get in, for not putting in all the effort that was required."

As de Kerckhove's luncheons progressed, he began to notice problems. "The government's position on the Israeli-Palestinian conflict started hurting them considerably. And also the lack of personal investment on the part of the prime minister made it a more difficult thing to run," he said. De Kerckhove said he wasn't aware of any high-level political phone calls – from the prime minister or foreign affairs minister to potential supporters – in those early days. He also said the government could have demonstrated "a bit less harshness on some positions to allow a bit of space so countries could vote for you."

The UN had faced no shortage of criticism after too many corruption and mismanagement scandals in the previous decade, particularly the oil-for-food scandal that undermined the sanctions it imposed on Iraq. In what was widely viewed as the biggest threat to the UN system, more than 2,200 reputable firms had been caught making more than $1.8 billion in payments to Saddam Hussein's regime, a scam that exploited a program that was designed to lessen the effects of the sanctions on innocent Iraqi civilians.[4] When he first took to the General Assembly podium on Canada's behalf in 2006, Harper, the new kid on the block, told the institution that it needed to shape up. "Earlier this year, Canada's new government was given a mandate to make our national government more accountable, to ensure taxpayers get full value for their money, and to pursue a clear, focused agenda that produces tangible results," he told the assembly. "The United Nations should accept nothing less. This organization must become more accountable and more effective. Management reform must continue, and at an accelerated pace. The taxpayers of member nations, Canadians among them, make significant financial contributions to this organization," he said. "They have the right to expect stronger, more independent oversight mechanisms, more robust accountability for how funds are spent, and human resources practices that are based on merit."

When on 23 September 2010 Harper addressed the General Assembly for the second time, it was to win support for Canada in the Security Council vote nineteen days away. This speech didn't help, said Stairs, because "he made a public, crudely transparent, and unprecedentedly self-serving pitch in support of the Canadian cause."[5] Moreover, his return to the assembly came one year after he decided to take part in a photo-op at a Tim Hortons donut factory in Oakville, Ontario, instead of speaking at the UN. On paper, Harper had a strong argument that Canada was a worthy candidate: not only was it the UN's seventh-largest funder at the time, it was contributing to global security through the Canadian Forces in Afghanistan. Harper reminded the assembly of Canada's role in the founding of the UN in 1945, and described his government's commitment to improving the plight of pregnant women, young mothers, and their newborns in the developing world – his signature foreign-aid initiative – and how that dovetailed with the UN's Millennium Development Goals. Most of all, he talked about the sacrifices of the Canadian Forces, as casualties continued to mount.

"Canada continues to pay, for instance, a heavy price to fulfill our UN obligation to support the lawful government of Afghanistan," the prime minister said. "We pay it in both the resources of Canadian taxpayers, but also with profound sorrow in the priceless lives of our young men and women who serve there in the Canadian Armed Forces, as well as, sadly, civilians who have also given their sweat and their lives in the service of both our country, and of the people of Afghanistan." Without mentioning it specifically, Harper was evoking Article 23 in the UN Charter, which placed a premium on a country's contribution to peace and security when vying for a temporary Security Council seat. Harper kept the anti-UN rhetoric out of this speech, saying Canada remained committed to the founding principles of the UN, "through peace and development, to build a better world. To prevent war and conflict, yet at the same time, to uphold what is right and to protect the weak and the poor from those who prey upon them."

The argument failed. Stephen Lewis said the loss fell squarely at Harper's feet for his "negative, contemptuous dismissal of the United Nations as a useful forum." But Ian Brodie, Harper's first chief of staff, has rejected the notion that Harper abandoned the UN. He pointed out that Harper addressed it three times during his time in power, not a bad record for any prime minister, even though "the Security Council is at a low point in its history." Brodie said the council was ineffective in preventing the "illegal actions" by Russia in Ukraine.[6]

When the General Assembly reconvened in September 2011 with the Conservatives fully entrenched in a majority government, Harper unleashed his new pit bull of a foreign affairs minister on the UN. John Baird arrived at the General Assembly guns blazing and teeth bared, ready to relay to the international community the same message that Harper gave to Conservative supporters in Ottawa earlier that summer. "Just as fascism and communism were the great struggles of previous generations, terrorism is the great struggle of ours. And far too often, the Jewish state is on the front line of our struggle and its people the victims of terror," the new foreign minister said. "Canada will not accept or stay silent while the Jewish state is attacked for defending its territory and its citizens. The Second World War taught us all the tragic price of 'going along' just to 'get along.'" And just as Harper had done in 2006, Baird blasted the UN for allowing countries with dubious rights records to be members of the Human Rights Council where they could sit in judgment of more upstanding countries.

Canada's new, more robust foreign policy sparked heated domestic debate that pitted seasoned politicians, diplomats, and academics against each other. Detractors – and there were many – as well as supporters of the Harper government agreed on one thing: the conduct of Canada's foreign policy, particularly its multilateral engagement with the UN, had been fundamentally altered since the 2006 arrival of the Conservatives.

Robert Fowler was Canada's longest-serving ambassador to the UN and a public servant with strong bipartisan credentials: he was a foreign policy adviser to both Pierre Trudeau and Brian Mulroney. In a 2013 opinion column, he characterized the Harper government's "'we won't go along to get along' mantra" as smug and simplistic. He said the underlying attitude cost Canada its 2010 Security Council bid, and he predicted that unless there was a fundamental change in foreign policy, Canada would remain on the sidelines.[7]

Former prime minister Brian Mulroney also heaped scorn on Harper in September 2014 during a CTV interview. Mulroney said Harper had essentially undone decades of work at the United Nations. "When Canada, for the first time in our history, loses a vote at the United Nations to become a member of the Security Council ... to Portugal, which was on the verge of bankruptcy at the time, you should look in the mirror and say: 'Houston, I think we have a problem.'" Mulroney said Harper's foreign affairs policy "has to be enveloped in a broader and more generous sweep that takes in Canadian traditions and Canadian history in a much more viable way." He said Canada had to start acting like it was in the "big leagues" and to stop being "out-riders" on the international stage.[8]

One of Mulroney's former U.S. ambassadors and top advisers was far more impressed with Harper's tougher attitude towards the UN. Derek Burney, Mulroney's former chief of staff and one-time envoy to the United States, was also the head of Harper's transition team in early 2006. Burney and his writing partner, Fen Hampson, one of Canada's leading international affairs analysts, said it was about time Canada started addressing the problems with the UN head on, the way Harper was doing. "The UN is hobbled by an out-of-date structure, ineffective governance and misplaced values and ideals," Burney and Hampson argued, and they lamented the "second-rate efforts" of the UN member countries to fix it.[9] They defended Harper's various snubs of the UN General Assembly, most notably his decision to attend the donut shop photo-op as well as skipping the assembly again in 2012 in favour of accepting an award from the Appeal of Conscience Foundation at a New York hotel just a few blocks away. Burney and Hampson insisted that "the government has good reason to be frustrated with the UN."[10] They said the professors and former Canadian diplomats who were "in a lather" over this "should be directing their wrath at the UN, not the prime minister."[11] They called the 2010 Security Council loss "a stinging rebuke to a country that has long done yeoman's service in defence of freedom and the maintenance of international peace and security."[12]

They also argued that the Responsibility to Protect doctrine, championed by the Liberals under Paul Martin, adopted by the UN in 2005, and then jettisoned by the Harper Conservatives, had become "laughable" because of the UN's inability to halt the bloodshed in Syria.[13] "Syria's civil war is a clear indictment of the world's multilateral security architecture, and a clarion call for Canada to lead efforts to reform a system that has strayed from the principles of humanitarian intervention," Burney and Hampson wrote. They described the ineffectiveness of UN sanctions, saying that "barely 20 per cent of UN sanctions have had any impact at all and only 10 per cent have actually changed the behavior of their intended targets."[14]

Moreover, Burney and Hampson offered a sharp rebuttal to critics who accused the Harper government of not supporting the UN: "In spite of all the criticism directed at the Conservatives, Canada continues to be the seventh largest contributor to the UN's budget," with a bigger contribution than Russia and China, who are permanent Security Council members.[15] Canada, they argued, should push for UN Security Council reform, and should also advocate for Japan, Germany, India, and Brazil to become permanent members. And if there were no progress, Canada should start cutting back its financial support by as much as 10 to 20 per cent a year. "Such a move would send a strong signal that we are serious about UN reform and, since we are the seventh-largest contributor to the UN regular budget, others would take note and perhaps even follow our lead."[16]

For all their tough talk on the UN, Burney and Hampson did not advocate that Canada should turn its back on the institution. "Make no mistake. The world and Canada need viable and effective multilateral institutions," they argued.[17] But Canada can't keep on "drifting" at the UN; it needs to push for reform because this is urgent.[18]

They clearly advocated Canada playing an active role within the institution to make it better.

Harper would find a theoretical framework to back his wholesale rejection of all things liberal – or Liberal – in Canadian foreign policy in Roy Rempel. Since 1998, Rempel had been a policy advisor and researcher in the Canadian Alliance and the Conservative Party of Canada. In his 2007 book *Dreamland: How Canada's Pretend Foreign Policy Has Undermined Sovereignty*, Rempel argued the Liberals and the Progressive Conservatives erred by embracing the UN. Rempel wrote that "the centre of gravity of any state's international policy should be wherever the livelihood and well-being of ordinary citizens are most affected by international events."[19] He called Canada's adherence to multilateralism "pathological."[20] He argued that the UN could not be at the centre of Canadian foreign policy because it had proven ineffective at preventing genocide in Rwanda and the Balkans, and had given a forum to dictators such as Robert Mugabe and Vladimir Putin.[21]

This criticism of Putin would come years before the eruption of the 2014 Ukraine crisis. But it clearly foreshadowed the hardline rhetoric that Harper and Baird would direct at Putin after Russia's annexation of Crimea and the unrest caused by Russian-backed militias in eastern Ukraine. Rempel was unequivocal about where the UN fit in terms of Canadian foreign policy: "Where the UN is incapable of supporting Canadian interests, it should not be permitted to exercise a veto over the conduct of Canadian international policy."[22] Along with Burney and Hampson, Rempel offered the Harper government serious ideological support for its criticism of the UN. Three years after Rempel wrote his book, he was back working at Harper's side: he was hired as a policy adviser in the Prime Minister's Office in 2010.

*   *   *

From the moment he won power, Harper began challenging the traditional assumptions at the heart of Canada's foreign policy. As far as his first non-political foreign policy adviser was concerned, that wasn't necessarily a bad thing. David Mulroney was a seasoned public servant who became deputy minister in charge of the

Afghanistan Task Force during the height of the war and ambassador to China in 2009, when relations between Beijing and Ottawa were at a particularly low ebb. Harper was determined to challenge a way of thinking about foreign policy that "had grown very cozy with identifying Canada's interests with the interests of the multilateral system at the UN," Mulroney, who retired in 2012, told me. "He felt we were too ready to take positions at the UN that didn't reflect what he'd see as the true direction or necessary direction of Canadian foreign policy." The prime example was repeated criticism of Israel at the UN while other countries – totalitarian regimes that didn't respect the rule of law or, often, their own civilians – avoided censure. This was a hard pill to swallow at the Foreign Affairs Department where the "high priests" of multilateralism looked down their nose at those who promoted bilateral, country-to-country relations, said Mulroney.

"In the past, Conservatives had been as invested in the multilateral consensus. Brian Mulroney's government was like the old Republicans in the U.S. – internationalist, links to business, a very strong vision of Canada in the world. And it took the bureaucracy a long time to figure out after 2006 that this is an entirely new government," said David Mulroney. This new Conservative government, he said, "had been on the outside, resenting the elites in both the Liberal and Conservative parties."

Harper wanted his diplomats to stay on message, so he imposed what ultimately became a stifling control. He wanted to avoid precisely the sort of thing that happened in June 2011, when his ambassador to the United Nations in Geneva, Marius Grinius, warmly welcomed the North Korean ambassador into his new appointment as the rotating chair of the UN's Conference on Disarmament. It was the standard welcome that accompanies such a passing of the torch on UN committees. But those diplomatic niceties were poorly timed. Just a week earlier, foreign affairs minister John Baird had denounced the appointment as unacceptable because North Korea was an international pariah whose nuclear weapons status was universally opposed as a danger to world peace. In an editorial, the *Toronto Sun* told Baird to fire Grinius, calling him an "absolute twit."[23] To Harper it was "the ultimate icing on the cake," said Mulroney, but the prime minister overreacted by putting all his senior diplomats on a tighter leash. "It was micromanaged at the political level," he said. "The diagnosis wasn't entirely wrong, but the prescription was way too strong."

Micromanagement of the foreign service from Ottawa stifled the creativity and morale of its members. It extended as far as seeking permission from home in the middle of delicate negotiations abroad, he said. "You have a kind of command and control diplomacy where people check in: Can I do that? I want to go to this meeting. Can I go to that meeting? Can I give this speech?" Mulroney said that created a new generation of diplomats that shied away from doing anything creative, filled with "people who are really scared they'll get in trouble if they say just about anything."

* * *

The overriding imperative of the new direction in foreign policy was to perpetuate the rule of the Conservative Party of Canada. Before 2006, this was about winning power from the Liberals, which Harper viewed as the natural governing party of Canada. Afterwards, it was about consolidating power by smashing the Liberal brand and redefining Canada. Harper left no doubt about this in 2008:

> My long-term goal is to make Conservatives the natural governing party of the country. And I'm a realist. You do that two ways … One thing you do is you pull conservatives, to pull the party, to the centre of the political spectrum. But what you also have to do, if you're really serious about making transformations, is you have to pull the centre of the political spectrum towards conservatism.[24]

Harper wanted to break with the Liberal past and reconfigure Canada's position on the world stage. In his first major foreign-policy speech after he won power in 2006, the prime minister told an audience at the Wilson Center in Washington, DC, that he planned for Canada to play a more influential role on the world stage – but not necessarily in multilateral organizations, such as NATO, the G8, *La Francophonie,* and the Commonwealth: "To accomplish such a goal will require more than membership in the various multilateral bodies I have just talked about." For Harper, this meant breaking with the way things had been done in the past, primarily under the Liberals: "Previous governments have had all those club memberships, but they haven't always been leaders."

Harper arrived in office facing "a severe shortage of experience on the front bench," wrote Canadian diplomat Louise Frechette, who served as the first UN deputy secretary-general between 1997 and 2005.[25] To compensate, the Conservatives fell back on ideology. "The new government's foreign policy priorities – few in number and sketchily defined – seemed to respond both to genuine ideological differences with the Liberal party and an intense desire to appear to be different." Frechette said she noticed domestic political considerations gaining influence on foreign affairs near the end of Liberal era, as her term at the UN was winding down. In 2004, the country embarked on a period of "prolonged political uncertainty" with seven years of minority government, she said.[26] Kim Richard Nossal, the director of the School of Policy Studies at Queen's University, said Harper's foreign policy was driven by "the primacy of the ballot box ... international policy shaped first and foremost by electoral considerations, and in particular the broader strategic goals of the Harper Conservatives to become Canada's 'natural governing party.'"[27]

After serving under Harper in a number of capacities, David Mulroney retired and became a senior fellow at the University of Toronto's Munk School of Global Affairs. He came to the conclusion that the Harper Conservatives really didn't care what the UN thought of them. "The fact that they would go and say those things and rattle the furniture as much as they did suggested they weren't overwhelmed by the institutions." Harper behaved that way to appeal to a core constituency inside Canada: one that helped bring his party to power. "The people that they wanted to reach reflect those positions. And that again gets to this notion of domestic politics," said Mulroney. "You don't want to be hypocritical and ignore what people believe domestically, but sometimes you have to say, the world is a complicated place, we have to compromise sometimes."

* * *

The Conservative government demonstrated a particular disdain for an important UN function: the crafting of international treaties. Under Harper, Canada managed to avoid signing the UN Arms Trade Treaty (ATT) to regulate the global trade in conventional arms – from guns to tanks. It also became the only country in the world to withdraw from the UN Convention to Combat Desertification in 2013. On the ATT, the Conservative government faced pressure from recreational firearms users in Canada, who believed the UN treaty would somehow meddle with their lawful rights to possess weapons. The evidence is clear that the Harper government's decision not to join the ATT was based on a domestic political calculation: it did not want to be offending a core group of supporters – rural gun owners and sport-shooting enthusiasts. Harper's longest-serving foreign affairs minister, John Baird, explicitly stated that the ATT could lead to a revival of the federal long-gun registry, which the Conservatives managed to abolish in 2012 because it was hated by rural gunowners, a core constituency for the party. "If you look at the listing of treaties that were not ratified, signed or otherwise, you will always find a direct link to the ideological proclivities of the present government," said Ferry de Kerckhove.

Two of the top players in Canada's gun lobby told me that it was in the Conservatives' domestic political interest to stay away from the ATT. Tony Bernardo, head of the Canadian Shooting Sports Association, said he had been working hard to oppose UN gun-control efforts since the mid-1990s, and that he had found a great ally in Baird. "Minister Baird has been very thoughtful and intelligent on the Arms Trade Treaty right from Day One," Bernardo said in an interview. "At the beginning of the process he asked the United Nations to remove civilian firearms from the scope of the treaty. He's seen the writing on the wall. He's not a dumb man." Sheldon Clare, president of the National Firearms Association, said, "I think they also recognize there would be some significant ramifications in their voting base were they to approve this." Clare said he was worried that the ATT would lead to higher prices on the imports of firearms, ammunition, and accessories. "We rely heavily on imports."

Industry Canada data showed that the imports of guns, rifles, shotguns, ammunition, and accessories nearly doubled during the first seven years of Conservative rule. From 2006 to 2012, they totalled $2.84 million. During the final seven years of Liberal rule, between 1999 and 2005, weapons imports to Canada totalled $1.56 million. Meanwhile, Baird's office door remained open to the gun lobby. According to a heavily censored briefing note released under Access to Information, Baird agreed to Clare's request for a meeting on 9 May 2012 in his Centre Block office. One of Baird's key messages was that Foreign Affairs "will continue to find efficient ways to facilitate the lawful importation of firearms and their accessories."

With a late summer conference at the UN on small arms and light weapons looming, associate deputy minister of foreign affairs Gerald Cossette prepared a briefing note for Baird that proposed "Canada play a low-key, minimal role at the Review Conference (RevCon)." Cossette wrote in the 11 July 2012 memo, released under Access to Information, that the conference was taking place three weeks after the ATT negotiations were set to wrap, and there were "similar issues at play." Canada's position should be to ensure "(1) no new burdens are imposed on law-abiding, responsible Canadian firearms owners; and (2) that Canada does not enter into any new commitments that are inconsistent with its domestic laws and regulations on firearms."

The senior bureaucrat made it clear this was controversial. "The Canadian delegation is likely to face criticism or questioning by some delegates on this approach ... and Canada could be isolated from traditional friends and allies," Cossette wrote. "Critics may view any attempt by Canada to seek voluntary language in an outcome document as further evidence that Canada is attempting to undermine all forms of gun control, including at the international level." Cossette also suggested that the Conservatives might be able to avoid controversy because the conference was essentially taking place during the dog days of summer, and would be "unlikely to generate a lot of interest among Parliamentarians." The "proposed Canadian delegation" to the UN was to include four people: three officials from Foreign Affairs, and Steve Torino, president of the Canadian Shooting Sports Association. In a clearly legible handwritten script at the top of the memo, it read: "Approved by the Minister on August 23, 2012. JB."

Just as quietly, the Harper government decided to withdraw from another UN treaty to which it was already a party. The decision to

leave the Convention to Combat Desertification shocked the
German-based secretariat that administers it, and represented a blatant snub of the UN treaty system. In 1995 Canada ratified the convention, which created a UN body that researches ways to stop the
spread of droughts that destroy farmland across the globe, especially in Africa. But with the minimum of public notice required,
the federal government posted a cabinet order online in 2013 that
authorized "the Minister of Foreign Affairs to take the actions necessary to withdraw, on behalf of Canada, from the United Nations
Convention to Combat Desertification, in those Countries Experi-
encing Severe Drought and/or Desertification, particularly in
Africa." The government forgot one other important thing: it did-
n't bother telling the UN any of this. The UN secretariat did not initially find out from the Canadian government that Canada was, in
fact, withdrawing.

   I told them. On 27 March 2013, after I phoned the UN secretariat
in Bonn, the spokeswoman there told me: "We cannot comment on
something that is not communicated officially to the secretariat or
to the United Nations." The woman said she was going to be calling
the secretariat's lawyers.

   The next day, Morris Rosenberg, Canada's deputy minister of foreign affairs, sent Baird a one-page briefing note recommending
"that you sign the attached letter to the UN Secretary-General in-
forming him of Canada's withdrawal from" the treaty. An X was
penned through the "I concur" box, and the top of the page was
marked with the same clearly legible handwritten script as the earlier Arms Trade Treaty signoff: "Approved by the Minister on March
28, 2013. JB." With that stroke of the pen, Canada became the only
country in the world outside a convention designed to combat the
global threat of increased droughts and lost farmland. The UN called
that "regrettable." Baird defended the desertification pullout, saying
it was a waste of taxpayers' money – Canada contributed about
$300,000 annually to the convention – to support what was essen-
tially a "talkfest." The convention was admittedly obscure, but following the government's earlier decision to withdraw from the
Kyoto Protocol climate change treaty in 2011, the move raised more
than a few eyebrows internationally.

Canada's allies noticed the shift in relation to UN treaty bodies, but few diplomats were willing to speak on the record about it. France was one exception. A former French ambassador to Canada, Philippe Zeller, questioned the desertification pullout directly. "When it's such a question as to how to deal with desertification – well it's difficult to accept, to see a leader like Canada, countries that are known for having developed aid policy since the 1960s, to decide to go out. But we have to respect that," Zeller said in an interview at the French embassy, a week prior to his departure from Canada in early 2015. Zeller also questioned Canada's decision not to join the Arms Trade Treaty, and the long-delayed ratification of the Convention on Cluster Munitions. He suggested his government had been quietly urging Canada to take action on these fronts.

Shortly after Harper was defeated in the autumn of 2015 another diplomat from a Western country told me, on condition of anonymity, that there was a behind-the-scenes push to get Canada on board with the treaty. The diplomat said that their country's foreign ministry had instructed all of its embassies to lobby hard for the treaty, and to urge countries that had yet to sign to do so. When it came to Canada, however, this diplomat simply threw in the towel. "We used to say, 'it's a waste of time in Ottawa as long as Harper is around.'"28

There was also agreement among some of the country's closest allies that Canada should take another run at the Security Council. Former Australian prime minister and foreign minister Kevin Rudd held this view, even though he generally supported the tough stand Harper had taken towards the UN. Rudd had a label for Baird: "He is a practical internationalist." Rudd coined the term when I spoke with him during his visit to Ottawa in January 2015 to meet with the Foreign Affairs Department in his new job as the head of the Independent Commission on Multilateralism. Baird and Norwegian foreign minister Børge Brende had been named co-chairs of the commission in September 2014, an initiative launched by the International Peace Institute, a non-profit New York think-tank, to help reform major international institutions, including those of the UN.

"I don't think he (Baird) is the sort of guy who wants to go to conferences for the sake of going to conferences," said Rudd. "He speaks with a high degree of credibility from a realist perspective; he wants to see the UN function and function effectively." Three days after that conversation, in February 2015, Baird abruptly announced he was quitting politics. His connection to Rudd's commission also ended.

Rudd was also impressed with the deep institutional knowledge that Canadian diplomats seemed to possess about the inner workings of the UN, calling them "a senior band of officials who know the UN system backwards." Senior managers, foreign service officers, and other department officials spent several hours listening to a presentation by Rudd on the future of the UN. He came away convinced they could help reform the UN. "The particular expertise that could bring about credible reform lies with so many of the folks who have literally decades of experience," Rudd said. "I think Canada is one of the great repositories of – let's call it multilateral knowledge – in the world."

All of that begged the question of whether Canada should be licking its wounds as Australia had done, and mounting another campaign to serve on the UN Security Council sometime soon. After all, Australia had just finished its two-year stint on the council in December 2014, after suffering its own bitter failure to win a seat in 1996. Rudd himself launched and led Australia's campaign for the seat in 2008, calling the three-and-a-half-year battle "tough and taxing," but worth it in the end. "It's a bit like global Tammany Hall," he said, laughing, "not to be undertaken lightly." Australia, along with tiny Luxembourg, was able to push the yardsticks forward slightly on the Syria crisis with a pair of resolutions that made "modest improvements" to the access humanitarian groups were able to secure to help bring relief to war-torn areas of the country.

Rudd insisted he didn't want to give advice on what Canada should do, but quickly added: "Apart from the question of UNSC membership and candidatures, all I'd say is Canada is a strong, credible voice in the world historically, and is into the business of global problem solving. And we need more and more countries like that."

*   *   *

Canada's UN history showed just how much of a bridge-builder it had been, especially on the Security Council. On 6 January 1948, under-secretary of state Lester Pearson took the seat for Canada's first appearance on the Security Council, saying it was a great honour for Canada, and one he hoped the country could live up to.[29] One month later, Canada's new ambassador to the UN, retired general Andrew McNaughton, was chairing the council for Canada's first month-long stint in that leadership role. McNaughton, a Second World War army commander, took the initiative to help resolve the four-year-long Kashmir dispute between India and Pakistan that culminated in a deal on 1 January 1949.[30] On 27 December 1949 – more than seven months after McNaughton proposed a peace conference between the two factions – the Netherlands signed a sovereignty agreement with the Indonesian Republic, giving birth to what is now the world's most populous Muslim country.[31]

"He loved the experience of being in the formative stages of an organization that was essentially set up with the cry of 'never again,'" McNaughton's grandson, Andrew Leslie, who would become Canada's army commander for the fiercest fighting of the Afghanistan campaign between 2006 and 2010, recalled in an interview. Leslie was only nine when his grandfather died, but his parents told him how McNaughton and his Canadian contemporaries felt. "I'm told that they saw this as a calling, they saw it as an opportunity to try and help, using instruments other than the nuclear weapon," Leslie told me. They realized that the UN was created "to prevent the real protagonists from going at it and killing the rest of us."

Historian Norman Smith recalled McNaughton chairing one particularly raucous session on Kashmir in February 1948. Smith watched from the public gallery when India's Sheikh Abdullah "hurled his defiant threat that no force on earth save his own people could take him from power in Kashmir." Two women from Brooklyn were settling into seats near him when all of this was happening. "Look," one of them said, "a Canadian is chairman." Her friend replied: "Good for Canada, I didn't even know they were here."[32] Sixty-six years later, Stephen Harper arrived in New York to address the UN for the first time in four years, following his failed effort in September 2010 to persuade the General Assembly to grant Canada a seventh Security Council term for Canada. A UN staffer, who was overheard by Canadian reporters, said, "So nice of him to show up."[33]

Harper's last UN visit in 2014 also contrasted with the hero's welcome his Progressive Conservative predecessor Brian Mulroney received in September 1988, when he made one final push for what would be Canada's fifth Security Council stint. Yves Fortier had only been in New York a few weeks, after his good friend Mulroney appointed him to be Canada's ambassador, succeeding New Democrat Stephen Lewis. "He made it very clear that number one on my agenda was going to be lobbying ... the other ambassadors in New York to secure their support for Canada's election," Fortier told me. For Mulroney, partisan politics were not part of the equation once he was in the international arena. "He was a disciple of Lester Pearson," Fortier recalled. "The political colour of these two men, again from Mulroney's perspective, mattered not. What mattered was the fact that Pearson had been an exemplary representative of Canada at the UN."

Canada had been campaigning for years, and even though he was parachuted in for the final weeks, Fortier was determined to make the most of it. When a new ambassador presents his credentials at the UN, he pays courtesy calls to his fellow diplomats, so Fortier turned those visits into campaign stops. "I combined my courtesy visit with a plea for their support, that country's support. I was encouraged by the reaction by the majority of my new colleagues," he recalled.

Fortier was also encouraged by a private visit with UN secretary-general Pérez de Cuéllar. He told Fortier, "When I want to give an example of how a country should behave if it is a member of the United Nations, I always refer to Canada." As he walked back to the Canadian mission afterwards, Fortier thought, "he probably says that to every UN ambassador."

But Fortier realized Pérez de Cuéllar just wasn't blowing smoke when on 26 October 1988, Canada won a first ballot victory in the General Assembly. Looking back, Fortier said support from African countries played a key role because of Mulroney's leadership fighting against apartheid. "No question, no question. The African countries were very grateful to Prime Minister Mulroney for the leading role that he played in ridding South Africa of apartheid."

The Pearson era of foreign affairs from the mid-1940s to the late 1950s is routinely referred to as Canada's "Golden Age" of diplomacy. But when Fortier thinks back on the 1989–90 term at the UN, "those were the golden years of the United Nations. It was at that time that the UN Security Council truly functioned as it was envisaged in 1945." The Berlin Wall fell. The Soviet Union collapsed. Nelson Mandela walked free after twenty-seven years in prison. The eight-year Iran-Iraq War ended, and the world's geopolitical chess pieces were reconfiguring themselves for Saddam Hussein's quickly thwarted invasion of Kuwait in 1990. And Canada had a front row seat for it all.

Fortier recalled the day the Soviet Union became the Russian Federation. "I thought I was being fed a speech by the American ambassador. I thought I had the wrong translation, the wrong channel," he recalled. "It was that revolutionary a change."

On 19 December 2000, Paul Heinbecker, then Canada's ambassador to the UN, offered what would be the last utterance by Canada as a full-fledged Security Council member. Heinbecker told the council that Canada supported new sanctions on Afghanistan because it continued to be a backer of terrorism, but he stressed precautions were needed to protect civilians who had lived through two decades of war. "We believe that the Security Council has an important role to play in eliminating terrorism, and we welcome its continued determination to do so," he said. "We encourage the Council to address the conflict itself and to consider ways to hasten the end of the interminable war and the desperate conditions endured by the people of Afghanistan."34

Less than ten months later, al-Qaida terrorists, who had found safe haven in Afghanistan, hijacked four American commercial airliners and turned them into suicide missiles, two of which destroyed the twin skyscrapers of New York's World Trade Center while one blew a hole in the Pentagon and the last was driven into the ground of a Pennsylvania field by its rebelling passengers. Canada has been absent from the deliberations of the Security Council since then. In April 2013, Baird ruled out another bid for a Canadian run to win a Security Council term, telling a House of Commons committee that the country was "focusing on other priorities."

Harper and Baird made brief cameo appearances at the Security Council in September 2014, during its deliberations on the world's response to the Islamic State of Iraq and the Levant, or ISIL, the al-Qaida offshoot that had created an oppressive and violent Islamist caliphate. Canada was on the verge of contributing special forces commandoes and six CF-18 fighter jets to the American-led coalition about to go to war against ISIL. At the invitation of U.S. secretary of state John Kerry, Baird and Harper were asked to speak. On 19 September, in a short intervention, Baird pledged Canada's support to the cause, saying: "We must defend the firm and unyielding principles of human liberty and dignity that have withstood the tests of fascism and communism, and now terrorism. That is the test facing us today. We cannot afford to fail." Five days later, Harper pledged Canada's support to the Council in an even shorter speech. "We will also continue to work with the government of the United States, the government of Iraq and our other friends and allies on a range of humanitarian, political and military assistance to those fighting this phenomenon in the region."

And with that, Baird and Harper were gone. The permanent five of the United Nations General Assembly continued their weighty deliberations with their ten temporary partners: Argentina, Australia, Chad, Chile, Jordan, Lithuania, Luxembourg, Nigeria, South Korea, and Rwanda.

It's nice to be invited, said Fortier, but guest appearances like those simply can't compare to the access a temporary member gets during its two years on the Security Council. What's incontrovertible is that in the post-9-11 era, Canada has been "outside the tent" of the world's most powerful body. "These are very difficult times on the geopolitical stage, whether you're looking at Ukraine, whether you're looking at Iraq, Syria, whether you're looking at the situation of Russia vis-a-vis the member states of the European Union – there's a lot that's going on in the Security Council where Canada's voice is not being heard," Fortier said.

"It's like night and day ... you have daily meetings with the five permanent ambassadors – the big boys. That is worth its weight in gold, I assure you."

CHAPTER FIVE

Recession Warrior
and Trade Crusader

AUGUST 2012

The Harrington Lake summer retreat, which has served prime ministers since the late 1950s, is arguably the best perk of being Canada's leader. It is nestled in the secluded greenery of the Gatineau Hills, less than a half-hour drive from Ottawa. A few minutes here will leave you feeling a world away from a G8 capital – or a G20 one. On a warm summer day like this one, its manicured green lawn is one of the most privileged places one could hope to find, in these parts, for a late afternoon stroll. That's one reason why Stephen Harper and Angela Merkel seem so content in each other's company.

The prime minister and the German chancellor are smiling and talking amiably. Quite clearly, they are getting along. The fact is, Harper and Merkel really do like each other. As it's been said of Harper many times, he'd rather stay at home alone with a good book than hobnob with people outside his immediate circle. Merkel is different. During his time in power, Merkel became one of Harper's greatest allies in the battle to save the global economy after the 2008–09 Great Recession. Harper's relationship with her exemplifies his role as a financial statesman. Harper loves to talk economics. It comes naturally to him, a product of both formal education and personal passion.

As the leader of the country that was the engine of Europe's economy, Merkel wholeheartedly supported the Comprehensive Economic and Trade Agreement (CETA), a sweeping free-trade deal between the European Union and Canada. Harper also looked westward to Asia and pushed hard for Canada's inclusion in the twelve-country Trans-Pacific Partnership (TPP) that encompassed 40 per cent of the global economy. Much of the groundwork for these deals, liberalizing trade and strengthening the economies of new markets, took place in the G20. It was in this realm of global finance that some of Harper's most active international engagement took place. Harper used the G20 to argue the merits of freer trade and extoll the evils of protectionism. Harper and Merkel would become the two longest-serving leaders of the G20. Before Harper hosted it in 2010, the G20 leaders had met three times before in Washington, London, and Pittsburgh, in what was a SWAT-team response to the world's financial crisis. The leaders decided to make it a permanent institution to guide global economics, so the 2010 Toronto gathering became, in effect, the inaugural summit of the newly created G20.

On this August 2012 day there was no summit, and no need for a sweeping declaration to speak to the economic problems of the world. There was, in fact, "no political reason whatsoever" for this meeting in the Gatineau Hills, a top German government official told me on condition they not be identified. Merkel had finished her summer holidays two days earlier, and her office and Harper's had been talking about finding time to get together. The German official said Harper and Merkel had lots in common. They were both conservatives, they shared the same values, they'd both been around a long time, "and obviously like each other."[1] As Harper's spokesman Andrew MacDougall put it, "Whether it has been at summits or international meetings, the prime minister has always valued the chancellor's view on matters. And I think the reverse is true as well."

During this trip, Merkel also spoke at a reception at the Westin Hotel in Ottawa to her travelling entourage of German business people and journalists. In Harper she had an ally for her belief that austerity was the key to tackling the ongoing economic turmoil in Europe: Greece was due to report on the progress of its bailout, while Italy and Spain were floundering and thinking of reaching out to the EU for help. Merkel told the crowd she liked Canada's promotion of economic growth, its budget discipline, and the fact it was "not living on borrowed money," and that Europe could learn a few lessons about that.[2]

*   *   *

JANUARY 2010

Stephen Harper is in the Alps, addressing the world's rich and powerful at the World Economic Forum in Davos, Switzerland. On this day, he quotes former U.S. secretary of state Cordell Hull, who won the Nobel Peace Prize in 1945 for his role in helping create the United Nations and the World Bank. "He had this to say about international institutions: 'to be sure, no piece of social machinery, however well-constructed, can be effective unless there is back of it a will and a determination to make it work.'"

Harper also endorses the relatively new international club – the G20 – but not before offering some caveats on how he thinks it ought to work better, for the betterment of everybody, not just the rich and powerful. "It doesn't matter what global structures we devise for our mutual betterment, if we don't have the right global attitudes, they will not work," he says. "Our ambition – the necessary condition for success as the G20 moves forward – must be a shared belief that the rising tide of recovery must lift all boats, not just some.

"This is the exercise of sovereignty at its most enlightened. And I don't believe, by the way, that this is all about the structure of global institutions. It is more a matter of attitude."

The speech – and his subsequent actions in the G20 – was in many ways Harper's answer to his harshest critics. It showed that he had not entirely written off the ideals that brought the world together in San Francisco in 1945 to create the United Nations. But he was tired of the architecture of the institutions that Lester Pearson, General Andrew McNaughton, and their contemporaries fought so hard to create and support. He was weary of the internal flaws evident in those organizations, including the mother ship of multilateralism, the UN.

Harper impressed Klaus Schwab, the German economist who founded the WEF. "You come as the prime minister of a country which has relatively very well weathered the storms," Schwab told Harper at the 2010 gathering. "According to my knowledge, you have best managed of all the G7-G8 countries in the present economic crisis. Thank you for giving a good example."[3]

Some point to Harper's January 2010 speech at Davos as a rare occasion during the Conservative era when the country's multilateral foreign policy roots were evoked, if only for a fleeting moment.

The world had emerged from the Great Recession of 2008–09, and Harper expressed hope in the long tradition of multilateralism because of how world leaders, particularly through the G20, first responded to the crisis at an emergency summit in Washington that year, and its subsequent meetings in London and Pittsburgh.[4] "I saw world leadership at its best, a glimpse of a hopeful future – one where we act together for the good of all. The world we have been trying to build since 1945. The world we want for our children and grandchildren," Harper told his Davos audience. "It can be done if we act together. This is 'enlightened sovereignty.'" Harper further defined this notion as "the natural extension of enlightened self-interest."

Harper's affection for the postwar multilateral institutions may not have extended to the United Nations, but it certainly embraced the Bretton Woods financial system. Preserving the stability of the world's financial order and strengthening its performance were necessary for Harper to pursue his other main goal: transforming Canada into a more robust free-trading nation. Harper would lose power and would be deprived of any opportunity to personally preside over the ratification of the two major free trade deals he pushed with Europe and the Pacific Rim: CETA and the TPP. But he created momentum that seemed irreversible.

"Harper has put to good use his post-graduate degree in economics, his family familiarity with accounting, and his Paul Martin-like commitment to balanced budgets in the medium term, rather than rely on the sugar highs of serial stimulus spending sprees that produce cancerous deficits and debts all too soon," wrote John Kirton, of the University of Toronto's G8 Research Group. "And he has practiced as well as preached his free-trade principles, concluding more full free-trade agreements abroad than any other Canadian prime minister."[5]

Harper's former chief of staff, Ian Brodie, has said history should award Harper a partial victory for his role in the battle to save the world's economy. "Harper has governed during a severe global economic crisis. His government has focused on building the G20, the IMF, and other multilateral forums for economic coordination. And while it is too early to assess the results, the effort cannot be denied," Brodie wrote in 2014.[6]

Harper may have had little patience for indulging what he saw as a club for dictators at the UN. But he was clearly willing to roll up his sleeves and sit at the G20 table with its dictatorial component (China and Saudi Arabia) to help the institution perform better, to make it an effective vehicle for making the world a fairer place in which to do business, and to create the necessary conditions for people to prosper with as little government involvement as possible. The way to accomplish this, in his view, was to find a method to hold the G20 and other institutions to account – to move the institution beyond the plague of international summitry that saw leaders meet, issue vague declarations and promises, and then disappear without ever honouring any of them.

Harper was tired of the decades of broken promises at the G8 and was determined to prevent that from happening in the G20 six months later on his turf. "We must be pragmatic, focused, and above all, encourage accountability. The G20 nations must fully deliver on the commitments they have made. The Group of Eight must live up to their promises," he told his Davos audience. "Accountability, ladies and gentlemen, is the prerequisite for progress. As host of the G8 and G20 meetings this June, Canada will use its leadership role to focus on these key challenges."

Harper had already done some legwork on accountability six months earlier at the G8's July 2009 summit in L'Aquila, Italy. With the support of Britain and the United States, he pushed for the adoption of an accountability and "transparency" report that would monitor past commitments made by the G8 in food security, water, health, and education. The L'Aquila summit set up a senior-level working group to develop a way to measure promises and progress. Harper made sure the accountability report would be delivered at the G8 he would be hosting in Ontario's Muskoka region in June 2010 in tandem with the G20 in Toronto.

*　*　*

They're called "sherpas" for a reason. Like their Himalayan namesakes – who are renowned for guiding others up dangerous mountain terrain while carrying most of the gear – the senior public servants who do the preparatory work for international summits, including the G20, perform most of the heavy lifting. Their elected bosses get the credit, the blame, the spotlight, and the smile-filled family photo with fellow leaders. Behind the scenes, each political leader has their sherpa, a person who toils in the shadows, carrying out the complicated and disagreeable pre-summit work.

Prime Minister Stephen Harper's sherpa was Len Edwards, the deputy minister of the Canada's Foreign Affairs Department. In March 2010, Edwards led his nineteen counterparts at a closed-door meeting in Ottawa. It was over those two days of private discussion that they would hash out the issues facing the world's still sputtering economy, and more or less decide what it was their leaders were going to say about it at their summit in three months' time in Toronto.

There was a lot riding on the Toronto G20 summit of 2010. It was the first permanent summit of the emerging world leaders' club after its three emergency sessions. The G20 had been around since 1999, but had largely been a vehicle for finance ministers to meet. Former Liberal finance minister Paul Martin was a big backer of this group. The collapse of Lehman Brothers in 2008 and the economic meltdown it triggered across the globe pushed the leaders to take over the G20 themselves. They decided to make the G20 the main multilateral vehicle for dealing with the global economy, a role that had previously fallen to the G8 before it expanded its mandate to security, climate change, food safety, and international development. With increasing frequency, the international crisis on any given day would trump the G8's carefully scripted plans.

Harper was driven by a sense of urgency, deeply concerned about protecting Canada from the spread of the worst effects of the recession, and determined to play a leading role in helping fix the situation globally. "This was very much in his sweet spot," Edwards told me. "He felt that Canada could play an important role in the G20 at a time of the emergency because of some of the policies that his government and indeed his predecessor's government had played in ensuring that Canada had a strong banking sector for one."

Edwards said the previous Liberal government laid the "ground work" for Harper's success. It was Paul Martin who blocked the two proposed mergers of Canada's four big banks back in 1998, and who cut spending and managed to slay the deficit the Liberals inherited from the Progressive Conservatives in 1993. But when Harper embraced the challenges of the 2008–09 recession, Edwards said "he spoke of his policies as the prime minister of Canada and the head of the Conservative government."

As Edwards and his fellow sherpas were getting down to business in March 2010 in Ottawa the worst of the recession had been weathered, but they were still very worried about the possibility of another big downturn if the G20 didn't rise to the occasion. The possibility of a "double-dip recession" was discussed at length in the four-page memorandum that Edwards brought to the meeting to frame the discussion. It was not a public document, but I obtained a copy from a confidential source. "As we prepare to meet in March in Ottawa, here is how Canada views the state of play on deliverables for Toronto, according to the main themes we will discuss," it said.

First and foremost, Canada wanted to ensure there was no "premature withdrawal" of stimulus spending. That was Canada's top priority for avoiding another financial calamity. The memo stated that modest growth and increased business and consumer confidence could be viewed as positive signs of economic recovery, but it warned that "output still remains below pre-crisis levels" and credit remains "relatively" tight. "As such, there remains a risk that premature withdrawal of stimulus could jeopardize the current recovery. As growth recovers, there is also a risk that unemployment will continue to lag behind," it said. Ending stimulus spending too soon "could risk a double-dip recession and higher unemployment." This is interesting because Harper was no fan of stimulus spending. He was no Keynesian, but the stark reality of the 2008–09 meltdown forced him to temporarily change his economic stripes. It was a tough pill to swallow, especially for finance minister Jim Flaherty. Still, the Conservatives brought in their temporary $6 billion stimulus plan in 2009. It was set to expire in 2011, as Edwards was leading a broader closed-door discussion about the risks associated with that.

"We were trying to ensure that the impact of the global downturn didn't have undue negative effects in Canada," Edwards recalled. "So yes, it required a bit of a 180-degree shift in terms of how he regarded and I'm sure how Mr Flaherty regarded the need for fiscal prudence. But it was certainly what needed to be done and he did not hesitate in doing it."

The memo outlined Canada's other priorities heading into the summit. It made clear that Canada believed that nothing less than the future credibility of the G20 was at stake. Canada wanted to sustain the momentum that was started by the G20's "New Beginning" framework the previous fall at its Pittsburgh summit that emphasized the importance of promoting sustainable and balanced growth. "In Canada's view, the G20's future credibility and effectiveness will be judged by its ability to move forward on this key commitment," the memo said.

It also underlined the importance of Harper's sacrosanct economic principles: resisting protectionism and promoting free trade and investment. It urged the sherpas to "consider where there may be opportunities for Leaders to support and demonstrate further measures towards liberalization of trade and investment flows."

It called for the strengthening of the financial and regulatory system, because Canada saw that as an essential way to avoid future crises. "We must fully implement all G20 commitments on enhancing sound regulation and strengthening transparency in order to avoid a return to the excessive risk-taking that caused the crisis," the memo said. It went on to say that there had been substantial progress in strengthening oversight, risk management, transparency, and international co-operation, but that there could be no let-up in the commitment to "develop by year-end strong international rules on capital and liquidity" among other things.

The document also revealed that the sherpas would have a surprise visitor: Harper himself planned to drop in for the opening day of the meeting and speak to the group directly. Harper's visit was to follow an opening session of experts from the International Monetary Fund and World Bank. It was unusual for a leader to put in an appearance at a sherpa meeting, but it underlined Harper's personal commitment to making sure the summit that he was about to host would be a success.

Harper didn't overstay his welcome, joining the meeting for fifteen to twenty minutes.

"It was the symbolism of it that was important," Edwards recalled. "He was a prime minister that was meeting with the senior representatives of the other leaders and letting them know what his preoccupations were, and just giving them a bit of the time of day."

Edwards said Harper's cameo paid dividends later. "I think it stood us in good stead through the final stages when I was chairing meetings and we were trying to come to agreements and so forth; they certainly knew where my prime minister stood because he'd come to that meeting."

When the world arrived at Harper's doorstep in June 2010, he was in his element. After ending the G8 summit in the Muskoka town of Huntsville, Ontario, he and his fellow leaders helicoptered to downtown Toronto. Harper took a seat at the head of a large round table at the Toronto Convention Centre and opened the G20, the second half of this unprecedented round of back-to-back summits. The prime minister set the tone immediately. With the "recent skittishness of markets" facing them, Harper told his fellow leaders that the time had come for coordinated, balanced, and decisive action. "Here is the tightrope that we must walk: to sustain recovery it is imperative that we follow through on our existing stimulus plans," he said, encapsulating his take on the closed-door discussion of the sherpas three months earlier. "But at the same time, advanced countries must send a clear message that as our stimulus plans expire, we will focus on getting our fiscal houses in order."

There had been some tough discussions in the intervening months leading up to the summits, but in terms of the economic agenda Harper wanted to pursue, everything was pretty much on track.

Harper and Merkel found themselves allied at the G20 as they called for more focus on deficit reduction and the winding down of government-funded stimulus projects. But U.S. president Barack Obama, who wanted to keep the stimulus taps turned on, opposed them. In the end, there was compromise. Harper's success came in the summit's final communiqué that committed the countries to cutting their deficits in half by 2013, and ensuring their debt loads were on the road to being lowered by 2016.

"It was a very strong performance, and it showed itself at the summit table," Edwards recalled. "He was very forthright as you would have guessed from the way he is as a man, and the way he deals with other problems ... Not everyone agreed with him at the table but he was certainly one of the leading voices throughout this economic crisis."

The 2010 G20 leaders' summit acknowledged that some countries might not be able cut their deficits as fast as others. "At the same time, recent events highlight the importance of sustainable public finances and the need for our countries to put in place credible, properly phased and growth-friendly plans to deliver fiscal sustainability, differentiated for and tailored to national circumstances," said the summit's final communiqué.

A year later, Harper carried on with confidence at the next G20 in in the south of France. He stood in a boardroom looking down on the wealth of Cannes. The luxury yachts anchored along the French Riviera shoreline below spoke to a wealth that did not exist in other parts of Europe.[7] French president Nicolas Sarkozy, the summit's host, was all gloom and doom, warning that Europe was on the verge of being ripped apart. Greece's economy was on the verge of default, imperilling its continued membership in the European currency, as well as the greater EU itself. "If the euro exploded, Europe would explode. And in fact it's the guarantee of peace on the continent where there were terrible wars – fiercer than anywhere else in the world – not in the fifteenth century but in the twentieth century."

Harper countered Sarkozy with the voice of reason. He said Greece's exit from the eurozone was a topic of discussion, but he believed that simply wouldn't come to pass. "My expectation is that cooler heads will prevail and the (bailout) package will be accepted and we'll move forward on that basis."[8] He also said Greek prime minister George Papandreou was given a stern message: "If you don't accept the (bailout) plan, you're going to be outside the euro."[9]

The fears of another recession still lingered. Europe needed a bailout, but Harper held firm against contributing any Canadian cash to the cause. Back home, Canada's own unemployment rate was rising.[10] "It is the government of Canada's conviction that Europe remains fully capable of dealing with its own European problems," Harper told reporters travelling with him. As the yachts bobbed in the harbour below, he added: "There is a lot of wealth here. There is a lot of firepower here."

Harper's journey through G20 summitry continued, and he gradually found himself off side in arguing that austerity was key to economic recovery. At the November 2013, St Petersburg, Russia summit, Harper could count on the support of fewer fellow leaders. Russian president Vladimir Putin was one of those who actually shared Harper's view. Flaherty, who was travelling with Harper, said growth was all about finding the right balance. "We are spending money on job creation and on job training, very substantial long-term infrastructure projects, so that's one part of the balance," Flaherty said. "The other part of the balance is making sure you're back to balanced budgets, and addressing the debt-to-GDP ratio in the medium term."[11]

In November 2014, Harper won positive international headlines at the G20 summit in Brisbane, Australia, for famously telling Putin to "get out" of Ukraine. But that summit also saw the G20 evolving beyond austerity. It set a target to raise global output by 2 per cent over the coming five years. It recommended a major global infrastructure spending push to stimulate stagnating growth. The International Monetary Fund recommended governments run deficits to do this, saying they could take advantage of historically low interest rates.

The Liberals under Justin Trudeau would unseat Harper from power less than a year later running on that exact platform, while Harper held firm to his no-deficit policy. When Trudeau made his G20 debut in November 2015, he found himself in lockstep with the new consensus taking shape there. "I'll be talking about the fact that in order to create more global growth, particularly in support of the middle class around the globe, we need to be investing," Trudeau said ahead of the trip. "I believe in investment rather than austerity."

Edwards said Harper earned his stripes as an "economic statesman" who made a lasting, positive contribution to the world at a time of great financial crisis. Harper was a serious man who read voraciously and came to meetings prepared. He understood complex subject matter and always asked the right questions. In their private moments, usually sharing a ride in an automobile, Edwards said he and Harper usually gravitated towards three topics of discussion when they had a little down time: music (Harper had an encyclopedic knowledge of the Beatles, and Edwards grew up in a musical family and had a daughter, Kathleen, who became a successful Canadian recording artist), hockey, and a shared love of history.

When it came to dealing with other leaders, Harper dove in head first; he just wasn't one for interpersonal niceties. "Mr Harper was never, I felt, extremely comfortable in these social situations, but he engaged in to and fro that you see at the meeting table. Between the sessions when they circulate and talk to each other and so forth, he was always playing that game very effectively – talking to people he needed to talk to," Edwards said. "I think he will be remembered for his economic leadership. I don't think there's any question about that."

To the very end, Harper defended his approach towards guiding Canada through the Great Recession, including his deeply held belief that the country's books had to be balanced. The day before he was defeated, on 18 October 2015, the prime minister spoke with *Bloomberg* in Mississauga, Ontario. It was his last day on the campaign trail, before he would head off to Calgary to meet his political fate the following evening. Looking back, Harper was clearly proud of how he had steered Canada through the recent years of global economic upheaval. And he blasted Trudeau's plan for running deficits to pay for a new stimulus as being part of "some imaginary future of rainbows and unicorns."[12]

"Canada's growth has been more consistent and steadier than other developed major economies and should continue to be so in the next few years given the strong economic fundamentals we've created in banking and housing and ... federal government balance sheets," Harper said.

"I often tell people when we look back at the financial crisis the government did some important things, we actually did run a large stimulus program, we did it right, we didn't build new bureaucracy, we sped up existing infrastructure, got the money out the door, supported the Canadian economy," Harper added. "But often I think what is underestimated is what we did not do. We turned down the request to permanently expand government bureaucracy, to permanently expand entitlement programs, to really take us down the path of a structural deficit.

"So I think looking back, had other people been there we would not have come out of the recession quickly, would not have come out with a balanced budget, would not have had the good fundamentals we have, we would be on the same deficit, debt, zero growth track that you see most European countries on."[13]

The day before his defeat in the 2015 election, *Bloomberg's* Ottawa bureau chief Theophilos Argitis asked Harper to look back ten years and imagine what that decade would have looked like for Canada economically if he had never been elected, and the Liberals had carried on in office. Harper was emphatic about one thing: Canada would not have become the ardent free-traders that they had become had it not been for his government. "One thing we'd know for sure would be different is that Canada would continue to be the most significant trading economy in the world with virtually no trading agreements. One of the big transformations this government has made has been building our free trade network across the world," Harper said.

"We're going to have as consequences of the agreements we've concluded, obviously the European Union and most recently the Trans-Pacific Partnership, Canada is going to have virtually tariff free access to two thirds of the global economy, making Canada one of the best – not just good for global supply chains – but one of the best countries in the world from which to be a platform to do global business in the Asia Pacific, the Americas and in Europe."[14]

The Harper government boasted that it had increased the number of countries with which Canada had free trade deals by ten times. Canada reached fifty-one, up from five before they took power, two weeks before the 19 October 2015 federal election when an agreement by the twelve Pacific Rim countries negotiating the TPP was reached. Canada's new Liberal government would sign the deal in February 2016, but formal ratification would have to wait. The Liberal government professed to be free traders too, but this wasn't their deal. They needed to actually read the 6,000-page text and present it to Canadians – in both official languages – before consulting with its long list of supporters and critics and putting it to a vote in Parliament. As for CETA, the free trade deal with Europe, the timeline on getting that signed and eventually ratified – or implemented in some practical form – extended years past Harper's departure from 24 Sussex. As for the other free trade deals, some were with big fish like South Korea or moved the goalposts forward into emerging Western Hemisphere markets such as Peru and Colombia. But others were with economies that were decidedly low-volume – Israel, Jordan, and that bastion of economic corruption, Ukraine. Meanwhile, there were no deals with China and India, despite their obvious importance. There had been lots of talk of one

with Japan, but Japan simply relegated a bilateral deal with Canada
to the back burner in favour of engaging with it through the TPP.
But with the two biggest prizes – CETA and the TPP – while Harper
could not legitimately claim, to borrow a metaphor from his
beloved sport, hockey, that he had put the puck in the net by himself, he could certainly say he moved it up the ice. The actual goals
would be scored on the Liberal watch, or not at all.

Still, Harper's pursuit of trade deals had its own share of daunt-
ing hurdles. Canada's ambitious free trade deal with Europe had a
particularly epic and tortuous timeline. Negotiations started in 2009,
with the hope of reaching an agreement within three years. After
four years of negotiations, Harper announced with great fanfare that
he was flying off to Brussels to trumpet victory.

"This is a big deal. This is the biggest deal Canada has ever made.
Indeed, it is an historical achievement," Harper declared in Brussels
on that October 2013 day. The deal would give Canada greater access
to a market of 500 million consumers.

Earlier that morning, I sat, classroom-style, with a bleary-eyed
group of Canadian reporters in a room inside our country's Brussels
embassy after our impromptu transatlantic flight on the prime minister's plane. At the head of the class was the man who was going to
brief us – a person we could not identify by name but had to refer to
as "a senior government official." After all, this was Harper's big moment. The prime minister's photo-op and press conference with European Commission president José Manuel Barroso would take place
later in the day at the commission's large press theatre. The government clearly saw no point in letting a "senior government official"
share the spotlight on this auspicious day with the prime minister
who had invested so much political capital in securing what was,
without a doubt, a major trade deal with a very rich group of countries, notwithstanding the periodic economic meltdowns of some of
its more fiscally backwards members. It should also be noted that at
no time during our twenty-four-hour trip to Brussels with the prime
minister did the journalists travelling with Harper receive any on-
the-record briefing from Canada's chief negotiator, Steve Verhuel.

So there we sat in Canada's Belgian embassy, waiting to be briefed,
waiting to see a text of the agreement that had been negotiated in
secret and had sparked no end of controversy and criticism.

We got the briefing. But there was no text.

The senior government official gave us a forty-four-page Canadian government summary that outlined what Canada had won in this deal. The main one was greater access for Canadian pork and beef in Europe. There was still "drafting and fine tuning" of the text that would take place, and there would need to be a "scrub" of it as well to make sure it was "legally coherent." Naturally, the senior government official was peppered with questions about the concessions Canada made at the bargaining table, which, by the way, are completely par for the course in any negotiation. Europe won some big concessions, which weren't outlined in the government's forty-four-page highlight package: European companies won the right to bid on contracts at the provincial and municipal levels, which would put them in the running for billions of government procurement dollars. Not even the North American Free Trade Agreement afforded Mexican and American companies that right. Drug patents for brand-name European pharmaceuticals were extended by two years, which would delay the introduction of cheaper generic drugs into the market, which was estimated to increase the cost to Canadian consumers and provincial health plans by an extra $1 billion a year. CETA also eliminated tariffs in the auto trade, which would make luxury European cars more affordable and more competitive with North American vehicles. The brochure declared: "Under CETA, not only will world-class Canadian products enjoy preferential access to the EU, Canadians will also have the tools and support they need to succeed in this lucrative market ... The vast benefits will be shared by Canadians across the country, from those who produce primary products – for example minerals and agricultural products – to those who turn them into value-added processed and manufactured goods."

Harper was back in Ottawa on the same calendar day. From Brussels he brought with him a signed "agreement in principle." The negotiations continued for almost another year.

A camera-ready text was ready for public consumption on 26 September 2014. Barroso flew to Ottawa with European Council president Herman Van Rompuy for another round of handshakes and photo-ops with Harper. Barroso predicted all parties would ratify the deal in 2015 and that it would be in force by 2016. But 2015 came and went with no ratification. Instead, opposition was simmering in parts of Europe, beginning in the summer of 2014, about a controversial provision of the deal on how to settle disputes between companies and the various levels of government. Opposition to a key section on an investor-state dispute settlement mechanism, known as ISDS, began to grow in some French and German political circles, along with a growing number of anti-trade activists in Europe, who were joined by the Council of Canadians. The clause gave companies the power to sue governments. The ISDS opponents believed this could give companies a legal club with which to beat foreign governments if they didn't think they were reaping enough profit. This also fed anti-trade activists' narrative that big multinationals were intent on bulldozing the laws and regulations of sovereign countries in a broad range of areas including food safety, the environment, and labour. German economy minister Sigmar Gabriel lit a fuse that followed Barroso and Van Rompuy to Ottawa. "It is completely clear that we reject these investment protection agreements," Gabriel said during a debate in the German parliament.[15]

The European politicians insisted there was no serious problem, and so did every French and German official I spoke with. The discontent may have been rooted in domestic German politics because the objections were from the Social Democratic Party, which was backing Merkel's Christian Democratic Union in Germany's governing coalition. But those domestic German ripples lapped Canadian shores, complicating Harper's goal of finalizing his mega trade deal. By the end of 2014, Barroso and Van Rompuy finished serving their terms and moved on. Harper, of course, went down to defeat in October 2015.

In January 2016 I sat down with Marie-Anne Coninsx, the European Union's ambassador to Canada, at her high-rise Ottawa office, and asked her for her best estimate of when CETA would come into force. Her answer? "Early 2017." Coninsx appeared slightly weary of the topic, describing that when she first arrived in Ottawa in 2013, all anybody wanted to talk about was the free trade deal.

But Coninsx was actually able to shed some light on how the complex deal, which presumably had to pass muster with twenty-eight European countries, might actually come to be ratified. She removed the possibility that any one European country with a grudge against Canada possessed the power to reject ratification. That was a lingering possibility, particularly in Romania and Hungary, because their citizens required visas to come to Canada. Opposition by Belgium's Wallonia region also had to be overcome.

"The most important stage in order to start implementation will be the agreement of the European Parliament, the consent of the European Parliament," Coninsx explained. "If the parliament says yes, at that moment, the agreement can start its provisional implementation."

According to Coninsx, provisional implementation meant that pretty much the entire deal would apply to all areas that are the "exclusive competence of the European Union, which means more than 90 per cent." And in her view, that would likely happen in early 2017.

By the end of February 2016 there were indications things might be moving a little more quickly than that. International trade minister Chrystia Freeland announced that the government's review of CETA was done. The deal was signed on 30 October in Brussels, with the Liberals thanking Harper for his work. The ISDS problem had been ironed out. The revised section gave governments greater power to pass labour and environmental regulations. "The core notion of having a dispute-resolution process is not to supersede that right to regulate – it is to ensure that governments don't discriminate against foreign investors," the minister explained. Freeland also gave her seal of approval to the deal. "This is really a gold-plated trade deal," she said. "It is going to bring tremendous benefit to Canadians and to Europeans. We are going to feel it all in a real increase in prosperity and I'm confident this is going to become the landmark trade agreement."[16]

It would have been hard to imagine Harper saying it any differently.

*　*　*

As for Harper's role in getting CETA done, this much can be said: he went down swinging. Harper used his last trip to Europe in June 2015 to mount one final effort to get it approved. The main purpose of this excursion was to attend the G7 leaders' summit in Germany's Bavarian Alps. It would also be the last time he would speak face to face with Angela Merkel, now carrying the weight of the world on her shoulders. Germany was facing an influx of an estimated one million Syrian refugees, and after an initial welcome it started closing its borders in an ugly backlash against foreigners. Aided by the fact she was fluent in Russian owing to her East Berlin upbringing before the fall of the Wall, Merkel was also the West's best chance for talking sense to Russian president Vladimir Putin, who not only was making mischief in Ukraine but may have held the key to talking sense into his despotic ally, Syrian president Bashar Assad, who was busy killing off tens of thousands of his own people in a civil war that had reduced great swaths of his country to rubble. Like Harper, Merkel was finding out that her international financial performance, especially her support of austerity, was becoming very much offside. Former German foreign minister and Green party leader Joschka Fischer tore a strip off Merkel earlier in the year, declaring her policy officially "in tatters" with the victory of the leftist Syrzia party in Greece and anti-austerity sentiment growing in France, Italy, and Spain. Fischer declared that Merkel's policy of "saving your way out of a demand shortfall" was threatening the very existence of the euro.[17]

Just before his last meeting with Merkel, Harper made one more pitch for the European free trade deal by meeting the new European Council president Donald Tusk and the new European Commission president Jean-Claude Juncker in the castle of Schloss Elmau, the main G7 summit site in the beautiful, secluded, and heavily fortified Bavarian Alp village. Tusk, the former prime minister of Poland, was a good friend, and the prime minister congratulated him on his new appointment. Forty-five minutes later, Harper had made his way to the adjacent building, a luxury resort with floor-length glass windows that gave onto a stunning mountain vista. Large panels of bulletproof glass lined the balcony, leaving the view unspoiled. In terms of setting, Merkel had more than returned the favour for her trip to Harrington Lake three summers earlier. Harper and Merkel were standing, smiling, and chatting amiably like the old friends that they were. Merkel moved her hands describing how something in the room or the area was "much larger" than it had been. Harper beamed a warm smile back at her, paying close attention to her every word. And then he looked over at us, the pool of journalists that had been swept into the room to observe the start of the meeting.

"Merci, tout le monde," Harper said.

His right hand then arched upwards, in a weary, dismissive wave. We had our picture, and now he wanted us gone. It was time for the battered austerity allies to have one more face-to-face conversation. Harper dropped onto a couch and faced Merkel, who was seated on another directly opposite. We were ushered swiftly out of the room by grim-faced German handlers, but not before Harper was seen flashing one more smile at Merkel and heard to say:

"It's going well so far."

CHAPTER SIX

Saving Mothers, Children, and Dollars

MAY 2014

United Nations secretary-general Ban Ki-moon is addressing a packed ballroom at Toronto's Royal York Hotel, where some of the world's leading health professionals are meeting to find ways to prevent the unnecessary deaths of newborn babies and their mothers in the poorest countries. So far, everything is going well for Prime Minister Stephen Harper at the big international aid conference he is hosting. But before this day is done, the UN chief will pull the rug out from under the prime minister.

Ban thanks the prime minister for his new five-year commitment of $3.5 billion, announced a day earlier, to help improve maternal and newborn health in poor countries. It is known by the acronym MNCH, and the secretary-general urges other world leaders to pony up as well. This is Harper's signature foreign-aid initiative. In addition to the UN chief, the prime minister has brought together a wide range of international players in health, development, and politics, including the philanthropist Melinda Gates, the Aga Khan, and Queen Rania of Jordan, as well as the heads of several major UN agencies and the World Bank. They all laud Harper for showing leadership on an important issue. For Harper, it is crucial to have the UN's stamp of approval for this project.

Harper's Muskoka Initiative, as it was known, was aimed at accelerating progress towards two of the UN's eight Millennium Development Goals, or MDGs, that had been established at its turn-of-the-century summit: reducing child mortality (MDG4) and improving maternal health (MDG5). Harper introduced this initiative in 2010 when he hosted the G8 summit in Ontario's Muskoka region. He made an initial five-year, $1.1 billion pledge on top of $1.75 billion already being spent on the cause, and hoped to encourage visiting world leaders to contribute more. Later, in September 2010, Ban appointed Harper and Tanzanian president Jakaya Kikwete as the co-chairs of the new UN Commission on Information and Accountability for Women's and Children's Health, an oversight body charged with ensuring MNCH funds were properly spent. Harper elevated MNCH to the status of Canada's "flagship" development priority.

But this flagship aid initiative was not without controversy. Harper also slashed overall aid spending, plunging Canada well below the UN target for rich countries, and he banned all funding for abortion, triggering a firestorm of criticism. Canada's aid history has been troubled since the government started giving money to poor countries in 1950, but Harper found new ways to cut foreign aid while attempting to maintain the image of a benevolent donor. His government clawed back aid commitments by simply letting hundreds of millions of dollars in funding lapse – or die – as projects sat unapproved on a minister's desk.

Early on, Harper decided that none of Canada's MNCH money would go directly to funding projects that provided abortions as part of a family-planning strategy. Those options would be aimed at preventing the deaths of hundreds of thousands of women in pregnancy and childbirth each year, as well as annual deaths of nearly seven million children under five years old. The abortion ban sparked criticism from the leading British medical journal, *The Lancet*, and former U.S. secretary of state Hillary Clinton, among others. "You cannot have maternal health without reproductive health. And reproductive health includes contraception and family planning and access to legal, safe abortion," Clinton said. As well, the Conservatives imposed a five-year freeze on aid spending from 2010 to 2015 in order to slay the deficit resulting from billions of dollars in stimulus spending after the 2008 global financial meltdown. That meant Canada's overall aid spending had sunk well below the UN target of 0.7 per cent of gross national income, to 0.24 per cent by 2014, according to the annual survey by the Paris-based Organisation for Economic Co-operation and Development.

But at this moment in May 2014, with Ban at the podium, those controversies are forgotten. Ban breaks into a story that he says he has never before told in public. It is a poignant departure from the formal tone that usually characterizes the South Korean diplomat's speeches. "I have been known in my family, and everybody knows I am the eldest son ... in fact I should not have been. I should have been the third child. I had an elder sister, an elder brother, according to my mother, but unfortunately they died soon after their birth," Ban tells Harper's assembled audience. When he was young, Ban explains, it was quite normal to see women and children in his poor village die in childbirth. "People accepted this as a fact of their life. Our food was not sufficient; women feared giving birth. What should have been the most joyful day was often the scariest or often the saddest day instead."

Ban says that is what drives him to fight for the eradication of such needless deaths. That's why, he says, he launched his own UN initiative in September 2010 to improve maternal, newborn, and child health after seeing so many more needless deaths across Asia and Africa. The crowd bursts into applause. In that moment, Harper is able to bask in the approving glow of the chief of the world's largest multilateral organization – one that he and his ministers have often criticized. But what the secretary-general gives, he will soon take away.

Three hours later, Ban and Harper are standing next to each other at separate podiums for a final press conference to close the three days of meetings. As the first reporter to the microphone, I ask the two men whether Canada needs to increase its overall commitment for international development – notwithstanding Harper's generous promise of $700 million per year for the next five years for the MNCH program – to bring it closer to the 0.7 per cent of GNI target. Canada adopted the 0.7 per cent target in 1970 as part of Pierre Trudeau's foreign policy review. As Trudeau was assuming power, his predecessor Lester Pearson was chairing the World Bank's 1969 blue-ribbon Commission on International Development, which made the recommendation that national governments should spend 1 per cent of GNI on foreign aid. Pearson's foreign minister, Paul Martin Senior, had made the same commitment in 1966.[1] Trudeau eventually settled for a slightly lower 0.7 per cent target. In 1970's

Foreign Policy for Canadians, Trudeau wrote: "The values of Canadian society, as well as the future prosperity and security of Canadians,
are closely and inextricably linked to the future of the wider world
community of which we are a part. It is thus important for Canada
that we accept our fair share of responsibilities of membership in the
world community."[2]

Meeting that target has since proven elusive for most developed
countries. Only six countries, including Britain, have reached it.
Canada never has, reaching an all-time high of 0.53 per cent of GNI
in 1975 under the Trudeau Liberals.[3] Aid spending sank like a stone
under the Chrétien Liberals, plummeting to 0.25 per cent of GNI by
2000 after several years of austerity.[4] Despite having an economy
worse off than Canada's, Britain became the first G7 country to commit to meeting the target in 2013, something I point out to Harper
and Ban in the preamble to my question.

Harper deflects the question, saying Canada targets its foreign aid
spending to programs that produce results. "It's the philosophy of
our government and, I believe, of Canadians more broadly that we
do not measure things in terms of the amount of money we spend,
but in terms of the results we achieve."

Then it's Ban's turn. He prefaces his remarks by saying he is grateful for Canada's continuing support in addressing humanitarian
crises such as the civil war in Syria, which by any measure has been
generous. However, Ban points out that the 0.7 target was also one
of the 2000 Millennium Development Goals, and says he believes
Canada has the ability to live up to that commitment as well. "This
overall agreed target should be met," he says, standing next to Harper. "I sincerely hope that the countries of the OECD and particularly
G7 should lead by example."

Ban's comment was a bit of a wet blanket over Harper's presentation of Canada as benevolent. Harper may have presented the
Muskoka Initiative as a way of kickstarting the stalled effort to reduce the deaths of children and improving the health of mothers.
But he selectively ignored another component of the MDGs by re-
fusing to commit to the 0.7 per cent development target.

The Lancet also took Harper to task for his overall lack of aid
spending, despite the $3.5 billion MNCH investment. In a commen-
tary published one week after the Toronto conference, it called on

Canada to live up to the 0.7 per cent commitment it had made both in the 1970s and later when it committed to the MDGs in 2000. "It has been many years since Stephen Harper had so much unconditional love poured over him," said the commentary. "But there are good reasons to ask questions about Canada's magnificent promise."[5] First, *The Lancet* criticized Harper for not including reproductive health issues in its MNCH initiative – specifically abortion, saying they "had been dropped by a conservative government that, for example, saw the toll of over 20 million unsafe abortions as too 'divisive' to discuss." Secondly, the commentary said Canada "remains a long way from fulfilling its promise of 0.7 per cent" of GNI in aid funding. It said Canada's overall level of spending on aid had declined sharply since the government introduced its MNCH initiative, falling from 0.34 per cent of GNI in 2010. "Prime Minister Harper's commitment to mothers and children is generous and sincere," the commentary concluded. "But we should also say firmly and respectfully that the scope of his commitment remains too narrow, that he needs to deepen his financial promise still further if he is to meet the international commitments his nation has signed up to ..."[6]

While the Harper government was making high-profile aid announcements to specially chosen international guests, less transparent aid cuts were taking place inside the newly amalgamated Department of Foreign Affairs, Trade and Development in 2014. Not only was overall aid spending being slashed, the government wasn't even spending the money it had allotted to help poor countries. In 2013, it failed to spend 13 per cent of its budget, $419 million of the $3.14 billion that Parliament had authorized it to spend on grants and contributions to poor countries and UN organizations.[7] In November 2014, the first performance report was released for the newly amalgamated Foreign Affairs Department, which had absorbed the Canadian International Development Agency the previous year. It revealed that of the $917 million that was available to spend on alleviating poverty abroad for the year 2013–14, only $792 million had been spent. That left more than $125 million in lapsed funding, 14 per cent of funds budgeted.

That money is not simply kept by the department and rolled over into the next year's budget – it is returned to the central treasury. Like a twenty-dollar bill discovered in a pair of pants on laundry day, this is found money for the federal government. In this case, it could be used to help the government pay down its deficit in an election year to show taxpayers how well it was managing the economy. The NDP's development critic, Hélène Laverdière, was one of several people I spoke to who suggested that "The Conservatives are trying to balance the books on the backs of some of the most vulnerable people who need our support."

New Democrat foreign affairs critic Paul Dewar challenged foreign affairs minister John Baird over the lapsed funding during testimony at a House of Commons committee in November 2013. "Why is it taking so long for the approvals from the department to get to you? Why aren't these being approved? The approval process from your bureaucrats seemingly gets stuck with you," Dewar asked the minister at the Standing Committee on Foreign Affairs and International Development. Baird replied: "I don't make any bones about that. I don't wake up every morning with a desire to spend every single dollar that I can possibly spend."

Roger Earnhardt, who retired after a twenty-seven-year career at the now-defunct Canadian International Development Agency, said the phenomenon of lapsed funding was something he had never seen until the latter portion of his career when the Conservatives were in power. Based on the department's internal procedures, the only way to do that is with political direction, he explained in an interview. From 2000 to 2010, Earnhardt was CIDA's director general of multilateral development institutions, responsible for the flow of Canadian dollars to UN organizations and regional development banks. One thing he learned in all those years was to spend every last penny on what Parliament intended it to be spent on.

"There was always mechanisms in place to make sure we'd spent the money that was allocated to us," Earnhardt said. The concept of hundreds of millions of development dollars going unspent was simply not something that was allowed to happen in the department. "You can only do that if you deliberately want to because the agency is so good at spending money we're always within a couple of million dollars of our budget."

Department officials would monitor the pace of spending, keeping a close eye on the five months leading up to 31 March, the end of the government's fiscal year. The agency's management committee

would meet and indicate the projects for which money was likely to
go unspent, he said. The plan was to give those funds to a United Nations agency ahead of schedule, taking advantage of the fact that
Canada's fiscal year ended in March while the UN operated according to the calendar year.

"We would owe them a payment for the calendar year and we would
just make it in March rather than in June, for example. It was a benefit
to them because the earlier in the calendar year they got the money,
the better it is for their planning," said Earnhardt. The key to doing that,
without breaking any rules, was for department officials to get their
minister's approval in advance. Suddenly, said Earnhardt, the approvals
stopped coming. "It hadn't been done before. It was really a deliberate
manoeuver to cut back spending in an underhanded way because it's
not announced in the estimates, it's not approved by Parliament. It's
sort of reducing spending through a back-door mechanism, which isn't
necessarily a legitimate way to go about it. It's not open."

University of Ottawa political scientist Stephen Brown told me
that while he believed spending money on young pregnant mothers and their babies in the developing world was a worthy cause,
Harper's overall development strategy was fundamentally flawed.
That was because the government was not increasing its aid budget, which meant that its big-ticket MNCH spending initiative would
only reduce what could be accomplished in other areas. "We're focusing on symptoms and we're abandoning the underlying causes,
which are poverty and inequality."

Dewar, the NDP's foreign affairs critic, said the government was
deliberately showcasing MNCH to mask the fact it had cut overall
development spending. "Overseas assistance development should be
done in a way that has high impact with people we're trying to help,"
Dewar told me. He said the Conservatives were using development
assistance "for the promotion of the government."

International development minister Christian Paradis acknowledged that one of the goals of the MNCH initiative was to promote
Canada's brand outside of its borders. During an interview in the
spring of 2014, Paradis was enthusiastic and sincere about the need
to tackle the problem. "We want to be a leader in this and we can do
more," Paradis told me. "This is important for the taxpayers to fully
appreciate how Canada is well-branded all around the globe."

Earnhardt said he started seeing cracks in Canada's reputation, particularly in Africa, where he was once posted and visited regularly for CIDA. "I took part in numerous multilateral meetings over ten years. I would say by the time of the end of that period, around 2010, our reputation was much weaker than it had been earlier on," he said. "I had people that I'd been in meetings with four or five years in a row, and they'd take me aside and say, 'What's wrong with Canada here? Why aren't you being supportive on this?'" Over his last decade at CIDA, Earnhardt regularly represented Canada at the replenishment meetings for the world's regional development banks, particularly in Asia and Africa. Deciding each country's contribution for what would usually be a three-year spending commitment required attending two or three meetings before a gathering where countries were expected to come up with a final figure in order to set the bank's budget. Around 2007, Canada started showing up without a number, Earnhardt recalled.

"People would say, 'Why can't you come up with a number? Everybody else has done it.'" Eventually Earnhardt and his team would "muddle through" by offering up a figure with the hope they'd get it approved in Ottawa, which they usually did. Earnhardt recalled a 2009 meeting in Paris when that short leash became particularly uncomfortable. He had arrived at the final meeting without an actual pledge. His team managed to muddle through, but not before he was pulled aside by a senior World Bank official. "He wasn't terribly pleased that we weren't able to deliver," Earnhardt recalled. "Privately, he wasn't pleased."

✻ ✻ ✻

Respecting taxpayers' money became a growing concern in international development circles at the turn of the twenty-first century, as corruption and waste made donor countries increasingly skeptical. Two of Harper's Canadian neoconservative predecessors also gave the prime minister ammunition to pursue a harder-edged aid policy. Former Ontario premier Mike Harris and founding Reform Party leader Preston Manning co-authored a foreign policy treatise in 2007 as part of a series of books under the banner "Canada

Strong and Free." They viewed aid as part of a weak foreign policy that needed to be toughened up: "Canadians work hard for their money. They do not mind paying taxes for good purpose – and most would agree that alleviating poverty is such a purpose."[8] With a fondness for italics to stress their argument, Harris and Manning questioned the need to fund the MDGs, which the UN Millennium Project estimated would require "$70–$80 billion *each year*" to meet the targets. "This in turn requires donor countries such as Canada to approximately *double* the amount they give as a share of GNP." They said the hundred billion spent annually across the globe on development "*cannot be proven* to be effective in relieving poverty."[9] They said aid should be about providing "tools of wealth creation" and "promoting economic freedom" with more public-private partnerships and less reliance on governments. And they asserted: "As we have already said, the evidence showing that development aid has any effect in alleviating poverty or producing prosperity is inconclusive at best."[10]

Finally, Harris and Manning took aim at the UN's call at the 2000 Millennium Summit for rich countries to meet the 0.7 per cent of GNI target for aid spending. "Why adopt a random, analytically arbitrary monetary target rather than a seasoned, evidence-based target keyed to results? In addition to the oft-noted absence of any fiscal, macroeconomic, or empirical basis for this 0.7 per cent target, it is flawed from a deeper perspective," they wrote. "The commitment targets money *to be spent*; it says nothing of how, or how well, it is *used*. Where is the incentive to improve, or even achieve poverty reduction or development when more aid money flows each year regardless of its effectiveness? This is the epitome of the preference for activity over results."[11] The arguments of Harris and Manning gave Harper the theoretical template to support his views.

Canada had a troubled history of delivering foreign aid, and there was enough blame for the Liberals and the Conservatives to share. Canada's best intentions never lived up to the expectations of Canada's foremost advocate of foreign aid, Lester Pearson. In 1950, when he was Louis St Laurent's external affairs minister, Pearson pushed for Canada's involvement in the Colombo Plan, the blueprint for economic development in India, Pakistan, and Ceylon (now known as Sri Lanka). The decision to participate was controversial and divided St Laurent and Pearson.[12] But Pearson eventually convinced St Laurent to participate.

When John Diefenbaker drove the Liberals from power in 1957, he entrenched the idea of marrying foreign aid to domestic economic interests. With the support of Saskatchewan wheat farmers, he found a way to get rid of their massive surpluses. In 1956–57, food accounted for 3 per cent of overseas development assistance. Two years later, it mushroomed to 50 per cent.[13]

When the Liberals returned to power in 1963 with Pearson as prime minister, the notion of "humane internationalism" was born. The idea was simple: helping the world's poorest rather than finding outlets for Canadian exports. Canada's aid budget doubled on his watch. Pierre Trudeau continued the focus on the world's poor in 1968 when he succeeded Pearson. But the newly created Canadian International Development Agency, first led by young entrepreneur Maurice Strong when it was founded in 1968, was under pressure to focus on more advanced countries that would be better able to buy Canadian goods and services.[14]

"The commitment to poverty alleviation added substance to Canada's claim to be a responsible and constructive member of the international community," wrote political scientist Elizabeth Riddell-Dixon.[15] "Having a foreign aid program dedicated to humane internationalist objectives helped Canada, especially in the later 1960s, to distance itself from the United States and its war in Vietnam. In short, Canada's policies on issues of peace and economic development were geared first and foremost to forwarding Canada's own immediate interests." This 1960s and 1970s tension between humane internationalism – acting altruistically – and using aid simply as an extension of Canada's economic interests anticipated the debate over the Harper government's approach. But there was a growing consensus emerging among international observers that the pendulum swung much farther towards Canada's self-interest under Harper than in previous decades.

In 1975, the Trudeau government's five-year development strategy emphasized helping the poorest of the poor. It declared that Canada "would harmonize various external and domestic policies which have an impact on developing countries ... in order to achieve its international development objectives."[16] The government also decided "the development assistance program will direct the bulk of its resources and expertise to the poorest countries of the world." In doing so, Trudeau also endorsed the 0.7 per cent target.[17] His government also decided that the United Nations would play the deciding role in determining which countries received support.

Canada's internal debate over foreign aid continued into the 1980s under Brian Mulroney's Progressive Conservatives. In 1987, the House of Commons External Affairs committee issued a report that tied aid to human rights for the first time, and called on the government to never let foreign aid dip below 0.5 per cent of GNI.[18] But Mulroney and his external affairs minister, Joe Clark, ultimately rejected that spending floor. The year 1989 marked the beginning of the end of robust foreign aid funding, a decline that continued under the Liberals; it also essentially marked the abandonment of the 0.7 per cent target, which would also be ignored throughout the Chrétien and Martin years.[19] By 2001, Canada posted its lowest foreign aid ratio, 0.21 per cent of GNI.[20]

"In the end no one really expects many countries to meet the targets anymore except for the Nordic countries and the Netherlands. They're not bad things to have, they're aspirational," said Earnhardt. "You can use it to keep a lot of countries from sliding back."

The twenty-first century dawned with new possibilities to alleviate poverty in underdeveloped countries. The economies of Canada and its Western allies were rebounding from the cutting and slashing of the deficit fighting of the 1990s. After years of stagnation and decline, development policy appeared to be moving in new directions. Public concern about transparency and accountability meant a new approach to aid and development had become mandatory.

When Canada hosted the Kananaskis 2002 G8 summit in Alberta, the Liberals decided to double aid spending in 2002 for each year to 2010, something that finance minister John Manley said "reflects the understanding that you cannot have a world of peace unless you address the world of need."[21] Chrétien appointed Robert Fowler to be his G8 sherpa to deliver his new Africa Action Plan to the attendees. Chrétien pledged $500 million for the Canada Fund for Africa, Canada's contribution to the broader international plan. This was focused on several areas: economic growth, market access and public sector investment, governance and institutions, health, nutrition, agriculture, water, and education.²² Canada also made huge, billion-dollar commitments to Afghanistan and Haiti, transforming them into its two largest bilateral aid recipients in the years to come.

Harper cut and reconfigured those Liberal aid initiatives after he won power in 2006. The Harper government dined out on the Liberals' aid spending increases for their first four years in office, adopting them as their own before slashing the budget altogether. Harper's ministers, then–CIDA minister Bev Oda in particular, regularly took credit for the Liberal commitment at Kananaskis in 2002 before the Muskoka Initiative was unveiled in 2010. Harper may have answered the growing calls in development circles for more accountability and transparency, but he simultaneously ignored the calls for broader multilateral coordination or boosting overall aid spending to meet the UN's 0.7 per cent target. In 2010, after eight years of Liberal-promised aid spending increases had come to an end, Harper froze aid spending and ramped up his own marquee MNCH project.

Harper still won support from some the world's leading development advocates. They were some of his A-list invitees to the May 2014 conference in Toronto, including Melinda Gates of the Gates Foundation, Queen Rania of Jordan, and the Aga Khan. But as big a fan as she may have been of Harper, Gates could not mask her concern when I reminded her of Canada's falling aid numbers in an interview. "I think Canada has honestly done a great job in some of these areas," she said. "But we'd never want to see a country go back down or slide backwards (on overall aid spending) because it's just not the right message."

One of the main beneficiaries of Harper's MNCH initiative was a small Ottawa-based non-governmental health organization called the Micronutrient Initiative (MI). It was one of the four main multilateral partners chosen by the government to receive MNCH funds. In 2010, it was given $75 million over five years to deliver important supplements such as vitamin A to poor countries to make young mothers and pregnant women healthier. At the November 2014 Francophonie summit in Senegal, Harper doubled that to a new five-year, $150 million commitment until 2020. Despite how well his organization had done under this initiative, Joel Spicer, the head of MI, attempted to take the measure of the man when he and a dozen other aid executives got privileged access to Harper in April 2014, a month prior to the big three-day Toronto conference. Spicer's long career had included stints at the United Nations and the World Bank, taking him from West Africa and South Asia to Washington and Geneva. He said it was rare for a world leader to make a commitment on a development issue and follow it through years later.

"What struck me – because I was really looking for it – is that he's actually sincere; he's personally committed to it," Spicer told me. "He was saying, 'I deal with so many issues on a daily basis and this is one of the ones I actually think is important.'"

Spicer recalled how others around the table were asking themselves what was in it for Harper. "There was some discussion about to what extent was this opportunistic. It was very clear he was personally committed, that he felt a sense of injustice," he said. "The fact of the matter is: this is not something that would win an election."

Whether Harper used MNCH for domestic political gain did not matter to Anthony Lake, the chief of the United Nations Children's Fund (UNICEF). "I do not know his (Harper's) motives. I'm sure parts of them are of genuine passion for children," Lake said in an interview. "And a part of it is probably political. And that's a good thing. We are all trying to make these issues part of the political scene because there should be a popular demand for dealing with the welfare of children around the world."

Earnhardt said it is hard to criticize a government for championing the cause of underprivileged women and children. But at the same time, "It's an easy one to champion." He aligned himself with other critics who said that the Conservatives were trying to soften their image with voters to reach new supporters beyond their traditional base. "I think there's a recognition that if you're going to get beyond a certain percentage of the population, they needed to show another side of the government. MNCH was one area that allowed them to do that." But by deciding that none of the funds for the initiative would go to projects that included abortion, the Conservatives were also pandering to their grassroots base, he said. "Somewhere in the government they decided this was a time where they could show their credentials to those who were opposed to abortion and include that in the program," said Earnhardt.

The Conservatives didn't immediately trumpet that part of the package when they announced their plans for this signature initiative in early 2010. Rumours abounded regarding the abortion issue in the months leading up to the June 2010 G8 leaders' summit in Ontario, but the government said little. On a visit to Ottawa on 31 March 2010 with her fellow G8 foreign ministers, U.S. secretary of state Hillary Clinton addressed the simmering controversy head on. "I do not think governments should be involved in making these decisions. It is perfectly legitimate for people to hold their own personal views based on conscience, religion or any other basis," Clinton said when asked about the issue by a Canadian reporter. "But I've always believed the government should not intervene in decisions of such intimacy." Clinton's host, foreign minister Lawrence Cannon, remained silent beside her.

Almost a month later, on 26 April 2010, Bev Oda, the cabinet minister for the Canadian International Development Agency, confirmed the abortion-funding ban at a meeting of G8 development ministers in Halifax. Harper was forced to defend it the next day in the House of Commons. "Canadians want to see their foreign aid money used for things that will help save the lives of women and children in ways that unite the Canadian people rather than divide them," Harper said. "We understand that other governments, that other taxpayers, may do something different."

One month later, and with just a month to go before Harper welcomed his fellow G8 leaders to Canada, the British medical journal *The Lancet* sharply criticized the government in an editorial. It lamented the absence of emergency obstetric care in Harper's plan, along with any provisions aimed at improving access to safe abortion. "Sadly, this omission is no accident, but a conscious decision by Canada's Conservative Government not to support groups that undertake abortions in developing countries. This stance must change," the editorial said, pointing out how 70,000 women across the world died each year from unsafe abortions.[23] "The Canadian Government does not deprive women living in Canada from access to safe abortions; it is therefore hypocritical and unjust that it tries to do so abroad." *The Lancet* called on Canada's fellow G8 leaders to stand up to the abortion ban, but in the end they did not. "Although the country's decision only affects a small number of developing countries where abortion is legal, bans on the procedure, which are detrimental to public health, should be challenged by the G8, not tacitly supported. Canada and the other G8 nations could show real leadership with a final maternal health plan that is based on sound scientific evidence and not prejudice."[24]

Senior public servants inside CIDA also opposed the no-abortion policy. Internal briefing documents prepared for Oda made it clear that access to safe abortions could save the lives of numerous women in developing countries. "How can we make it happen?" was the heading of the document that was released under Access to Information. Then–CIDA president Margaret Biggs approved it. It listed "safe abortion services (when abortion is legal)" under a series of family-planning services that might lower the number of women who die each year during pregnancy or childbirth – about 500,000 – as well as the nine million children who die before their fifth birthday. "Globally, complications after unsafe abortions cause 13 per cent of maternal deaths," the document said, adding that an initiative promoting safe abortion methods would lead to "a significant decrease in the global number of unwanted births and of half the number of unsafe abortions."[25]

For Stephen Lewis, Harper's position on abortion was proof positive that he was not sincere about his signature project. "Canada's reluctance to provide money for family planning, or any kind of sexual or reproductive health, and the ban on providing money on abortion, that diminishes significantly the validity of the initiative," said Lewis, who remains active in the UN system. "People are very, very suspicious about a northern country that doesn't take contraception seriously and doesn't take abortion seriously. These are two factors that plague maternal health."

*   *   *

After winning his long-sought majority in 2011, Harper allowed his foreign minister, the notoriously pugnacious John Baird, to trumpet his own aid project, this one also designed to generate a warm glow. Baird's personal cause was the proliferation of child brides and forced marriages in poor countries, a problem that the UN said affected 400 million women or girls in Latin America and the

Caribbean, South Asia, and sub-Saharan Africa. These teenaged brides were not only abused but when they became pregnant, they and their babies faced life-threatening consequences. In poor countries, complications during childbirth had been found to be the leading cause of death in girls between the ages of fifteen and nineteen.

Like the prime minister's MNCH initiative, this project appeared suddenly. Baird announced it in his 2013 General Assembly address, with the government's new foreign policy mantra. "Here at the UN, Canada targets its efforts on securing tangible results for the human family," he said. "Canada's government doesn't seek to have our values or our principled foreign policy validated by elites who would rather 'go along to get along.'" He called early forced marriage "abhorrent and indefensible" and declared, as if there was some other alternative, "We condemn it."

In December 2013, I interviewed Baird at his Ottawa office. It had been three months since he had announced the priority at the UN. Surprisingly, he had no specifics on what Canada would be doing to combat the child-bride problem. He vaguely offered that there would be money for programs on some form of advocacy.

"We're just really starting from the ground on this," Baird told me. "There's room for government action, but it will require societal change from the ground up. We're just at a very, the early stages of this." Like Harper's MNCH plan, the one thing Baird could say categorically was that pregnant child brides wouldn't have access to abortion. "The reality is, what this initiative is about is stopping this from happening in the first place. It's like fire prevention," Baird explained. "In your fire prevention budget, you don't hire firefighters. You do prevention work."

Susan Bissell, a senior United Nations official who was well aware of the abortion controversy, was still extremely positive about the overall initiative. A Canadian who worked as the associate director of the child protection branch at UNICEF in New York City, she told me she didn't think Canada's abortion ban diminished its international leadership on the issue because there were other ways for the government to make a difference. "We're trying to leave that off the table. We're talking about everything but that, frankly," she said, calling the issue "an obstacle to negotiate around." She had come to Ottawa to meet with policy-makers a few days before my own interview with Baird, and left genuinely impressed with the deep level of understanding. To Bissell, they understood the overlapping complexities that encompassed health, justice, and education. "Canada is the first government that I've talked to that sees those connections," she said. What Bissell was really hoping to see was a multimillion-dollar contribution to the fight against the exploitation of girls.

Within a year Baird delivered $30 million in new funding, but when he announced the last batch in November 2014, Canada's lack of commitment to the 0.7 per cent target once again reared its head. Baird was honouring Princess Mabel van Oranje of the Netherlands with the government's John Diefenbaker human rights award. Her organization, Girls Not Brides, was helping lead the fight against child brides in sixty countries. Like those invited to attend Harper's MNCH conference earlier in the spring, van Oranje heaped praise on Canada for being a world leader on an important child welfare issue during an interview about her visit to Ottawa. But when asked about Canada's overall aid commitment, she told me, "I think it's wise for rich countries to spend 0.7 per cent of their GNI on international development." She called that "a smart investment, and the amounts involved are not enormous." After all, she said, "We're talking about less than a per cent of all the wealth that we have, on development."

*   *   *

FEBRUARY 2016

UN secretary-general Ban Ki-moon is back in Canada standing next to a new prime minister in the foyer of the House of Commons. He clearly likes Justin Trudeau. Ban has heard Trudeau's "Canada is back" slogan and he has an emphatic answer of his own: "I am here to declare that the United Nations enthusiastically welcomes this commitment." Ban says Canada has always been "one of our most important partners" since the founding of the UN and he mentions Lester Pearson's Nobel Peace Prize "for helping to pioneer United Nations peacekeeping."

And then I ask Ban the same question that I asked him in front of Harper nearly two years earlier: "Do you want Canada to meet the 0.7 target?" Ban essentially gives the same answer he gave in 2014. "Canada is one of G7 and G20 member states, very important as well as very wealthy rich country," he says. "I believe that Canada has capacity and resources. I know that the prime minister may have all different priorities but I'm sure that Prime Minister Trudeau and his government will pay more focus on this matter. I count on your leadership."

Melinda Gates told me the same thing a couple of weeks later. "I would like to see them moving in that direction," she said. "It's important for a country like Canada to do it as it shows leadership, particularly in these very tough economic times." And in fact, finance minister Bill Morneau reversed the aid decline with a modest, two-year $256 million increase in his first budget the following month. Canada's contribution to the Global Fund to Fight AIDS, Tuberculosis, and Malaria was also boosted by 20 per cent with a three-year, $785 million replenishment. The government also hosted the Global Fund's fifth replenishment conference in Montreal in September 2016 to show that Canada was serious about international aid. The event raised $12.9 billion.

The new international development minister, Marie-Claude Bibeau, embarked on a review of Canada's development priorities, planning to present her findings to cabinet in the fall of 2016. "I think the 0.7 is too ambitious as a target," she said, because it would force Canada to spend an additional $10 billion a year. She said Canada would have to be "ambitious but realistic, considering the Canadian fiscal framework." Trudeau reiterated this reluctance to aim high, telling the *Toronto Star* that the target was "too ambitious for this year and probably next year as well."[26]

Aid agencies, such as CARE Canada and Oxfam, wanted to see more. The heads of their Canadian branches each told me they wanted to see a ten-year plan from the government to reach the 0.7 per cent target, which the UN once again restated as part of its new fifteen-year plan, the 2030 Sustainable Development Goals. Instead, Trudeau decided to extend Harper's commitment to maternal and child health – with one significant change. He reversed Harper's decision to forbid the funding of projects or agencies that performed abortions. Trudeau said his government would recommit to helping the world's most vulnerable based on "science" and not "ideology." He made this clear in his mandate letter to Bibeau, telling her to ensure "that Canada's valuable development focus on Maternal,

Newborn and Child Health is driven by evidence and outcomes, not ideology, including by closing existing gaps in reproductive rights and health care for women."

Gates told me in a February 2016 interview that Harper's ban on abortion needed to go, even though he deserved much credit for advocating so hard for MNCH. "What I will say about Prime Minister Harper is: he put MNCH on the agenda not just for Canada, but for the world," she said. "This was the component that was really still needed ... and it sends the right message to women all over the world," especially the 200 million women in poor countries who wanted more access to contraception. Despite his stand on abortion, Gates said she had no problem giving Harper a very public endorsement for what he was trying to accomplish. "That's OK, that's how you work together and find common ground. So to me, Prime Minister Trudeau saying that's still really, really important and it's a yes, and I'm going to open up this other piece, to me that's just a win-win." she explained. "That's great politics on both sides of the aisle. And I would love to see that in more countries."

Trudeau's election victory was partially premised on making Canada a more "compassionate" actor on the world stage. But this did not extend to boosting Canada's overall aid spending to eventually reach the 0.7 per cent target to which his father's government aspired before he was born. Trudeau won power by taking another daring fiscal position; he said he was willing to run small deficits to fund his ambitious infrastructure program to kickstart domestic growth. This meant building roads, bridges, and other "green" infrastructure to end the urban gridlock that was preventing middle-class families from reaching each other at the end of their workdays, or taking their children to soccer or ballet, where they could thrive. Voters agreed to let Trudeau bleed a little red ink, but their understanding was that this was to fix their First World problems. Directing their attention to the plight of the world's poor simply wasn't part of the program.

The Liberals wanted to bring Canada "back" to the world in a variety of ways, including working better with the UN, and returning the country to its Pearsonian roots. But not when it came to evoking Lester Pearson on the tricky question of foreign aid. That was definitely off the table.

CHAPTER SEVEN

Cluster Bombs

JANUARY 1991

British flight lieutenant Richard MacCormac is in the cockpit of a
Jaguar fighter jet streaking across a clear blue sky towards the coastline of tiny Kuwait. Iraqi army radar technician Moaffak Alkhafaji
is in a truck travelling in convoy across the last expanse of his country's southern desert towards its border with Kuwait. Four months
earlier, President Saddam Hussein's army invaded their neighbour,
so a thirty-five-country coalition mounted a military campaign to
repel the Iraqi forces. The coalition is operating under a United Nations mandate led by the United States, and including a modest contribution from Canada.

MacCormac and Alkhafaji may be separated by the Kuwaiti-Iraqi
border and serving with opposing forces in the first Persian Gulf
War. But at different moments during this pivotal month, both will
experience the effects of a weapon that causes indiscriminate human
carnage. When this war ends they will join together in a common
cause: ridding the world of the horrific weapon that changed their
lives forever.

MacCormac is flying alongside a handful of British RAF bombers.
He zeroes in on a series of zigzagging trenches laden with Silkworm
missiles, part of an air-defence network that Iraq has embedded along
Kuwait's Gulf coast. MacCormac and his comrades pull the trigger
on a weapon they have never used before – not even in training – a
volley of cluster bombs. Each cigar-shaped missile contains dozens of
smaller submunitions, the size of baseballs, which spray over the
ground below when their furiously spinning carrier missiles open

mid-air to unleash them. A generation later, MacCormac recalls being "thunderstruck" by the massive plume of dust that rose up from the ground below. "Most of the guys in the formation were rather taken aback. I was struck by the amount of damage that was being done and the area that was being covered," he told me. "We were quiet on the way back home because we were having a good think about what we'd seen. Somebody wrote in the authorization sheets, when we got back, 'That's a pretty nasty weapon.'"

On another January day, Alkhafaji hears the sound of jets screaming overhead as his convoy continues its southward advance. Seconds later, his truck is rocked by a series of explosions. Alkhafaji struggles out of his vehicle and staggers momentarily, emerging onto a burning landscape littered with dead and wounded comrades, before he collapses, clutching his bloodied left leg. What remains of Alkhafaji's leg is removed the same day.

Years later, Alkhafaji told me he had been the victim of "a very dirty weapon" because "its effect is random. It doesn't care if the target is civilian or military."

A generation after they were first exposed to cluster bombs in a war in which they were enemies, MacCormac and Alkhafaji came together to rid the world of the weapon. MacCormac retired from the Royal Air Force after twenty-five years, and in 2011 joined the Danish non-governmental organization DanChurchAid, leading its efforts to clean up the remnants of cluster bombs in several countries. Alkhafaji formed his own NGO in 2003, after Saddam was driven from power in the Second Gulf War. Alkhafaji called his organization the Iraqi Alliance for Disability.

Canada also took part in the 1991 Persian Gulf War, deploying CF-18 fighter jets to the Iraq coalition, but did not use cluster bombs. In fact, Canada has never used cluster bombs. The government announced in September 2014 that it had destroyed its unused stockpile of them, a remnant of its Cold War arsenal.

Cluster bombs are wildly inaccurate and unreliable weapons that have a track record of maiming and killing innocent civilians. They were first used during the Second World War but were more extensively used by the United States in the bombing of Vietnam, Cambodia, and Laos in the 1960s. They were used in later conflicts by Israel in Lebanon, Western countries such as the U.S., France, and

Britain in the 1991 Gulf War, by coalition forces in the subsequent wars in Afghanistan and Iraq, and most recently by combatants in Syria and Ukraine. A single large cluster bomb spreads hundreds of smaller, baseball-sized bomblets over a wide area. An estimated 10 to 40 per cent of them fail to explode immediately, which can leave them littering the landscape for decades. They are an irresistible draw for children because of their bright colours. Farmers in poor countries inadvertently stumble upon them. That's how thousands of innocent people in two dozen countries have been maimed or killed.[1]

Under the Conservative government of Stephen Harper, Canada was oddly, almost inexplicably, slow to back the UN treaty process to outlaw cluster bombs and stigmatize their use. It was a curious position for Canada to occupy, given that it helped lead the world towards a ban of a similar weapon, the anti-personnel landmine, in the 1990s. Canada signed the UN convention to ban cluster bombs in December 2008 but would wait until March 2015 to ratify the treaty. Canada did not ratify the treaty until well after Iraq and other war-ravaged countries such as Afghanistan, Congo, Lebanon, and Laos had done so. That included most of Canada's NATO allies, the most notable exception being the United States. China, Russia, and Israel took a pass on joining the convention.

Canada's delay exposed it to widespread international criticism. Like many international observers, MacCormac and Alkhafaji were concerned that the legislation Canada used to ratify the convention was flawed. They cited a controversial provision that allowed the Canadian Forces to be involved in the use of cluster bombs in joint military operations with countries that were not signatories – specifically with its closest ally, the United States. MacCormac said he had issues with "the way the legislation appears to provide opportunities, loopholes if you like, even for Canadian involvement in acts that the Convention on Cluster Munitions itself expressly tries to suppress or forbid."

Alkhafaji agreed. "It's not good that Canadians collaborate with other countries like the United States on support, or use … or transfer cluster munitions because it's against the humans all over the world."

The cluster bomb saga was a case study in just how much the Conservatives had distanced Canada from its traditional acceptance of the UN treaty process – especially given that in 1997, the Ottawa

Convention outlawed anti-personnel landmines and made some of world's most war-torn places discernably safer. The international drive to ban landmines was closely associated with Liberal foreign affairs minister Lloyd Axworthy, who brought together his own coalition of international NGOs and civil society groups to lead what was known as the Ottawa Process.

The Harper government faced widespread international criticism over the law that it enacted to ratify the United Nations Convention on Cluster Munitions. One of Canada's most notable critics was the International Committee of the Red Cross. Lou Maresca, a senior ICRC lawyer for the scrupulously neutral organization, took the unusual step of going on the record with me about Canada's inadequate legislation. "The biggest concerns we have about the legislation are linked to the provisions on interoperability," Maresca told me from the ICRC's hilltop headquarters above Lake Geneva. "For us, that raises serious questions about the legislation and how that goes in parallel with the object and purpose of the convention, which is to eliminate any use of cluster munitions."

Norway assumed the lead on cluster bomb eradication, just as Canada did with landmines in the 1990s, so the campaign was dubbed the Oslo Process. "We all observe that Canada has, over the last years, had different priorities, so there is less emphasis on multilateral work and also on disarmament," Norway's ambassador on the cluster bomb initiative, Steffan Kongstad, told me in an interview in Geneva. Kongstad also had questions about the framing of the bill for Canada's ratification of the treaty. "We would normally not comment on the internal processes in other countries," he said. "But I can say that we would not present such a law in the Norwegian parliament. It seems somewhat inconsistent with the purpose of the convention."

Foreign affairs minister John Baird confronted the controversy when the Senate Foreign Affairs and International Trade committee opened its hearings into the bill on 3 October 2012. As its first witness, Baird testified that the government did not want provisions of the treaty to prevent senior Canadian military officers from being invited to join high-profile U.S. military exchange programs. This was particularly relevant for Canada because it gets a privileged level of access to military exchange programs with its powerful neighbour, one that no other country can claim. For example, two retired Canadian generals who served as chiefs of the defence staff, Rick Hillier and Walt Natynczyk, both served as deputy commanders of the U.S. Army's III Corps in Fort Hood, Texas. The sprawling U.S. army base is the size of a large suburb. The posting allowed the Canadian generals to help command 60,000 U.S. personnel, about as many men and women as there are serving in the entire Canadian Forces. Baird said it was in the government's interest to see that nothing got in the way of those top-level exchange programs.

"I simply think it would be rather presumptuous of Canada to say, 'We are sending one person to work with these other 60,000 people, and here is a long list of things that we want to impose on you,'" Baird testified. As few as those opportunities were, Baird said the government was determined to protect them. "In our existing military co-operation, obligations in NATO, we have a small number, less than 0.001 per cent of Canadian Forces, on secondment or training missions with non-party state convention countries."

However, Steve Goose, the chair of the Cluster Munitions Coalition and the head of the arms division of Human Rights Watch, said nothing in the convention would have impeded Canada from participating in joint operations with the United States. Canada just had to swear off the use of cluster bombs the same way it did with the landmines treaty in 1997. "Canada's implementing legislation is nothing short of a disaster. It's by far the worst implementing legislation of any country that has signed the convention," he said in an interview in Geneva.

American political scientist and anti-landmine advocate Ken Rutherford considered Axworthy and his fellow Canadians to be heroes, and he said those fighting to ban cluster bombs owe Canada a debt of gratitude because of their groundbreaking work with the landmines treaty. "Everybody was modeling the negotiations based on the Ottawa negotiations," Rutherford said. "Unfortunately on cluster munitions, Canada abdicated its moral leadership."

*   *   *

In the Vietnam War's dying days, the drive to ban landlines took root. The movement began in the 1970s with an attempt by the

International Committee of the Red Cross (ICRC) to update international humanitarian law.[2] It started in the United States, which demonstrated support for anti-landmine efforts even though it would eventually stay out of the 1997 Ottawa treaty. Still, there was early support for a landmine ban from both Republicans and Democrats.

The ICRC was joined by several civil society groups in the United States, particularly the Vietnam Veterans of America Foundation led by Robert (Bobby) Muller who, along with U.S. senator Patrick Leahy of Vermont, persuaded Congress to pass a law that placed a moratorium on the export of landmines. Republican president George Bush Senior first signed the moratorium legislation in 1992, and it was extended several times before Democratic president Bill Clinton signed it into law. The NGO coalition grew under Muller's leadership and expanded, incorporating the ICRC and the International Campaign to Ban Landmines (ICBL) headed by American activist Jody Williams.[3] She joined forces with ICRC president Cornelio Sommaruga to lobby world governments to ban landmines. In 1994, Clinton used his UN General Assembly address to call for a worldwide ban on landmines. Meanwhile, at the 1995 G7 summit, Prime Minister Jean Chrétien informally discussed a landmine ban with fellow leaders, though Canada had not officially joined the coalition.[4]

A twist of fate led to Canada's much deeper involvement in the cause in 1995, when the UN mistakenly included it on a list of countries that had placed a moratorium on landmines.[5] The mistake forced Canada into the anti-landmine camp, which did not faze the Liberal government of the day. They quickly realized that any attempt to correct the record would do more harm than good to Canada's international reputation, so the momentum carried the country forward. In 1996, Axworthy took over the foreign affairs portfolio from André Ouellet, who was also an anti-landmine advocate. But Axworthy would take things significantly further, viewing landmines as an opportunity for "policy innovation" and a way to place his stamp on his new cabinet post.[6]

It was not a partisan issue: the Liberals held a firm majority in the House of Commons but they found support from Dr Keith Martin, a Reform MP who would later cross the floor to the Liberals, when he introduced a private member's bill that supported the ban. "The

Conservative party were supporters at the time of the treaty, when we brought all the parties together," Axworthy recalled in an interview. "It wasn't a matter that this was some kind of Liberal gambit. It was something the entire country got involved in." Ottawa eventually convened an international strategy conference in October 1996, which Axworthy brought to a memorable close by challenging all to return to Ottawa by the end of 1997 with a signed convention.

The Ottawa Process became a model for how to mobilize soft power and show international leadership, while costing the Foreign Affairs Department few actual dollars. The coalition of international actors rose to Axworthy's challenge when they returned to Ottawa to sign the treaty with great fanfare in Ottawa on 3 December 1997. Two months earlier, in September 1997, the details had been hammered out in Oslo, Norway.

* * *

Ten years later, Earl Turcotte found himself in Oslo on the cusp of another international attempt to rid the world of a weapon as heinous and indiscriminate as the anti-personnel mine. Turcotte had seen the effect of cluster bombs a decade earlier while working for the Canadian International Development Agency in South Asia. He'd met the civilian amputees, the peasant farmers, and the children who'd stumbled across the dormant bombs decades after they'd been dropped. The experience seared itself into Turcotte's soul, and set him on a life-altering path that would eventually lead to a bitter dispute with the Harper government.

It began in Oslo on 3 December 2007. Turcotte was Canada's lead negotiator and the head of its delegation to craft the Convention on Cluster Munitions. Canada was one of forty-nine countries that convened to discuss the creation of the treaty, similar to the Ottawa Convention. But the similarities ended there: "We were nowhere near the front of the pack on that one," Turcotte told me. But Canada was still making an active contribution at the outset, he said. In the months and years that followed, however, Turcotte would begin to gradually lose faith in his government's handling of the issue – so much so that he threw in the towel in early 2011, ending an otherwise successful public-service career that spanned nearly three

decades. He decided he had no choice but to quit working for a government that he believed had undermined both international law
and his country's reputation.

Turcotte had initially been thrilled to be a major part of the global effort to ban cluster bombs, which gained strength in response to
the Israeli bombardment of Lebanon at the end of the summer war
against Hezbollah in 2006. When the shooting subsided, southern
Lebanon was littered with an estimated 100,000 unexploded
bomblets. Jan Egeland, then the United Nations under-secretary-
general for humanitarian affairs, criticized Israel for its "completely
immoral" use of the weapon, saying 90 per cent of the bombing occurred in the last three days of the war, when a resolution was in
sight. UN teams identified 359 separate cluster bomb strike locations
with up to 100,000 bomblets, Egeland said.

Israel had also used cluster bombs in Lebanon in 1978 and 1982.
In fact, U.S. president Ronald Reagan imposed a six-year ban on cluster bomb sales to Israel after an investigation by Congress found
that Israel had used them in civilian areas during the 1982 Lebanon
invasion.[7] Ahmad Mokaled discovered one of the unexploded remnants of that war on 12 February 1999. It was the day he turned five.
Ahmad's father, Raed, brought him to a park in the town of
Nabatieh with his older brother, then eight, to celebrate. It was one
of the first sunny days of spring, and Ahmad sprinted into a group
of children to join the revelry. His eye was drawn to a tiny, brightly
coloured object that had been dropped on his country long before
he had been born. He reached down to pick it up, and the explosion instantly ended his short life. "I call this weapon – the cluster
bombs – a blind weapon," Ahmad Mokaled's father told me in
Geneva. "It cannot choose. They throw it everywhere ... Sometimes
the Israelis throw a cluster bomb that looks like a toy."

The Harper government was a steadfast supporter of the Israeli
military's campaign against Hezbollah in Lebanon during the 2006
summer war – the conflict that had broken out as I travelled on
Harper's airplane following his election victory. Mokaled had some
advice about the bill before Parliament. "I want to send a message
to the politicians of Canada," he said. "Think on our children, like
you think on your own children. Protect the children around the
world (from) war, like you protect your own children."

In May 2008, Turcotte was again leading a Canadian delegation, this time at a ten-day international conference in Dublin that was putting the finishing touches on the Convention on Cluster Munitions. Turcotte worked late into the night, helping craft the wording of what would become Article 21 of the treaty allowing parties to the convention to take part in joint military operations with those that were not. A little over six months later, on 3 December 2008, the convention opened for signatures in Oslo. Canada was one of more than ninety countries to sign the convention. As it turned out, it was the eleventh anniversary of the signing of the Ottawa Convention to ban landmines. But when Turcotte returned to Ottawa, he found the signed text did not sit well with his government.

Even though senior bureaucrats had approved the proposed Dublin wording, they started hedging when they began examining the text, he said. Military officials in particular questioned whether this new international convention would affect the Canadian Forces' ability to be part of a joint operation with the U.S. "As soon as we got back to Canada, we got involved in a heated debate about what the implications would be for joint operations," Turcotte said. DND proposed alternative wording that would permit Forces personnel to be involved in the use and transport of cluster bombs during joint operations. Turcotte said he saw that as contrary to the spirit of the convention. "We had interdepartmental debates. I had great support from my bosses at Foreign Affairs for two years," he recalled. What changed, he said, is that his senior managers came around to DND's position after two years of infighting. "I can only speculate that this decision – I am certain this decision – was taken at the political level," Turcotte said. "We lost and DND won. Simple as that." He asked that his name be removed as the department's contact on the draft legislation because he couldn't in good conscience support it.

This wasn't the first time the Defence and Foreign Affairs departments went to war over the ban of such a weapon. Foreign affairs minister André Ouellet and defence minister David Collenette had their own turf war in 1995 over whether Canada should ban landmines.[8] Collenette didn't want them banned until an "effective and humane alternative" could be found. But Ouellet decided to push ahead. He took advantage of the fact that the U.S. was going to submit a UN resolution on a moratorium on the export of landmines, and had asked Canada to be a co-sponsor. That coincided with the UN mistakenly including Canada on its list of countries that had already agreed to an export moratorium. On 11 October 1995, Ouellet wrote to Collenette saying that he wanted to announce a Canadian moratorium and co-sponsor the resolution. Collenette reluctantly agreed, but insisted this would be as far as the military would go.[9] When Axworthy took over the portfolio in 1996, his predecessor had laid the groundwork for the landmine treaty initiative that followed.

Canada's efforts to support a similar ban on cluster bombs moved at a snail's pace in the decade and a half that followed. In the fall of 2012, almost four years after Canada signed onto the convention, the Conservatives introduced the bill needed to ratify it. It was tabled in the Senate, not the House of Commons, the usual route for new legislation. Clause 11 of Bill S-10 outlined the interoperability provision that Turcotte and many others found so offensive. It allowed Canadian Forces personnel who were on joint operations with non-party states to the convention to:

- direct or authorize an activity by the armed forces of a non-state party that may involve the use of a cluster munition ...
- expressly request the use of a cluster munition ...
- use a cluster munition or undertake another prohibited activity while on secondment, attachment or exchange with the armed forces of a non-state party.[10]

Turcotte, who had formidable experience in the technical aspects of the convention that he helped create, testified in October 2012 as a private citizen before the Senate committee examining the bill. Free to speak his mind, he said Canada was poised to "set a dangerous precedent" that undermined international humanitarian law with Article 11. "This would be a betrayal of the trust of colleagues in other countries who negotiated the convention in good faith, a betrayal of Canadians who expect far better from our nation and, worst of all, a complete failure to do everything we can to prevent more needless deaths and suffering among innocent men, women and children," he testified. "I challenge the government to identify any other state party or signatory that is giving its forces carte blanche, in its own words, to aid, abet, conspire and assist non-party state forces with the commission of acts."

That raised the hackles of Senator Pamela Wallin, who kicked off her round of questioning by telling Turcotte: "I am a bit troubled by your tone. You suggested ... that somehow Canada's military men and women are looking for a back door to find a way to use these munitions." Turcotte held his ground, saying he had nothing but the greatest of respect for the Canadian Forces. He told the senator that his father served three years overseas during the Second World War. He said twenty of the twenty-eight NATO countries had signed the convention. "We have a piece of legislation that is radically different from what the U.K., France, Germany, the Netherlands, Belgium, Norway, and many other NATO allies have," he said.

But as Wallin pointed out, Canada was on the same page as the United States. Indeed, Wallin affirmed the notion that Harper had emphasized in the past: that Canada's foreign policy interests did not lie exclusively with a multilateral institution such as NATO, but also in its core bilateral relationship with the United States. "We are allowed, with our largest friend and ally, to view the world differently," she said. "As a Canadian, I do not want to forfeit that right to view the world differently or use my moral suasion to change their mind."

The cluster bomb bill passed through the Senate without amendments in late 2012, as the Conservative majority outvoted proposed changes put forth by the Liberal members on the committee and strongly supported by some witnesses. The International Committee of the Red Cross proposed specific changes to the wording in Clause 11. But Bill S-10 remained as it was drafted. It was referred to the House of Commons, where it would continue to languish.

*   *   *

Turcotte returned to Laos in 2012, where he would work for two years as a technical adviser on cluster bombs for the United Nations Development Program after quitting the Canadian government. Turcotte had worked for several years in the 1990s in the tiny, land-locked South Asian country for the now defunct Canadian International Development Agency. It was there and in neighbouring

Cambodia he first met the young victims of cluster bombs, and was deeply moved by their suffering.

Laos, a country of six million, suffers from the heaviest cluster bomb contamination of any country in the world, per capita. During the Vietnam War between 1964 and 1973, American B-52s dropped 270 million fist-sized bomblets on Laos, eighty million of which failed to explode. These "rolling thunder" air attacks saturated the Ho Chi Minh Trail – the communist supply route – a part of which snaked through the dense Laotian jungles. Decades after the covert American bombing campaign, cluster bombs remained a hazard in Laos. The weapons had wounded or killed 20,000 civilians in the forty years since the Vietnam War ended.

Six months after the Senate hearings ended in Ottawa, I was in the Laotian capital of Vientiane, speaking with a young victim. Phongsavath Manithong told me about the day he turned sixteen. He was walking to school in his home village of Vinegthong, in central Laos, when a friend handed him a small metal bulb that he'd found by the side of the road. When Phongsavath tried to pry it open, it exploded. He remains blind to this day.

"We are not angry at the American government," Phongsavath said, seated on a couch in the Cope Centre, a government-run health and rehabilitation centre that also houses a small but powerful museum that poignantly illustrated the reality of the cluster bomb problem. "Many American people, they did not know what happened in Laos."

Above us, mobiles depicting dozens of cluster bomblets dangled from the ceiling in a chaotic constellation amid forms of prostheses that had been used in Laos over the years – improvised wood and metal contraptions that looked more like artifacts from the Middle Ages. "We need more help from the American government. They are a rich country," Phongsavath said. "That's not enough to help the disabled people, the survivors." At the time, the United States was the leading international donor to the $30 million annual effort to help rid Laos of its cluster bomb infestation and help its victims cope.

In the spring of 2013, several government officials told me that they wanted Canada to do more to help clear the contaminated countryside of cluster bombs and address the needs of victims. They told me that Canada had contributed more than $2 million between

1996 and 2011, but in 2012 Canada had cut its funding. In Vientiane, the normally inaccessible communist government granted me hours of interviews. Top officials were generous with their time and provided voluminous amounts of background, history, and context. With unfailing politeness, they also emphasized this message: tell your country to start helping us again.

"I cannot say exact figures, but as much as possible as the government can afford," said Bounheuang Douangphachanh, chairman of the Laos unexploded ordnance agency. "We also would like to ask Canada to continue its support to the UXO sector in Laos." Over at UXO Lao, the country's national cluster bomb clearance agency, deputy director Wanthong Khamdala moved his index finger up and down a chart of figures, coming to rest on the column on Canada: "2007 to 2009, three years, there's no support," he said. "In 2012, we have no support from Canadian government, too," he said.

We strolled to the covered front porch of his office where a large decommissioned cluster bomb case sat on a set of stilts, as long as Wanthong was tall. He said the missile once held 670 bomblets – "bombies" are they're called in Laos – which likely means that as many as two hundred from this one bomb failed to explode. "Maybe there's some other internal issue the Canadian people consider more important to resolve," he said. "But I'd like to request to the Canadian government to consider again to support." This message was reinforced by international organizations including the British agency MAG, which had been active in Laos for two decades, as well as the head of United Nations operations in the country, Minh Pham. How long could it take to rid Laos of cluster bombs? "It might take a few centuries at this rate, at the level of spending," said Minh, a Vietnamese-born American whose family was evacuated from Saigon in 1975.

All of these Laotian voices were included in my reports for the Canadian Press in the summer of 2013. But there were no Canadian voices. While I was in south Asia, Ottawa banned Canadian diplomats based in nearby Bangkok, Thailand, which has jurisdiction for Laos, from talking to me on the record.

A few months later, in October 2013, Baird travelled to Laos with money in hand. He announced $1 million to help fund ordnance clearance operations. For his photo-op, he chose the Cope Centre. Who would get the money? It would be split evenly between

UXO Lao and MAG, the two organizations in my reports. The United Nations Development Program would administer the money in trust. The announcement was just in time for the resumption of hearings on the cluster bomb bill, this time before the House of Commons foreign affairs committee. Baird indicated a willingness to entertain opposition amendments to the bill.

Back in Ottawa, the minister conveyed some distress over his recent trip to Laos. Baird told me outside the hearing room after he had testified that he was deeply moved by his trip to the Cope Centre's medical ward. "There was a baby – a baby – who had lost its entire leg," he said, pausing briefly to answer some questions. "There was a seventy-two-year-old man getting rehabilitation therapy with his prosthetic leg, and then everything in between."

For all of his emotional rhetoric, Baird and the Conservatives would remain unconvinced by the coalition supporting amendments to the bill. In December 2013, the Commons hearings ended, and they only agreed to the removal of one word from Clause 11. This amendment was proposed by the Conservatives and agreed to by the NDP and Liberals after the government majority on the committee shot down opposition proposals. The amendment removed the word "using" in a key part of the clause, but retained it in other sections. That meant that Canadian military personnel were clearly prohibited from directly using cluster bombs, but it did not completely rule out their being indirectly involved in use of the munitions in a joint operation with the United States.

That final round of hearings exposed a divide within the Canadian Forces itself. Walter Dorn, a professor at the Royal Military College of Canada, urged the government in his testimony to amend the "obnoxious portions" of the bill. Dorn said that the interoperability clause "opens a gaping loophole, one big enough to fit planeloads of bombs." He said the legislation, as written, undermined the purpose of the treaty and set a bad example for other countries. "Canada should, instead, set a good example for the ratification of this important global arms control measure by closing the legislation's loophole and making sure no Canadians are authorized or forced to assist, direct, aid and abet or conspire with others to use cluster munitions," he testified.

Retired general Walt Natynczyk, one of the two former chiefs of defence who benefitted from the high-level U.S. exchange programs, testified in favour of the government's position. At the time of his 21 November 2013 testimony, Natynczyk was the president of the Canadian Space Agency, and about a year later the Conservatives appointed him deputy minister of the Veterans Affairs Department. As part of his U.S. exchange program at Fort Hood, Natynczyk deployed to Iraq as the deputy commander of American forces in 2004. That was the second war in which the U.S. had used cluster bombs on Iraq.

Natynczyk reminded the committee that in 2008, when he was the top Canadian soldier, he signed an order prohibiting the Canadian Forces from using them. Still, he said, the Canadian Forces personnel needed Clause 11 because it would protect them against criminal prosecution if they were involved in the use of cluster bombs during a joint operation. "From my perspective, I believe article 21 enables our forces to remain fully interoperable with the U.S. armed forces. This comprehensive level of cooperation is a unique strategic advantage for Canada," he told the MPs. "The interoperability clause of the convention strikes a fair balance between profound humanitarian principles on the one hand, and Canada's security realities on the other."

Natynczyk pointed out that certain Canadian allies – a clear reference to the Americans – were not in favour of the cluster bomb ban because they were dealing with "major geostrategic security concerns that we, in Canada, are not faced with." He specifically pointed to South Korea, where cluster bombs were needed to protect the frontier against North Korea. Natynczyk also declared, "I can say to you with confidence that I was never aware that cluster bombs were actually stocked in theatre, or that I participated in planning for their use or in fact authorized their use," Natynczyk said. "I had none of that experience whatsoever. However, unwittingly, I could have done so, and I could have participated in activities without my knowledge that assisted in the use of cluster munitions. But I would not have known it at that time."

U.S. Marine Corporal Travis J. Bradach-Nall likely didn't know there were cluster bombs around when he went out on a mission near Karbala, Iraq, on 2 July 2003. The twenty-one-year-old corporal had joined his comrades for what his family was later told was a "mine clearing operation." He was killed in an explosion. After obtaining his service records from the U.S. Department of Defense a year later, his family found out a weapon that was manufactured in his own country and dropped by his own comrades had killed him.

"I knew nothing about clusters, but had two brothers that know about this. One is an attorney, and he decided he wanted to get all the paperwork on what happened. He went through FOI (Freedom of Information). He got the accident report, the pictures and everything," Louise Bradach, the deceased Marine's mother, told me in a telephone interview from her home in Palm Springs, California. In 2007, Bradach joined the international coalition to ban cluster bombs. She was aware of Canada's position, the one espoused by Natynczyk, that its military must remain interoperable with the U.S. "That's just a piece of garbage," she said. "Look at the percentage that are civilian casualties, look at what it does to the troops – the weapon is hideous."

Canada should be upholding higher standards than the U.S. and should not allow any "loopholes" to stand in the CCM, she said. Canada should tell its allies: "We will not use it, we will not transport it and we will not hold it for you, we will have nothing to do with it – no loopholes. You open it an inch, it opens a mile." In her years of activism, Bradach said she learned a few things about Canada, including how it led in the global ban on landmines, and how it had gone from leader to laggard in the way it has dealt with cluster bombs. "I always think of Canada as the nobler country in a way," Bradach said. "We (the United States) are a really great country, but we seem to be so frightened of anybody taking things from us or treading on us. It just seems like Canada is less damaging to other countries.

"I don't want to see you going the way we've gone."

The Conservatives cleared the last major legislative hurdle when Bill C-10 received royal assent in late 2014. On 16 March 2015, they served notice that they were ratifying the Convention on Cluster Munitions by issuing a press release that said Canada was helping to "save lives" with a contribution of $2.4 million to mine clearance. Turcotte said the bill did not live up to the spirit and letter of the convention, and that Canada would be "held to account by the international community, other states parties, civil society and UN agencies" on how it performs. In the fall of 2016, the Liberals said they had no intention of amending the bill, disappointing many anti-cluster-bomb campaigners, including Turcotte.

There may have been a long delay in ratifying the treaty but in one way the Harper government was active – behind the scenes – on the cluster bomb file: it was working to keep the Palestinians from joining the CCM. On 23 January 2015, the UN filed notice of Canada's formal objection to a decision by the Palestinian Authority to join the Convention on Cluster Munitions. "Canada considers the declaration made by the 'State of Palestine' to be without any legal validity or effect," stated the notification of Canada's position when it was posted online by the UN. The Palestinians had won non-member observer state status at the UN General Assembly in November 2012, an initiative that Canada deemed provocative and voted against. The Palestinians decided to join the CCM, and Canada opposed that move one week later in keeping with its steadfast opposition towards enhanced Palestinian status within the UN.

New Democrat foreign affairs critic Paul Dewar questioned how the government managed to find the time to object to the Palestinian action – which he defended as legal – when Canada had other international business on its plate. "The Conservatives should focus on ratifying Canada's commitments on the Convention on Cluster Munitions," he said, "rather than trying to keep others from joining this important international treaty."

CHAPTER EIGHT

Israel and the Middle East

25 JULY 2006

Israel's war on Hezbollah in Lebanon is in its fourteenth day. For nine of them, bombs have been falling in a belt of land no wider than five kilometres at Lebanon's southern border. The Israeli Defence Forces has designated this patch of land a "Special Security Zone." Three dozen Lebanese villages, two dozen United Nations observation posts, and several Hezbollah positions lie within the zone. The UN Patrol Base Khiam is one of them. The fortified two-storey building with an underground bunker sits in a compound ringed by razor wire and perched high atop a hill looking down on Lebanon and, four kilometres further south, on Israel itself. The base was established in 1978 by a UN Security Council resolution confirming the withdrawal of the Israeli military from Lebanon. A pair of Hezbollah positions sits two hundred metres from Khiam, one to the north, another west.

The Hezbollah-Israel war began two weeks earlier, after the militants started shooting rockets into Israel and then killed three Israeli soldiers and captured two more along the border. On that day, Prime Minister Stephen Harper sparked heated criticism in Canada when he called the Israeli response – a massive aerial bombardment – "measured." The Conservative government was accused of favouring Israel in its ongoing, unresolved conflict with the Palestinians. Now Harper was about to spark controversy again. This time it would be over his initial reaction to the death of a Canadian peacekeeper and three of his UN colleagues on this day.

A bomb dropped by an Israel Defence Forces warplane crushed
the bunker where forty-three-year-old Major Paeta Hess-von Kruedener was watching the war. "Wolf" was a gregarious, mustached
paratrooper with the Princess Patricia's Canadian Light Infantry, the
married father of a grown daughter and stepson.[1] His two decades
in the Canadian Forces brought him to Cyrus, Bosnia, and Congo,
and he'd trained with the U.S. Green Berets.[2] Hess-von Kruedener
had arrived in the Middle East the previous autumn to work with
the UN Truce Supervision Organization based in Jerusalem. He was
part of a four-person team assigned to Patrol Base Khiam along with
officers from China, Finland, and Austria.

They all died together on 25 July 2006.

The sixty-six-page report of the Canadian Forces Board of Inquiry
told the story of his final hours. It noted that the "clashes between the
IDF and Hezbollah escalated to the point that there was a large scale
protracted land incursion into South Lebanon by the IDF," with "no
traditional military front" and "pockets of operations."[3] On the day
of the fatal bombing, Hess-von Kruedener's base was hit by three
waves of Israeli bombardment, including four 155 mm artillery
rounds that landed in the base compound at 6:29 p.m.[4] UN peacekeeping leadership decided that they would withdraw their four people from Patrol Base Khiam the following morning at 7:00 a.m.
Meanwhile, rockets continued to fall. Radio transmissions from the
base reported "firing close" to it at 7:15 p.m., 7:16 p.m., and 7:17 p.m.
At 7:25 p.m., a nearby UN patrol base transmitted the evacuation details to Patrol Base Khiam. Five minutes later, according to the report,
"Patrol Base Khiam failed to respond to a scheduled radio check."[5]

Within forty minutes, a recovery team from a battalion of the Indian army was mobilized and on the way to Khiam, arriving at 9:55
p.m. They kicked down its locked gate, stormed the bombed-out
compound, and found "the near total destruction of the main building." They dug until the early morning hours of 26 July, finding three
of the four bodies in the rubble of the main building. Hess-von
Kruedener's corpse was one of them.[6]

"The Board finds that Major Hess-von Kruedener was not to
blame for his own death. The Board was unable to determine if a
specific individual was to blame for the death; the Board does

however find that, as an organization, the IDF is responsible for the death of Major Hess-von Kruedener," the Canadian inquiry ruled in its 1 November 2006 report. The board made clear that the IDF did not co-operate with its investigation, beyond providing a "Non Paper" summary of its own investigation. It concluded that a five-hundred-kilogram GPS-guided Joint Direct Attack Munition (JDAM) bomb delivered by an Israeli Air Force (IAF) aircraft caused Hess-von Kruedener's death.[7]

"The results of this incident were foreseeable to the IDF," the BOI report said. General Alain Pellegrini, head of UN operations for Lebanon, had a heated exchange with his Israeli liaison after the 6:29 p.m. bombings of the base.[8] As the BOI report stated: "More specifically, the effects of the direct impacts registered at 1829hrs were communicated to the IDF liaison network with clear and forceful intent and at several levels including the Force Commander stating, 'you are killing my people.'"[9] The board concluded that Hess-von Kruedener's death was "tragic and preventable." Its last word was this: "Ultimately, Major Hess-von Kruedener, along with his three colleagues, lost his life in the service of peace."[10]

On 26 July 2006, the day after the bombing, Prime Minister Stephen Harper questioned why Hess-von Kruedener and his comrades had remained at their post in the first place. He also reaffirmed Israel's right to defend itself against the Hezbollah militants inside Lebanon. "We want to find out why this United Nations post was attacked and also why it remained manned, during what is, more or less, a war, during obvious danger to these particular individuals," Harper said. The prime minister called the bombing a "terrible tragedy," and defended Israel's military campaign: "But that doesn't change the right of a country to defend itself against terrorists and violent attacks."[11]

Harper's comments put him at odds with UN secretary-general Kofi Annan, who blamed Israel for targeting the base. His spokeswoman, responding to Harper's remarks, said the dead peacekeepers were "posted in a well-marked area and the United Nations had assurances and reassurances that they would not come under attack." Israeli prime minister Ehud Olmert telephoned Harper to express his "deep regret" and to apologize to all Canadians.[12] In the weeks to come, as Hess-von Kruedener's body returned to Canada for his emotional funeral, Harper would temper his remarks and heap the sort of praise on the deceased paratrooper that he would offer to the many, many more Canadian military personnel who would die in the coming years in Afghanistan.

It would be another two years before the report into Hess-von Kruedener's death was released by the military in 2008. It was initially posted on the Defence Department's website, and then, sometime in 2009, it was gone. It disappeared from the Internet, spurring accusations that the Harper government was placating Israel once more. Hess-von Kruedener's widow, Cynthia, told the *Ottawa Citizen* in December 2012 that it was "embarrassing to the Israelis and, as we know, Prime Minister Harper has given his unconditional support to the Israelis."[13]

Hess-von Kruedener's story eventually faded from the public consciousness. But the Harper government's staunch alliance with Israel would grow ever stronger as the years progressed. Canada has always been a supporter of Israel, but the Harper government became a louder, much more unwavering friend of the Jewish state. In doing so, Harper took direct aim at the United Nations for fostering anti-Israeli sentiment, a stance that often left Canada among a small minority of nations. At the same time, the Conservative government also spent hundreds of millions of dollars on aid to the Palestinian Authority.

In Canada, the Harper government's Middle East policy sparked a bitter political cleavage. On one side, you have Canada's last ambassador to the United Nations Security Council, Paul Heinbecker, who said Canada's Middle East policy under the Harper government was "mindless." Heinbecker served as Canada's ambassador to the UN until 2003, three years after the country's final stint on the Security Council ended. Unlike some other retired diplomats, who joined Justin Trudeau's team, Heinbecker did not throw his hat into the political ring. He maintained he was not political, pointing out his past work as a non-partisan adviser to both Pierre Trudeau and Brian Mulroney.

He said Harper's initial reaction to the UN bunker bombing was simply unacceptable and one of many examples of a Middle East policy completely out of balance. "The first thing it says is it's a foreign policy totally without principle – one standard for our friends,

one standard for others," he told me. "I can tell you that senior officials in the UN were furious with us – that we seemed to blame the
UN for this thing."

Heinbecker said Canada never had a completely neutral foreign
policy that treated the Israelis and Palestinians equally. "We used to
have fair-minded positions – not balanced. Fair-minded means Palestinians exist too, they have rights, too, and they are owed a solution
to this situation as much as the Israelis are," he said. "We have taken
the view that the Israelis are right and the Palestinians are wrong, on
everything, all the time." And former prime minister Joe Clark writes
in his 2013 book that Harper's "fierce commitment to Israel also
guides Canadian policy on much broader international issues. For
example, the Harper government's hostility towards the United Nations is framed regularly in the context of solidarity with Israel."[14]

Shimon Fogel, the chief executive of the Centre for Israel and Jewish Affairs, Canada's largest Jewish-Israeli advocacy group, opposed
that view, saying that "the Paul Heinbeckers and the others who moan
and groan about Canada having marginalized itself" have it wrong.
"Canada has consistently been a strong supporter of Israel over the
years. This government first demonstrated some differences, more on
style and rhetoric, than substance," Fogel told me. "It didn't use the
kind of conventional language to gloss over its positions in ways that
would seem more nuanced." That meant loudly defending Israel when
it is under attack in the UN, he said. "It evolved into a more clarified
stand and tried to distinguish, as (foreign affairs minister John) Baird
tried to distinguish, the black hats and the white hats."

Fogel was referring here to a speech Baird made to the American
Jewish Congress's 2014 convention in Washington.[15] To an appre-
ciative audience of about one thousand, he recalled being a young
staffer in the 1990s, sitting in a briefing on the subject of attacks on
Israel. A federal public servant was saying how it was hard to tell the
good guys from the bad guys in the Middle East, or "the white hats
from the black hats." In response, Baird scribbled two columns on
his notepad, labelled "white hat" and "black hat." Under white hat he
wrote the words "Israel" and "liberal democracy" and "our best
friend." Under black hat, he wrote "Hezbollah," "international terrorism," and "our worst enemy." Baird won a round of applause from
the Washington crowd when he announced: "Twenty years later, we

don't have briefings like that anymore ... There is no room for moral relativism." The minister declared: "The days are gone when Canada's foreign policy was defined simply by taking the middle path, by testing the temperature of those around the table, and landing somewhere not too hot, not too cold," he added. "Relativism isn't leadership; it's the easy way out."[16] With that, Baird publicly redefined Canada's Mideast policy in black and white.

This vocal pro-Israel stance was a marked departure from the nuanced approach of successive Liberal and Progressive Conservative governments over the six previous decades. Canada endorsed the birth of Israel from a privileged position within the United Nations. It was one of the eleven countries on the UN Special Committee on Palestine (UNSCOP), which oversaw the partition of Palestine into Jewish and Arab states in 1947 after Britain's mandate came to an end.[17] The state of Israel was born in May 1948 with Canada's full support. McGill University political scientist Rex Brynen wrote that "cultural and historical factors rather than realpolitik" shaped Canada's endorsement of the new Jewish state, since Canada's political leaders viewed the creation of the "Holy Land" in the context of their memories of the Holocaust coupled with their "predominantly Christian heritage," while the "views of the majority of the indigenous Arab population in the territory counted for little."[18] Historians Norman Hillmer and J.L. Granatstein noted that Lester Pearson was a prime example of this, being "a minister's son raised on Bible tales of the Holy Land and sympathetic to the Jewish population."[19] But biographer Andrew Cohen maintained that Pearson, whose tenure as external affairs minister began in September 1948, was not a committed Zionist, contrary to what some suggested. "He was under more pressure from Jews than from Arabs, to be sure, but he was, as usual, a pragmatist."[20] In some ways, this was an early manifestation of the influence of domestic politics on foreign policy. As Hillmer and Granatstein noted, "The birth of Israel was an indication that ethnic groups in Canada had continuing interests abroad and that such interest could often pose difficulties for the government."[21]

Canada's Middle East policy evolved beyond domestic considerations to embrace a more nuanced understanding of the Palestinians. This occurred in the decades following Israel's creation, when the country went to war with its Arab neighbours. Canada was in the thick of it, serving its third term on the Security Council, when the June 1967 Six Day War broke out. Canada still remained mainly pro-Israeli as the Jewish state's powerful military crushed its Egyptian and Arab neighbours and seized the last remaining Palestinian areas – the Jordanian-held West Bank, the Egyptian-run Gaza Strip, and the Golan Heights.[22] However, some sympathy for the Palestinians could be seen in a July 1967 intervention at the UN Security Council when Canadian ambassador George Ignatieff called on the secretary-general to send a special representative to the region to start a peace process based on a "fair and balanced" resolution.[23] In November, Canada voted in favour of Security Council Resolution 242, which called for Israel's withdrawal from the occupied territories and a negotiated solution to the dispute.[24] Sheer economic necessity nudged Canada closer to the Palestinian cause after the 1973 Arab-Israeli War, because the Arab oil embargo sent fuel prices skyrocketing. "At the same time," wrote Brynen, "a number of Israeli actions – notably, illegal settlement activity in the occupied territories, as well as the annexation of east Jerusalem – eroded Canadian support for Israeli policies."[25]

After Canada started its fourth temporary Security Council term in 1977, Ambassador William Barton affirmed the importance of Resolution 242, which called for Israeli withdrawal from the occupied territories. He said that any peace settlement "would also have to take due account of the legitimate aspirations of the Palestinians."[26]

Privately, the Canadian government had reservations about whether the Security Council was having any effect on the Middle East crisis. A cable from the External Affairs Department to a dozen and a half foreign embassies on 22 September 1977 offered this sobering assessment. "It has not/not advanced prospects for peace in Middle East."[27] But it also indicated Canada wasn't giving up on the Security Council just yet: "On balance, Council has done little to enhance its position as UN organ with primary responsibility for maintenance of peace and security, although we are not unhappy with its actual performance."[28]

Canada's two-year term had expired by March 1979 when the Council adopted two more key resolutions, 446 and 465, which branded Israeli settlements illegal, and a violation of the Fourth Geneva

Convention that prohibits a country from transferring its own civilian population to land seized in war. Canada adopted that position and it remains the country's official foreign policy to this day. But when Harper travelled to Israel in January 2014, he steadfastly refused to restate the government's position on Israeli settlements, leaving it to his host, Israeli prime minister Benjamin Netanyahu, to tell journalists that the two leaders disagreed on this point – in private. Harper suggested his silence was meant to cut the Israelis some slack in a tough neighbourhood. "The one lesson I think we have learned is that when somebody is a minority, particularly a small minority in the world, one goes out of one's way to embrace them, not to single them out for criticism. That's a fundamental Canadian ethic," Harper said.[29]

Canada didn't begin to recognize the Palestinians as an entity until the late 1980s after their first uprising, or Intifada, of 1987, which occurred during the Mulroney Progressive Conservative government. Through most the 1980s, Canadian officials offered only "vague support for a Palestinian 'entity' or 'homeland' rather than a Palestinian state."[30] Canada began to accept the notion of Palestinian statehood after the 1993 Oslo Accords and the March 2002 Security Council resolution that affirmed the concept of a two-state solution.[31] Under the Harper government, that was still the stated policy – a negotiated two-state solution, in which a new Palestinian state peacefully coexists with Israel and recognizes its right to exist. Still, some saw a problem with that position, one that was simply not reflected by the reality in the region. "We're supposed to think these negotiations are among equals," said Heinbecker. "The Israelis are one of the most powerful military forces in the world."

Canadian policy took another major shift in 2004, when Liberal prime minister Paul Martin repositioned Canada more firmly on Israel's side at the United Nations. His ambassador, Allan Rock, put the UN on notice that Canada would be supporting Israel in upcoming votes on the Israeli-Palestinian question because of "longstanding concerns."[32] Canada had a long tradition of simply abstaining on the approximately two-dozen resolutions that would come before the General Assembly each year criticizing Israel. Martin decided that Canada would stop abstaining and join the United States and a handful of other countries in voting against resolutions perceived to be anti-Israeli.

Fogel said the Harper Conservatives "accelerated a process that really began with the previous Liberal government." The Martin government may have started a course correction, but it was Harper's that revved the country's political engines full speed towards Israel.

*   *   *

The newly elected Stephen Harper arrived at the United Nations General Assembly in September 2006 fresh from the controversy that his "measured response" remark had ignited during the summer war in Lebanon. The prime minister used his speech to take aim at an institution that had been anathema to Israel: the newly created Human Rights Council. It had replaced the troubled UN Commission on Human Rights earlier that year. "Will the new Human Rights Council become a forum where human rights are genuinely put above political maneuvering? Or will it emulate the fate of its failed predecessor organization?" Harper asked. "But I must tell you, the early signals suggest that too little has changed, that the page has not yet been turned." Harper had a point: at the time, Syria was the council's chair.

In 2008, the Canadian Senate human rights committee began hearings on the Human Rights Council and criticized it for being ineffective and discriminatory towards Israel. It said that Canada and the European Union found itself "pitted against" Islamic and Arab states, and the Non-Aligned Movement.[33] "The outcome of this political battle is more than evident in the fact that the human rights situation in Palestine and Occupied Arab Territories was put on the Council's permanent agenda, and that more than half of the Special Sessions have been held on issues surrounding Israeli actions," the report said. "NGOs in Geneva told the Committee that the 'bully' factor has become a fact of life on the Council."[34] The committee found that recent UN voting patterns "revealed that the Council continues to be a proxy for larger geo-strategic conflicts, such as the Israeli-Palestinian conflict."[35] Canada's decision to vote against anti-Israel resolutions, rather than abstain, often left the country standing alone as a "sole dissenter." It noted that while the European Union had tried to build a consensus on the Council, Canada found this to be a "time-consuming challenge" that was simply not worth it. "Canada's position with regards to Israeli-Palestinian issues has further left it marginalized, and according to some witnesses, exacerbated the bloc politics already at play."[36]

The spectacle of the poorly functioning Human Rights Council was on full display in September 2013 when Cuba, Russia, Iran, and Belarus – countries with poor human rights records – used the forum to pile on Canada. The council was conducting its Universal Periodic Review of Canada's performance on rights, measuring a wide range of issues including poverty, immigration, and crime. Canada rejected a series of resolutions that called on it to conduct a national review of violence against aboriginal women, a topic that had the Harper government under pressure domestically. Canada's ambassador to the UN in Geneva, Elissa Golberg, politely told the meeting that the country was proud of its human rights record, and that provincial and local governments were looking after aboriginal women's issues.[37]

Previous governments had also clashed periodically with the UN Commission on Human Rights, the precursor of the Human Rights Council. In 1981, Liberal solicitor general Robert Kaplan bristled at criticism that Canadian parole legislation breached a UN covenant and angrily said Canada was a sovereign nation and would not be bound by a committee finding.[38] In 1996, Canada ignored a finding that Ontario's funding of Roman Catholic schools was a violation of the United Nations International Covenant on Civil and Political Rights because it did not fund other faiths, such as Judaism.[39]

Jason Kenney, one of Harper's most versatile cabinet ministers, was a frequent, outspoken critic of the UN. In May 2012, the UN special rapporteur on the right to food, Olivier De Schutter, was making an eleven-day trip to Canada to research a report. "We have in this country more than 800,000 households who are considered food insecure," De Schutter said. "This situation is of great concern to me." Kenney said De Schutter was wasting his time in Canada. "It would be our hope that the contributions we make to the United Nations are used to help starving people in developing countries, not to give lectures to wealthy and developed countries like Canada. And I think this is a discredit to the United Nations."[40] Kenney was equally outspoken in defending Israel at the UN, most notably in November 2010 when he announced that Canada would once

again boycott its anti-racism convention in South Africa, known as
the Durban III conference, calling the widely criticized gathering
an anti-Israeli "hatefest."[41] He also accused the Human Rights Council of passing "dozens" of resolutions against Israel, "but virtually
none on brutal dictatorships like Iran and Syria."[42]

But as forceful as Kenney could be, it was John Baird who took
the lead in defending Israel after becoming foreign affairs minister in
2011. During the keynote address at the annual Negev dinner in November 2012, Baird explained why he felt so strongly about Israel,
describing how his "grandfather left Canada to fight the Nazis" sev-
enty years earlier. "I'm deeply influenced by his contribution to combating an evil, which sought to exterminate the Jewish people ... that
moment in history when the Devil almost drove a stake through the
heart of humanity," Baird told his audience. "The heavy spirit, the
knotted stomach, and the paralysis of shock I felt as I learned details
of the horrors of the Nazi era have been ingrained in my soul; they
shook me to my core and have become part of my DNA."

When he travelled to Israel later that year, Baird brought along an
ultra-orthodox rabbi from Ottawa's Hasidic community. "I have a
confession to make," Baird would say on several stops on this trip,
"I'm not Jewish ... But I do have a rabbi, and he's accompanying me
on this trip."[43] Baird also proudly displayed his pro-Israeli viewpoint
when he made his international debut at the United Nations in September 2011. He criticized the Human Rights Council, and equated
Israel's critics with the appeasers of Nazi Germany before the Holocaust. "Just as fascism and communism were the great struggles of
previous generations, terrorism is the great struggle of ours. And far
too often, the Jewish state is on the front line of our struggle and its
people the victims of terror," Baird told the General Assembly. "Canada will not accept or stay silent while the Jewish state is attacked for
defending its territory and its citizens. The Second World War taught
us all the tragic price of going along just to get along." Baird said
Canada was now "standing for what is principled and just, regardless of whether it is popular, or convenient, or expedient."

Baird's speechwriters also wanted him to say a few positive things
about the Palestinians, but the minister decided to leave those
suggestions on the cutting-room floor. For example, "Canada is a
leading supporter of the Palestinian people, having committed

$300-million over five years to assist the Palestinian Authority to build capacity in the key areas of justice sector reform, security, and sustainable economic growth, as well as providing humanitarian assistance to Palestinians in West Bank and Gaza, including refugees," said a paragraph from an early draft of Baird's speech, which I obtained under the Access to Information Act. Another passage that Baird rejected said: "Our support for the West Bank and Gaza demonstrates Canada's ongoing commitment to assist Palestinians in building the foundations of a viable, independent, democratic and peaceful Palestinian state living side by side in peace and security with Israel."

Stephen Lewis, Mulroney's first UN ambassador, said Harper's close friendship with Netanyahu poisoned the atmosphere against Canada at the UN "because Netanyahu is such an unprincipled scoundrel. So for Harper and Netanyahu to be seen as Tweedledum and Tweedledee is hard for people to take seriously." In the Mulroney era, and in the Chrétien years that followed, Canada displayed a nuanced position at the UN, especially towards the Middle East, he said.

For Heinbecker, Baird's 2011 UN speech was "a mixture of sour grapes and neo-con ideology." He said the loss of the 2010 Security Council election made the UN "more of a problem" than it had been previously for the Conservatives. "We sit on the sidelines in a kind of truculent sourness making judgments about things we scarcely understand."

Baird continued his criticism of the UN in defence of Israel. In October 2012, he called for the firing of Richard Falk, the UN's special rapporteur on human rights in the Palestinian territories. Falk called for a boycott of companies doing business with Israeli settlements in the West Bank and East Jerusalem. Baird said Falk's comments were "offensive" and "outrageous." A month later, on 29 November 2012, Baird returned to the UN General Assembly, this time to give a speech opposing the Palestinian bid for non-member observer status at the UN. The Palestinians won by a huge margin that day. Canada, Israel, the United States, and six small countries voted against the Palestinians, but Baird was the only foreign minister to make a speech in support of that opposition.

The U.S. chose not to speak publicly on the matter, trusting that its vote, coupled with its clearly stated and long-held policy of

supporting Israel, would speak for itself. Baird fully expected the
Palestinians to succeed but he said Canada had to "stand up for what
we believe is right." He said he was "tremendously disappointed"
with the Palestinian bid because he considered it an unproductive
way to negotiate peace with Israel. He said it would affect Canada's
relationship with the Palestinians, and added: "This government
makes no apologies for standing with the Jewish state."

Baird had identified two countries as top foreign policy priorities
– Indonesia and Turkey. But Baird's speech was sandwiched between
Indonesian foreign minister Marty Natalegawa and Turkey's Ahmet
Davutoglu. Natalegawa pointed out that Indonesia, as the world's
most populous Muslim country, was the co-sponsor of the Palestinian resolution. "The time has come for the international community to set things right. No longer can the world turn a blind eye to the
long sufferings of the Palestinian people, the denial of the basic
human rights and their fundamental freedoms, the obstruction of
their rights to self-determination and to independence." Davutoglu
said Gaza had become a place where "thousands of people live
through an inhumane blockade in an open prison." Flatly contra-
dicting Baird, Davutoglu said the UN recognition of the Palestinians would move the peace process forward, not hinder it.

Four months later, Baird elaborated on his efforts to block the
Palestinian statehood bid in a speech to the powerful U.S. lobby
group the American Israel Public Affairs Committee during its annual meeting in Washington, DC. Baird addressed his government's
critics once again, repeating that Canada would not "go along to get
along with some moral relativist crowd at the United Nations or
elsewhere." Enthusiastic applause followed.

In April 2013, Baird returned to Israel – and sparked another furor
for which he made no apologies – when he decided to have a cup
of coffee in East Jerusalem with Israel's justice minister Tzipi Livni,
because the Palestinians and the United Nations consider East
Jerusalem to be occupied land. Indeed, Canada's stated policy on
the Foreign Affairs Department website says: "Canada considers the
status of Jerusalem can be resolved only as part of a general settlement of the Palestinian-Israeli dispute. Canada does not recognize
Israel's unilateral annexation of East Jerusalem." As the criticism –
not to mention the surprise – mounted over the choice of location

for this meeting, the response from the minister and his staff was glib. To them, the sensitivities surrounding Jerusalem and international law, not to mention Canada's own policy, didn't seem to matter. Baird said he remained supportive of the Israelis and Palestinians returning to the negotiating table, as he brushed aside questions about the location for that cup of coffee as simply "irrelevant."[44]

"I'm just not interested in getting into the semantic argument about whether you have a meeting with one person on one side of the street, it's OK, and you have a meeting on the other side of street, and it's not," Baird said. "We're focused on trying to have an impact on the difficult and serious challenges, that being security for Israelis, an end to the conflict, and the legitimate aspirations for a state from those in the Palestinian side."[45] Baird's spokesman, Rick Roth, followed up in an email, saying: "As guests, we were pleased to meet our hosts where it was most convenient for them."[46]

Saeb Erekat, the chief Palestinian negotiator, saw it differently. He sent Baird a protest letter. "Your recent meeting with Israeli officials in East Jerusalem has the effect of attempting to legitimize the illegal situation on the ground and may be deemed as aiding, abetting or otherwise assisting illegal Israeli policies," he wrote. "As such, Canada's actions are tantamount to complicity in ongoing Israeli violations of the international laws of war."[47]

*   *   *

So much of the Conservative government's foreign policy was driven by domestic political calculations. The Middle East was different. Ideology, not domestic political considerations, was the prime driver there. This direction came from Prime Minister Stephen Harper himself, and it was rooted in his most formative experiences.

Stephen Harper's affection for Israel begins and ends with his father. As author John Ibbitson explained in his biography of the prime minister, Harper's loyalty to Israel was rooted in his deep reverence for Joe Harper.[48] "Harper's devotion to his father is deep and lasting," Ibbitson wrote. "But nothing that Joe Harper transmitted to his son could match the impact of his views on Israel." Polish immigrant Harvey Gellman, a pioneer in Canadian computing, befriended the elder Harper while they worked at Imperial Oil.

Gellman had come to Canada as a child survivor of the Holocaust, during which he lost many relatives. Ibbitson wrote that Gellman told Harper many stories about his family, and they "left a lasting mark on Joe, who had always hated intolerance, convincing him that the Jews had a right to their own homeland." Joe Harper passed that "fervent conviction" on to his three sons.[49]

In April 2008, the Holocaust became real for Harper when he paid a low-key but emotional visit to the Nazi death camp at Auschwitz. I watched as Harper silently toured grounds of the Auschwitz-Birkenau State Museum, where 1.5 million people, mostly Jews, were killed. He was the second prime minister to make the pilgrimage, after Jean Chrétien in 1999, and Justin Trudeau would become the third in the summer of 2016. Accompanied by the museum's director, Piotr Cywinksi, Harper walked from the small, red brick building that housed the gas chambers and crematoriums to the nearby Birkenau camp, before he arrived, alone, at a gray slate wall at the end of a rear courtyard: the Death Wall Memorial. Harper knelt at the foot of a wreath emblazoned with the name "Canada," and remained there for twenty seconds. He got up, turned, swallowed hard and walked on. Harper didn't say a word, and he didn't have to. In the museum's guestbook he wrote: "We are witness here to the vestiges of unspeakable cruelty, horror and death. Let us never forget these things and work always to prevent their repetition."

Shimon Fogel told me he knows Harper well and has no doubt that his stance on Israel was guided by an ideological moral certainty – one that still managed to generate some very real domestic political benefits. Any political party is going to want to score points with specific segments of Canadian voters, he said, but with the Harper government "it certainly wasn't the case that the government said, 'the Jewish communities are a ripe pool of support from which we can benefit, so let's change policies so we can attract their support.' I think it was exactly the opposite." That approach, Fogel said, allowed the Conservatives to unseat the Liberals as the party of choice for Jewish voters. That translated into Conservative victories in the Toronto area for finance minister Joe Oliver, former environment minister Peter Kent, and MP Mark Adler. These ridings, said Fogel, "typically would have gone Liberal."

Adler stole headlines from his prime minister during his January 2014 visit to Israel when he was caught on camera trying to bust into Harper's photo-op at the Western Wall in the Old City of Jerusalem. Adler was captured on video by a reporter travelling with Harper trying to coax Jeremy Hunt, one of the prime minister's aides, into letting him get into the shot. "Jeremy. Jeremy! Can I get in?" Adler pleaded. "It's the re-election! This is the million-dollar shot."[50]

One of the strongest pro-Israeli voices in the Liberal party, former Montreal MP Irwin Cotler, said that even he found the Harper government's support of Israel over the top. But Cotler conceded that it proved successful at the ballot box. In an interview in June 2015, during his final days in the House of Commons before retiring from politics, Cotler said the Conservatives had successfully transformed Israel into a wedge issue. "They have succeeded in winning the Jewish vote because as I've said they have been persistent in their support for Israel. And certainly in a declaratory way," Cotler explained. "The Conservatives are very effective in the short run in engaging that sort of targeting of voters. But in the longer run, this hurts the issues, and in the longer run, I don't think it's going to work."

Fogel's assessment was that Harper successfully swayed Jewish voters because they simply judged his views on Israel as sincere. Fogel pointed to Harper's 2014 speech to the Israeli Knesset, where he gave a nuanced analysis of how political opposition to Israel can sometimes cross a line and become anti-Semitic. "Now I understand, in the world of diplomacy, with one, solitary, Jewish state and scores of others, it is all too easy 'to go along to get along' and single out Israel," Harper told Israel's parliament. "But such 'going along to get along' is not a balanced approach, nor a sophisticated one. It is, quite simply, weak and wrong." Harper said criticism of Israeli policy is not necessarily anti-Semitic. "But what else can we call criticism that selectively condemns only the Jewish state and effectively denies its right to defend itself, while systematically ignoring – or excusing – the violence and oppression all around it?" the prime minister rhetorically asked. "What else can we call it when Israel is routinely targeted at the United Nations?"

Harper's speech was a reminder that sometimes criticism of Israel is not simply a policy disagreement, Fogel said. "Often it portrays

Israel as some kind of unique evil that, really, it just becomes the proxy for the Jew," he said. "And in those cases, it's hard to explain it as anything other than anti-Semitism."

David Mulroney, Harper's former foreign-policy adviser, had seen evidence of a clear link between the modern Conservatism that Harper embodies, and Israel. "If you've ever been in the office of a Conservative staffer in Ottawa, one of these young people who was in the young Conservatives in college, they generally have three kinds of symbols in their office: they have something to do with Ronald Reagan, they have a Margaret Thatcher picture and they have an Israeli flag," he told me. "Those are the touchstones of modern grassroots Conservatism – one of the main touchstones of modern conservatism as opposed to progressive conservatism as we know it."

* * *

For all of Harper's criticism of the UN over its treatment of Israel, his government quietly brought the Jewish state closer to the organization than any previous Canadian government. In his Knesset speech, Harper welcomed the fact that Israel had joined the Western European and Others Group of the United Nations. The UN divides member countries into five regional groups, which co-ordinate which countries can sit on committees and run for the Security Council. Arab states rejected Israel's membership in the Asian group, its natural geographic affinity, and that had prevented it from participating in a host of UN bodies including the Human Rights Council and the Security Council.[51] "Canada believes that Israel should be able to exercise its full rights as a UN member-state and to enjoy the full measure of its sovereignty," Harper said in his Knesset speech.

Israel's Canadian ambassador Rafael Barak told me that the Harper government helped persuade other countries in the Western group to accept Israel into its ranks. The veteran diplomat was able to explain the value of his country gaining entry into an international club that both Israel and the Harper government viewed with such deep-seated antagonism: it would enable the Jewish state to defend itself at the UN. "We were, in a way, in limbo," Barak said. "We don't want to be a one-issue country, dealing only with our political constraints." Barak said gaining fuller access to the UN would also allow Israel to play a more constructive role on the world stage, including allowing it to pursue its own temporary, two-year term on the Security Council, something Israel had never done.

Months after Harper left Israel, Canada found itself once again defending the Jewish state against the Human Rights Council. In July 2014, Baird expressed frustration and disappointment over the Council's decision to launch an international commission of inquiry to investigate possible violations of international law by Israel in its summer war in Gaza that year. "Canada is frustrated and deeply disappointed that the UNHRC decided to completely ignore the abhorrent terrorist acts of Hamas," Baird said, pointing out that the militant organization had been indiscriminately firing rockets into Israeli neighbourhoods where millions of innocent civilians lived. Baird said the failure to condemn the "reprehensible actions of Hamas has only emboldened its brutality and encouraged these terrorists to continue their inexcusable actions."[52] The fifty-day summer war, however, killed 2,100 Palestinians – most of them civilians – and seventy-two Israelis, most of them military personnel.[53]

Baird's last foreign trip before he suddenly quit politics in February 2015 included a five-day tour of the Middle East the previous month. He returned to Jerusalem and Tel Aviv, and also made one last memorable stop in Ramallah, the Palestinians' West Bank capital. Baird said the Palestinians had made a "huge mistake" and crossed a "red line" by joining the International Criminal Court and pushing for a war crimes investigation of Israel in the Gaza war of the previous summer. Baird said he communicated that message "in no uncertain terms" during his meeting with the Palestinian leadership in Ramallah. When Baird emerged from their meeting in Ramallah, his motorcade was pelted with eggs and shoes by an angry group of demonstrators.

The Conservative government's Middle East policy left a bitter divide in Canada. Heinbecker, Canada's former UN ambassador, said he was not the least bit surprised by the scene of Baird's motorcade being attacked. The Palestinians "go through decades of fruitless negotiations and they're supposed to behave as if everything is in fine." But Fogel brushed off the protest as internal posturing by the Palestinians. He recalled that former Liberal foreign affairs minister John Manley had been burned in effigy by the Palestinians a decade earlier. Fogel rebuffed the notion that Canada had lost respect in the region. "On the contrary," he said, alluding to the Canadian government's annual support of $300 million, "it's been able to demonstrate over the last nine years an ability to put its money where its mouth is."

That may have been the case, but behind the scenes, Canada was also forcefully opposing Palestinian statehood ambitions at the UN. In January 2015, Canada unequivocally opposed fifteen separate Palestinian attempts to join various UN treaties, conventions, and protocols. I downloaded the documents from the UN website. Canada objected to the Palestinians acceding to the Rome Statute that created the International Criminal Court and a host of other agreements, including the Convention on Biodiversity, the Basel Convention on the Control of Transboundary Movements of Hazardous Wastes and their Disposal, the UN Law of the Sea, a convention against transnational organized crime, a protocol on biosafety, and biological diversity and the convention on women's rights. Repeatedly, Canada's objections said, "'Palestine' does not meet the criteria of a state under international law and is not recognized by Canada as a state," adding that Canada considers any declarations "made by the 'State of Palestine' to be without any legal validity or effect." In its reply, "The State of Palestine" said repeatedly that it "regrets the position of Canada and wishes to recall" the resolution of 29 November 2012 that granted it "non-observer state status in the United Nations."

Said Hamad, who was then the chief representative of the Palestinian delegation to Canada, emailed a response when I asked him to comment on this development. I had met Hamad briefly on a handful of occasions during his tenure in Ottawa, and he was every inch the diplomat. During that time, he had refrained from making anything resembling a provocative comment, on or off the record. But on this occasion, he dropped the gloves. "It pains the Palestinians to know that Canada is trying to exclude us from our rightful place in the family of nations. It is awkward to see a great country like Canada relegated to the role of cheerleader for Israeli extremists at the UN," Hamad wrote. "When future Canadians look back at Canada's positions during this time they will be appalled that their country was so boldly opposed to justice and so far on the wrong side of history," he added. "We invite Canada to pursue a position of its own – rather than parrot policies developed by the Likud Party and its ultranationalist allies – on the matter of Palestinian freedom."

Yves Fortier, the former Canadian UN ambassador from the Mulroney era, said Canada under Harper had lost its credibility as a fair-minded participant in the continuing Middle East dilemma. "We're seen as: Israel can do no wrong, and the Palestinians can do no good. That doesn't put us on the side of any Arab country today."

*   *   *

Four days after Stephen Harper's government was defeated, Justin Trudeau and Benjamin Netanyahu spoke on the telephone. The so-called "Jewish vote" was among the many constituencies the Liberals had recaptured, sending Mark Adler and finance minister Joe Oliver down to defeat. The Israeli prime minister congratulated Trudeau on his win, and the prime minister–designate assured him that Canada was, and would remain, a friend of Israel. The affection that the Harper government had shown for Israel would be dialed down, but the substance of the relationship would be unchanged. As Trudeau's chief spokeswoman Kate Purchase told me, it was "a very positive call." But Trudeau also said "there would be a shift in tone but Canada would continue to be a friend of Israel's."

None of this caused a ripple of consternation with the Israelis. Rafael Barak, the Israeli ambassador, told me he had no doubt Canada-Israel relations would remain strong going forward. In fact, nothing leading up to that call had led the Israelis to be the least bit worried. "Mr Trudeau has been very consistent from the very beginning of his campaign in expressing his support for Israel," Barak told me. "I'm sure maybe the style will change. But I don't feel there will be a change on the substance. I'm really reassured."

So was Netanyahu. He invited Trudeau to visit Israel sometime soon.

Trudeau had also promised during the campaign to reestablish relations with Iran, which the Conservatives had severed in 2012. Israel wasn't particularly worried about Canada's plans to reengage with a country that was its bitter enemy. Barak said it wouldn't affect relations with Canada. "This is a Canadian issue," he said. "It is a domestic Canadian consideration of the security of their diplomats."

On Iran, Trudeau "has also been saying all the right things that Canada has been saying."

Some of Canada's allies had, in fact, been quite unhappy with some of the things the Harper government had been saying about Iran. It centred on what they saw as Canada's bellicose and relentless criticism of Iran while several of Canada's closest allies were trying to negotiate a deal with the country to prevent it from developing a nuclear weapon. They had grown tired of the Canadian government's carping from the sidelines. If Harper's support of Israel was full-throated, so too was his condemnation of Iran, which had become the Jewish state's existential enemy.

Canada's relations with Iran had deteriorated even before the Conservatives came to power. In 2003, Iranian-born Canadian photojournalist Zahra Kazemi, arrested for taking photos at a demonstration, died in Tehran after being tortured and sexually abused by her captors. That led to a swift diplomatic downgrade when the Liberals were in power. In September 2012, the Conservative government severed relations with Iran entirely, withdrawing its diplomats and closing its embassy in Tehran, while booting what was left of Iran's diplomatic corps in Canada out of the country. Concern for the security and safety of Canadian diplomats following an attack on the British embassy was cited as the main reason. In addition, Iran "refuses to comply with United Nations resolutions pertaining to its nuclear program. It routinely threatens the existence of the state of Israel, and engages in racist anti-Semitic rhetoric and incitement to genocide," Baird told a group of reporters, myself included, when he made the surprise announcement in Vladivostok, where we'd just landed for the Asia-Pacific Economic Co-operation forum.

Some of Canada's closest allies were in the midst of a long series of negotiations with Iran to curb its nuclear energy program and prevent it from secretly developing the capability to build a bomb. The Netanyahu government was scathingly critical of this effort, and it found a great supporter in the Harper government, which regularly expressed skepticism about the negotiations that the five permanent members of the Security Council – the United States, Britain, France, Russia, and China – as well as Germany were undertaking. In July 2015, the P5 plus one finally struck a deal that would call for international monitoring of Iran's nuclear program.

Rob Nicholson, the caretaker minister of the foreign affairs portfolio in the final eight months of Conservative rule, issued a statement that repeated, word for word, Canada's previous line towards the talks: "We appreciate the efforts of the P5+1 to reach an agreement. At the same time, we will continue to judge Iran by its actions not its words."

During the federal election's foreign policy debate in September 2015, Harper was unapologetic when pressed about being unsupportive of the Iran nuclear deal, saying his government's position was based on principle. "I fully admit that we don't always take the position of our allies." One Western diplomat, who spoke to me on condition neither they nor their country was identified, characterized that refrain as singularly unhelpful, if not insulting, to the efforts of Western negotiators. "We would welcome the prospect of a different approach on making the Iran deal happen," the diplomat said, days after Trudeau's victory. The diplomat added that the deal would not be easy to implement, and that the tough Western sanctions on Iran that had forced them to the bargaining table wouldn't simply disappear overnight. "To have Canada standing back, pounding out its skepticism – I'm glad that's over."[54]

In October 2016, Trudeau won approval from the Israeli government for the size and quality of the Canadian delegation he led to the funeral of Shimon Peres, the legendary statesman. Trudeau invited the leader of the Conservative opposition, Rona Ambrose; the leaders of two prominent Canadian Jewish organizations; his foreign minister; former Liberal prime minister Jean Chrétien; and Harper himself.

Harper declined the free ride on Trudeau's plane. He went to pay his respects, but took a commercial flight instead.

CHAPTER NINE

Standing with Ukraine
against the "Putin Regime"

JULY 2006

Stephen Harper sits facing the granite-faced, one-time KGB leader. They are in St Petersburg, Vladimir Putin's hometown, and in the ornate sitting-room of this resplendent palace, Harper is making his debut on the international stage. This is his first multi-country trip – the one that started with controversy when he commented on Israel's bombardment of Lebanon. Since then, Harper has been to London for a one-on-one meeting with one of the world's most seasoned statesmen, Prime Minister Tony Blair. Among other things, that visit allowed Harper to get a rundown of the other leaders he was about to meet in St Petersburg. Harper would eventually come to see the G8 – or more specifically its predecessor, the G7 – as Canada's preferred multilateral club. Where he had mistrust of the United Nations, Harper had more natural affinity for this group of likeminded countries.

In the years to come, this will mean paring down the club to its previous configuration – the G7, minus Russia. But at this first meeting with Putin, Harper is still trying to get along. He suggests they talk about hockey, but his host is unresponsive. Then comes the clunker: "And you will explain to me how to maintain my popularity at high levels." In the years to come, Harper would never again find himself demurring to Putin.

In 2006, Russia and Canada tried to get along even though neither had any illusions about the democratic distance between them. Senior Canadian government officials briefed journalists in Ottawa before Harper's trip. "It's an important opportunity for us to convey messages in terms of our expectations about human rights, good governance in Russia," said one official, who under the rules of those briefings remained anonymous. "These issues will also be subjects that leaders themselves discuss within the context of the G8. So that message will be conveyed directly, respectfully."

The Russians knew this was an issue too. Russian ambassador Georgiy Mamedov discussed the 2006 summit during a briefing at his embassy in Ottawa in June 2006, a few weeks before Harper was to depart. Mamedov extolled the positives of the Canada-Russia relationship – co-operation on energy and the Arctic, and the joint fight against terrorism. Canadians, he said, had sent partners to Russia to help it organize the large G8 gathering it was about to host. "We were a communist country just fifteen years ago," he said. "It can't change overnight. We appreciate any help you can offer us. The G8 process is an excellent opportunity for us to receive your help and assistance."

Eight years later, I interviewed Mamedov as he prepared to leave Ottawa after an eleven-year posting. He lamented the deterioration in Canada-Russia relations, and accused the Harper government of engaging in "propaganda" to suit its own needs. In the space of a decade Putin had become one of Harper's villains, a bad guy conforming to his Manichean worldview and his visceral loathing of all vestiges of Cold War communism. At one time, Harper would talk to Putin. But the more he listened, the more he watched him in action, the more he tried to reason with him, the more he decided he would be better off ignoring or even castigating him. This stance set Harper apart from many of his fellow G7 leaders, notably German chancellor Angela Merkel, French president François Hollande, and U.S. president Barack Obama, who didn't like Putin either but decided to keep the diplomatic dialogue going despite his unprecedented violation of Ukraine's – and Europe's – eastern border.

Two factors drove Harper's hardline attitude towards Putin: his own values and domestic political calculation. As with his strong support of Israel, this was value-driven. His hostility towards the "Russian aggression" by the "Putin regime," as he would come to call it, conformed to the worldview inspired by his formative readings as a young man, including Malcolm Muggeridge's accounts in the *Manchester Guardian* of the Stalinist-imposed Ukraine famine of the

1930s. And it was buttressed by the reverence in which Harper held his father, Joe. The prime minister himself revealed this connection nine years later on his final trip to an Eastern Europe grappling with Putin's sabre-rattling on Ukraine's borders.

*   *   *

JUNE 2015. WARSAW

Stephen Harper is marching solemnly to pay his respects at the Tomb of the Unknown Soldier, which sits under a stone enclosure in a massive open square from the Soviet era. Some of the Conservatives accompanying Harper and his wife, Laureen, are very excited to be here. Harper's staff was quick to point out that this was sacred ground in the long campaign that led to the demise of the Soviet Union. After Harper pays his respects, he lingers for a few moments on the gray drizzly day, which is a bit unusual for him. He likes to stick to his itinerary, complete his photo-ops, and move on. He's not usually one for small talk, but this time it's different.

Jason Kenney is accompanying Harper on this last trip before the 19 October 2015 federal election. He tells Harper and a group of Conservative MPs that this was the spot in June 1979 – sixteen years and ten days earlier – where Pope John Paul II gave the speech that historians view as having inspired the Polish Solidarity movement that contributed to the fall of the Soviet Union. "I remember it very well," Harper says. "There's very interesting history. My father was born and raised in Moncton, Canada, where much of the Polish air force trained during the war." And then he moved on. But not before evoking the memory, and the influence, of his father Joe. It was an unscripted glimpse into Harper's soul, and it was barely audible. But it spoke volumes about all the shouting he had been doing lately about someone else who was making people very nervous in this neighbourhood: Russian president Vladimir Putin.

For the second year in row, Harper made a point of travelling to Poland and Ukraine en route to scheduled G7 meetings in Europe to show Canadian solidarity with Ukraine, which was reeling from the March 2014 annexation of Crimea by Russian forces. Harper was the first G7 leader to visit Ukraine that month and returned three months later, and again in June 2015. He checked in on Poland on those two latter visits, assuring full co-operation with its NATO ally.

On those trips, Harper received very warm, friendly welcomes and performed like a natural statesman. All of this played well at home. In addition to the 1.3 million Ukrainian Canadians, there were also about one million citizens of Polish heritage. Harper's entourage on this trip included numerous influential members of these communities: the president of the League of Ukrainian Canadian Women, the president of the Ukrainian Canadian Congress, the president of the Ukraine Canadian Chamber of Commerce, and a representative of the Bloor West Village Toronto Ukrainian festival. He also brought along three Conservative MPs with links to Eastern Europe. There was Toronto-born MP Ted Opitz, son of Polish parents who suffered under Nazi German occupiers and their Soviet liberators. He was also a retired lieutenant colonel in the Canadian Forces who managed to knock off the Liberal incumbent in the Toronto riding of Etobicoke Centre by just twenty-six votes in the 2011 election. Manitoba's James Bezan received one of Ukraine's highest honours for his private member's bill that recognized the Ukrainian famine of the 1930s as an act of genocide imposed by Josef Stalin. Polish-born Wladyslaw Lizon, another Toronto-area MP, was a founding member of an organization called Tribute to Liberty, the driving force behind a controversial initiative by the Conservatives to build a large memorial to the victims of communism in Ottawa's main tourist district.[1]

Like Mark Adler, who talked about wanting to be in the "million-dollar shot" on Harper's 2014 trip to Jerusalem, images of these MPs had the potential to play well in their home ridings during the next federal election. After all, the prime minister's own camera crew was now well entrenched in the media delegation that travelled with Harper, recording everything the prime minister and his entourage did 24/7, including some events that did not happen in public. There seemed to be a fair amount of domestic politicking taking place in Eastern Europe. It was a premise that I put to one of Harper's spokespeople as the 2015 trip ended.

"These members have strong connections in foreign governments, helping to connect and grow Canadian business abroad," Harper's spokesman Stephen Lecce told me. "They also played an active role in promoting our economic and security interests, including Putin's aggression in Ukraine and the advancement of CETA," the free trade agreement between Canada and the European Union.

Harper's political opponents didn't buy that. "The prime minister is visiting countries with strong ties to Canada and large diaspora communities here," New Democrat foreign affairs critic Paul Dewar told me. "Canadians are left wondering what exactly he is hoping to achieve. It's all fine and well for the prime minister to stop by, but does he have an actual agenda beyond just visiting?"

The trip didn't help Opitz or Lizon. In the October 2015 election, they both went down to defeat, while Bezan held his seat.

*   *   *

In 2012, Margaret Biggs was an experienced hand at the helm of the soon-to-be-defunct Canadian International Development Agency. She was appointed in 2008 and would serve as its last president before the agency was formally folded into the Foreign Affairs Department as part of a controversial merger the Conservatives casually announced in an obscure paragraph in the 2013 federal budget. Typically, CIDA presidents had some autonomy, but in recent years Biggs, like all public servants, was feeling the squeeze as Harper's office slashed aid spending and started taking a more hands-on approach.[2] But she wasn't afraid to speak truth to power. On 3 April 2012 she offered some sharp criticism of a recurring and controversial practice of the Harper government: sending teams of election monitors to observe Ukraine's elections.

Ukraine's parliamentary elections were coming up at the end of May 2012, and Canada was intending to send a team of observers, as it had done two years earlier for Ukraine's presidential election. But as Biggs pointed out to Julian Fantino, the international co-operation minister, there was already more than adequate international monitoring in place – the time-honoured contribution by the Organizations for Security and Co-operation in Europe (OSCE) and its governance arm, the Office for Democratic Institutions and Human Rights (ODIHR). The office, based in Warsaw, had been created in the 1990s, and had dispatched tens of thousands of observers to hundreds of elections. In a March 2015 speech, Daniel Baer, the U.S. ambassador to the OSCE, called the "ODIHR's independent standards-based comprehensive assessment of the pre-election environment, technical preparations for voting itself, voting day and so on ... the gold standard for election observation."[3]

Biggs's memo was just one in a thick stack of internal government documents – the pile is several inches high – that Joan Bryden, my colleague at the Canadian Press, and I spent months poring over. Almost all of it was released under Access to Information. The paper trail is filled with recommendations by public servants telling the government that their own monitors simply won't measure up to the OSCE. The Harper government ignored this advice and sent hundreds of observers on multiple missions. Not only was this costly, it strained already limited resources within the Foreign Affairs Department. These missions also broke one of the cardinal rules of international election monitoring: they featured a large contingent of Ukrainian Canadians in defiance of an OSCE principle that warns against sending such diaspora observers because they will, at the very least, give the appearance of not being neutral.

The Liberals had also recognized the political value of being seen to be responsive to events in Ukraine, so they handed John Turner the job of leading the country's first monitoring mission back in 2004. It proved to be less than a stellar success, and the government concluded that the multilateral OSCE missions were the way to go. Its internal report stated that the Turner-led mission "should not be considered as a precedent but only as a 'last resort option' for future Canadian observer missions."[4] It also found that the Canadian mission was almost twice as expensive as the OSCE mission: it cost $9,335 per Canadian observer to send them to Ukraine for eight days, while a ten-day assignment through the OSCE cost only $4,981 per observer.

The report also raised concerns about the fact that 60 per cent of the delegation came from Ukrainian backgrounds. It was true that they were familiar with the country and could speak the language, but they lacked monitoring experience. In addition, the report noted "partisan behaviour" by some Ukrainian Canadians, because they were seen to be favouring Viktor Yuschenko, the pro-democracy candidate favoured by the West. In the end, Yuschenko beat his

Russian-backed rival Viktor Yanukovych. The 2004 election was widely seen as fair but had that not been the case, the report noted, it might "be more difficult to defend the mission as non-partisan." At the same time, the report extolled the work of the OSCE, saying it had a "respected track record of elections observation" and that its "multinational composition contributes to greater perceived neutrality." The report concluded that the OSCE mission was "more impartial, credible, professional, with experienced, well-trained observers and well-prepared and tested documentation and forms."

The Harper government ignored this report entirely, sending large delegations to Ukraine's 2010 presidential election and to its parliamentary elections in 2012. They also continued to contribute to the OSCE missions. The Conservatives never tried to hide the fact they were sending Ukrainian Canadians; in fact, they gave them senior roles on the missions. This greatly pleased the Ukrainian Canadian diaspora. Clearly, the move was a domestic political win for the Harper government. It was shown to be a caring defender of the freedom of Canada's friends in Ukraine. But behind closed doors, the bureaucracy continued to issue warnings against the missions.

As Biggs wrote in the spring of 2012, Canada was the second-largest contributor to the OSCE. "It is considered best practice for international election monitoring to be organized through multilateral election observation missions. Multilateral observation offers a host of advantages." This included the fact it was viewed as "impartial and trustworthy." She noted that the organization provides in-depth training to observers "and can hold observers to account in providing impartial and professional observation in line with OSCE standards." So she recommended that Canada send twenty-five long-term observers to the OSCE mission, the maximum it allowed any one country. The cost would be approximately $1.5 million. "This is where Canada can have the greatest value added and greatest impact in supporting transparent and fair elections," she said.

Her recommendation was rejected. Instead, the government decided to send more than 350 short-term observers on its own bilateral mission. On the eve of their departure, Harper himself gave them a big public sendoff at the Canadian Museum of History in Gatineau, Quebec, just across the Ottawa River from Parliament Hill. "Again the mission will be led largely by Ukrainian Canadians.

Thanks to waves of immigration going back more than 120 years, Ukraine's sons and daughters now number nearly a million and a quarter, or four per cent of all Canadians," the prime minister said. "We also understand that, for you, the situation in Ukraine remains deeply personal." And for good measure, he took a partisan shot at the current elected president of Ukraine. "We continue to call upon President Yanukovych to respect judicial independence, to cease the harassment of opposition voices and to conduct an election that is indeed free and fair."

In 2014, when the government's own lessons-learned report emerged on the 2012 mission, it was nowhere near as rosy as the prime minister made it out to be. Yet another internal assessment concluded that it wasn't a good idea for Canada to be sending its own monitors to the Ukraine election. Its conclusion: "This was a costly undertaking due to the large size and complexity of the various missions." It also cost a lot of time and effort on the part of CIDA and the Department of Foreign Affairs and International Trade staff to coordinate Canada's electoral support and ensure sound management of the missions. "Neither CIDA nor the Department of Foreign Affairs and International Trade have the in-house resources, or the required expertise, to perform this function on short timelines," it said. Like the earlier report, this one also concluded: "The Organization for Security and Co-operation in Europe was clearly perceived by the Ukrainian authorities, local media, and international media, as the leading and most credible international voice on the elections."

Despite this assessment, Harper considered pulling Canada out of the OSCE in 2012 because he believed Europe was at peace and the organization was no longer relevant. Three European ambassadors publicly disclosed the widely rumoured episode in February 2016, after the Conservatives had been defeated. The ambassadors of Germany, Austria, and Serbia revealed details of what had transpired to a small group of journalists, including me, who had been invited for breakfast at the German ambassador's residence. They said U.S. president Barack Obama had to persuade Harper to keep Canada in the OSCE. German ambassador Werner Wnendt said Harper subscribed to a widespread feeling that the organization had become irrelevant because there was no more conflict in Europe. "We all thought we defused tension in Europe," added Arno Riedel, the Austrian ambassador.

When the NDP's Hélène Laverdière confronted him about the
planned withdrawal during an April 2013 appearance before the
House of Commons foreign affairs committee, foreign affairs minister John Baird vehemently denied it. Baird accused her of "making
it up" and asked her three times "Who told you?" Baird said he was
"happy to clarify" that Canada had "no intention of withdrawing
from the OSCE." At the time, Baird was correct. But there was more to
the story. One of Baird's cabinet colleagues in 2012 was Treasury
Board president Tony Clement, who was overseeing a review of government spending and looking for ways to find savings. He said the
OSCE had actually been on the chopping block in 2012. "I guess we
looked at it for a little bit, realized it was valuable for Canada to continue to be part of that organization. And so, we didn't cut the funding," Clement told me in 2016. "We thought we were at the end of
history in Europe, but that proved unfortunately not to be the case."

When Ukraine later plunged into turmoil, the OSCE found itself
playing a pivotal role in monitoring its escalating conflict with Russia. The Harper government decided to send another large delegation of monitors to Ukraine's presidential election on 25 May 2014.
The world was watching this election because Ukraine had found itself in the centre of the worst crisis between the West and Russia
since the end of the Cold War. The Ukraine parliament announced
the May election in late February after its Russian-backed and democratically elected president, Viktor Yanukovych, fled the country
in the wake of a popular pro-democracy uprising. Moscow responded by annexing the Crimean Peninsula – an unprecedented
breach of Europe's borders that stoked widespread fears of a further
Russian invasion. Other cities in eastern Ukraine were mired in violent clashes with pro-Russian gunmen backing separatist forces.

Seeing Putin as the instigator of all of this, NATO suspended relations with Russia, while the G8 punted the Kremlin, reconfiguring
itself as the G7. The leaders of Germany and France decided to keep
the diplomatic lines of communication open, but the Harper government's rhetoric was noticeably harsher than that of its allies,
while its level of diplomatic engagement with what it now called
"the Putin regime" was virtually non-existent. In early March, Harper and Baird compared the Russian action to Nazi Germany's annexation of Austria in 1938.

With rhetoric in Canada and international tension in Eastern Europe at a fever pitch, the Conservatives were emboldened to send observers to Ukraine for the all-important presidential vote. Some 338 observers went as part of its stand-alone observer mission, and another 162 as part of the OSCE delegation, at a total cost of $10 million. Baird brushed off the critical report of the 2012 mission, saying "a variety of participants" assured him it was a success.

This mission was different from all others in one significant way: the government dumped Canadem, the non-profit agency that had been assembling them. Formed in 1996, this agency had recognized expertise in helping mobilize and manage big international missions on short notice. It had built up a roster of 20,000 experts. As far as CIDA was concerned, Canadem was the go-to agency to select monitors, even if they didn't agree with the concept of sending Canadian observers. In a January 2012 memo, Bob Johnston, a CIDA regional director-general, stated, "If this option is selected, Canadem would again be the only possible partner." His boss – Margaret Biggs – agreed. "Canadem, a Canadian NGO with a long track record of recruiting, training, and deploying election observers is the proposed implementing organization," she wrote in a July 2012 memo.

Instead, the Harper government gave Canadem's job to two organizations that had less experience doing this sort of work: the Forum of Federations and its subcontractor, CUSO International. The government also decided that the mission would be managed by a newly created organization called Canadian Election Observation Missions or CEOM.

Seasoned election observers were stunned. So was Canadem, which found out in late April 2014 – roughly a month before the Ukraine election – that it had lost the contract.

To experienced international election observers, the new arrangement smelled bad. But they were reluctant to speak on the record, because they made their living by winning these international contracts. They saw it as a move by the government to take greater control – in other words, to stack the mission with Ukrainian Canadians. They said that roughly one-half of Canada's 2012 observer team was of Ukrainian heritage. "You've got the gold standard with the OSCE, and we're sending the maximum contribution we can send anyway," one observer told me on the condition they not be identified. "On top of that, for domestic political reasons we're sending another however-many Canadians for no reason at all."[5]

Canadem's website made it clear that wasn't a good idea. "Regardless of how impartial and professional an observer is, the perception of bias or conflict of interest is a huge challenge, particularly for observers who are returning to their country of origin," it said. "Regardless of how good they are local voters will assume that they are not impartial. At a minimum, the standard practice is that the number of country-of-origin observers on an international mission must be relatively small."

In 2012, evidence of political favouritism emerged around the selection of the Canadian monitoring team when two former Liberal cabinet ministers said they had been unfairly excluded. Eleanor Caplan and David Anderson said they had both received telephone calls from Canadem telling them they hadn't made the cut. "You don't need to be a genius to figure this out. Obviously, this is seen as very political by the government," said Caplan, who had taken United Nations courses on election monitoring and served on a mission to Belarus. Caplan said she had been previously told that she was "good to go." All she needed was for "the minister" to sign off on her involvement. Then, she said, Canadem left her a telephone message saying that, "at the direction of the government of Canada, we've been directed to remove you from the delegation."[6]

The new observer mission went ahead as planned. Jason Kenney made no apologies, saying it was meant to send a signal to Putin and the Kremlin in Russia. "I hope that Moscow notices," Kenney said. "It is not Canada that is provoking the Russian Federation. It's the Russian Federation that is provoking the democratic world by so obviously undermining the sovereignty of an independent member state of the United Nations." And for good measure, Kenney offered his own prediction of how the election would turn out – the anti-democratic, Russian-backed slate would lose. "The government in Moscow continues with the laughable notion that Viktor Yanukovych is the president of Ukraine," he said. "These elections will demonstrate that there's a new Ukrainian leadership with a democratic mandate and that's why it's important that we be on the ground."

* * *

10 JUNE 2015. THE BALTIC SEA

It is a pristine day with not a cloud in the clear blue sky or the hint of land on the horizon. We are about fifteen nautical miles off Poland's northern coast. Defence minister Jason Kenney strolls casually out to the stern of HMCS *Fredericton*. It is the morning after I have set sail with the handful of journalists following Harper and his wife, Laureen, for an overnight trip on the Canadian warship taking part in a NATO "reassurance" mission. These maritime manoeuvres are designed to show solidarity with the alliance's Eastern European members while sending a message to Russia over its provocations in eastern Ukraine.

"There was flyover of NATO vessels by Russian fighters and helicopters on Monday of this week, including a helicopter that flew very close to the *Fredericton*," Kenney tells us. Clad in a black windbreaker, he keeps peering pensively out at the horizon through his binoculars. He points to two light-coloured vessels dotting the far-off horizon. They belong to Russia, he says. About half an hour later, as we are milling around the bow, Kenney re-emerges. Those two Russian ships, he tells us, were "tracking us east and this vessel corrected to go south."

None of it felt the least bit provocative. If anything, Kenney's updates were nothing more than a diversion on a beautiful, calm morning. When interviewed, the captain of the ship didn't sound worried either. In fact, Commander Jeffrey Murray seemed to be choking back a bemused smile as we peppered him with questions about the significance of those two Russian ships way out on the horizon. "Their interactions have been non-interfering and non-threatening, so we carry on with our exercises and our operations and there's been no impact," Murray told us, explaining that the closest they came to his ship was seven nautical miles. Yes, there had been that very close fly-by of a Russian helicopter earlier in the week. But that didn't seem to bother Murray. Up until two years ago, Russia took part in this military exercise with NATO. Now the alliance had severed relations because of the Ukraine crisis, but the Russians still had a naval base not far from Poland, so naturally they were staying curious. "I would say that they do what we do and they make sure they know what vessels were operating in waters near their areas of interest."

When we returned to the Polish port of Gdynia later that afternoon, Harper rattled the sabre one more time against Putin, as he had been doing all week in Ukraine, at the G7 in Germany, and in Poland. "The Royal Canadian Navy's presence here is the physical demonstration that Canada stands up for what is right and good in our troubled world," Harper said, flanked by sailors with a Sea King helicopter behind him on the stern of the *Fredericton*, now back at the spot where the prime minister had boarded twenty hours earlier. He accused Putin of invading Ukraine to "serve his own domestic political agenda": according to Harper, to mask the long-term decline of Russia that had taken place under his rule. "Mr Putin's recklessness threatens regional stability, and has spread fear among our allies. That, my friends, is why you, the men and women of the Royal Canadian Navy, are here."

One of Harper's last major interactions with Putin came during their fifty-five-minute discussion in September 2012 when he returned to Russia for the APEC leaders' summit. This was a more confident Harper than the one who had met Putin six years earlier in St Petersburg. The prime minister kept Putin waiting for more than fifteen minutes before he finally showed up. For the benefit of the cameras, they talked about hockey again – it was the fortieth anniversary of the first Canada-Russia series – and this time Putin appeared generally warm and actually had something to say. He said he'd met some of the Canadian team members on a recent trip to Russia and he was impressed with these "goodwill ambassadors." But behind closed doors the talk was serious, and it was mostly about the civil war in Syria that had broken out the previous year. Russia backed Syrian president Bashar Assad, and as a permanent veto-wielding member of the UN Security Council had blocked attempts to sanction his regime. Harper pushed Putin to be less obstructive and to appeal to Assad to stop the bloodshed. He didn't succeed, and neither had any other Western leader to date.

"Obviously, the government of Russia and ourselves have very different perspectives on this," Harper told us afterwards. "Obviously,

Mr Putin has a different perspective, but I urged Russia to play a more positive role than it's been playing."

As the G7 wrapped in Germany's Bavarian Alps almost three years later, Harper expounded on why he had downgraded diplomatic relations with Russia while some of his fellow Western leaders were still keeping the lines of communication open. As the prime minister explained it, he wanted Russia out of the G8 even before the Ukraine crisis erupted. "I came of the view, some time before the invasion of Ukraine, that his presence at the table of the G7 was not productive – in fact was inhibiting the kinds of discussions, the kinds of co-operation we could be having on a broad range of international issues," Harper said. "Even though Russia may objectively share security interests with us in the West, Mr Putin makes it his business to just deliberately be troublesome – to throw a spanner in the works wherever he can. And of course, the final outrage was actually trying to erase boundaries by force in Ukraine."

His remarks shed light on why he preferred the G7, and seemed to explain why he seemed cold towards the UN. "The G7 is not the United Nations. The G7 is not even the G20: the G7 is a group of countries that share fundamental values and objectives in the world," he said. "We also share similar values – deep, progressive and aggressive commitments towards democracy, freedom, human rights, and the rule of law – and of course we share security interests. We are all committed to each other's collective security. Mr Putin fits none of these definitions; none of them."

For Harper, it all came down to values. He said there was great hope that when Russia was admitted to the G8 in the 1990s, its exposure to the club's other members would help it grow democratically and economically. There was hope Russia would adopt the G7's values. But that never happened. Putin concentrated power in the hands of a few rich oligarchs, hanging his citizens' hopes out to dry.

In November 2014, Harper and Putin had their last meeting. The prime minister literally ran into Putin at the G20 in Australia. Harper said: "I guess I'll shake your hand but I have only one thing to say to you: You need to get out of Ukraine."[7] Harper's office was quick to share details of the moment with the media travelling with him. But the Russians were quick to the come back to the Canadian journalists with their spin. According to a Kremlin spokesman, Putin replied: "That's impossible, because we are not there."

So ended the intermittent, nine-and-a-half-year conversation between Harper and Putin.

Harper's strong views about Putin and his solidarity with Ukraine and Eastern Europe were held with the deepest conviction, but his partisan instincts were equally unshakable. This was evident when Baird paid a visit to Kyiv in late February 2014. It was only a week after more than fifty pro-democracy protesters had been shot dead by government forces demonstrating in Kyiv's main square, the Maidan. Baird toured the square, which was still smouldering from the violence. Baird took to Twitter to say it was an "emotional experience." The Tweet included a photo of a stack of tires with a white dove painted on it, draped by a rose. "I wish for peace upon the Ukrainian people, and mourn those lost," the minister added.

The Liberals and New Democrats wanted to accompany Baird to Kyiv, in an effort to show that all of Canada stood behind the Ukrainians in their time of need. Paul Dewar, the NDP foreign affairs critic, sent a letter to Baird asking that an all-party delegation accompany him. "Canadian parliamentarians of all parties should work together to show that our friendship with the Ukrainian people is a long-term commitment," Dewar wrote. It was a simple request, but the government denied it. The Liberal foreign affairs critic, Marc Garneau, told me: "This is not a way to communicate to Ukraine what multi-party democracies are like, because the reality is that all of the main parties share the same concerns about Ukraine."

Jason MacDonald, the prime minister's director of communications, told me that his government deemed the two opposition parties unworthy to be part of the Canadian delegation. MacDonald referred to a flippant joke that Trudeau had recently made on a Quebec television show, one for which he later apologized. As for the NDP, they'd criticized Baird's previous visit to the Maidan in support of the ongoing protest in December 2013. "Mr. Trudeau's comments about Russia and Ukraine were neither helpful nor did they contribute positively to Canada's efforts to assist the Ukrainian people, and as a result there's no role for the Liberals in this government mission," MacDonald told me in an email. "The NDP wouldn't pick a side, unlike our government, which has been steadfast in its support for the Ukrainian people. Until they decide on what they stand for they, like the Liberals, shouldn't be a part of the government delegation."

The explanation was firmly rooted in domestic politics. That much was evident based on the government's public response to the opposition request. As it turned out, there was more going on behind the scenes. Baird actually wanted his Liberal and NDP critics to join him on the trip – to walk alongside him in the Maidan – and leave aside their partisan squabbles. He pushed the Prime Minister's Office to let him bring the opposition but he was overruled.[8] This was a clear and unequivocal example that, for Harper, domestic considerations trumped foreign policy. He would not allow his political opponents to be seen favourably in the world.

Once in power, the Liberals proved to be as pro-Ukraine as the Conservatives. In November 2015, Justin Trudeau had his first encounter with Putin at the G20 summit in Turkey. They had a brief conversation during which Trudeau told Putin to honour the Minsk peace agreement for eastern Ukraine. "I pointed out that although Canada has shifted its approach on a broad range of multilateral and international issues, we remain committed to the fact that Russia's interference in Ukraine must cease," Trudeau recalled. That would mark one of the changes in how the Liberals would do foreign policy: unlike the Conservatives, they would talk to people they didn't particularly like. In February 2016, Stephane Dion, the new foreign affairs minister, travelled to Ukraine to visit the government of President Petro Poroshenko and pledge Canada's unequivocal support for the country. Dion also said the Liberals would begin talking to the Russians again, although they would not waver in their support for the territorial integrity of Ukraine. Dion said Russia and Canada had some legitimate shared interests, namely the Arctic.

Conservative MP Dean Allison accused the Liberals of "cozying up" to the "Putin regime." Allison wanted to know why Dion was "abandoning our Ukrainian friends." Dion shot back hard. "Today, the United States is speaking to Russia. Europe is speaking to Russia. Japan is speaking to Russia," he said. "In what way would it help Ukraine if Canada never speaks to Russia, even about the Arctic?" Canada's new top diplomat levelled a stinging partisan jab of his own. "Our foreign policy will stop being ideological and irrational, and will be effective for our allies and for Canadians."

In July 2016, Trudeau followed in Harper's footsteps by visiting Ukraine himself. For the third summer in a row, a Canadian prime minister was in Kyiv. Trudeau added the visit to his trip to Poland for the NATO summit. It was there that he demonstrated solidarity with Ukraine in no uncertain terms: Canada would command a multinational NATO brigade of 1,000 troops, 450 of which it would contribute to an open-ended commitment to deter Russia. Canada would join Germany, the United States, and Britain, who would lead similar brigades in Lithuania, Poland, and Estonia, part of a new NATO commitment to protect its eastern flank. As Trudeau said shortly before he arrived in Eastern Europe: "Canada will continue to defend Ukraine's sovereignty in response to Russia's illegal annexation of Crimea as well as its support to insurgents in eastern Ukraine."

CHAPTER TEN

ISIL
and the Politics of Terror

4 SEPTEMBER 2014. NORTHERN IRAQ

A brisk breeze blows over the flat, sunbaked plain. It is early morning and we are about thirty kilometres north of the Iraqi Kurdish capital of Irbil. The occupied city of Mosul lies another forty kilometres north of us up the road. In between, about one kilometre in the distance, sits a small village, a dark blot visible on the horizon. The Islamic State of Iraq and the Levant, known as ISIL, occupy this village as well.

It will be another half hour before foreign affairs minister John Baird arrives here, but in the meantime, the Kurdish Peshmerga fighters manning the sandbags of our bunker have plenty to say about the militant group that has captured huge tracts of territory in northern Iraq and in neighbouring Syria. Their commanding officer, Brigadier-General Magdeed Haki, a trim, clean-shaven man in a crisply pressed dark green uniform and wraparound sunglasses, gives the lay of the land as a hot sun beats down on the windwhipped plain. Haki says about 150 ISIL fighters are holed up the village, and there's no getting them out anytime soon. He's not sure if there are any civilians left there but, for the moment, launching an offensive seems to be a bad idea. "They (ISIL) take profit from the village and the mosques and the schools and these kinds of things," he explains. "They go inside to hide themselves from our attacks. That's why they keep inside the village. They won't come out."

Eventually Baird arrives, his convoy passing rows of empty white tents – an internally displaced person's camp that had to be evacuated to avoid an ISIL offensive. Baird makes for the bunker immediately, and starts scaling the sandy hill in his dark blue suit and black sunglasses. He pauses, and looks back. "Paul and Marc, come on," the minister says. This time, Baird has managed to bring the opposition to Iraq to present a united Canadian front. Over these two days Paul Dewar and Marc Garneau, the New Democrat and Liberal foreign affairs critics, will be at his side, whether here on the front line, touring displaced persons camps and meeting the victims of the ISIL onslaught, or in discussions with Iraqi government officials. Iraq's new government was to be sworn in the following week, and the Western consensus was that the incoming administration of Haider al-Abadi must lay to rest the sectarian quarrels that had hurt Iraq so badly over the previous years. Nouri al-Maliki, who was forced to step down as prime minister a month earlier, alienated Iraq's Sunni minority during his eight years in power by pushing a pro-Shiite political agenda. The divisiveness sowed the seeds that would give rise to ISIL's deadly insurgency and subsequent atrocities.

"I'm also very pleased to be joined by representatives of both the other political parties in Canada," Baird told his Iraqi hosts during a press conference in Irbil later that day. "I think we speak with one voice: we abhor the barbaric terrorist activity we see in the region and we really want to come and personally stand with you and the people of this great country." Dewar and Garneau left Iraq genuinely pleased with what they had accomplished. "This is a multipartisan trip to assess what's happening in Iraq, to assess what Canada can do," said Dewar, who was on his second trip to northern Iraq, after coming to Irbil on his own in 2007. Garneau said he appreciated that he and Dewar were active participants in all of Baird's meetings, and were invited to ask their own questions of Iraqi politicians. "From the Liberal perspective, we all have the same interests here."

But, of course, it was too good to last. Baird and his entourage were only hours out of Iraq when the government in Ottawa made a surprise announcement: Canada would be sending dozens of military advisers to Iraq. The timing seemed suspicious and all too convenient, and it raised questions immediately about whether the opposition had somehow been played by the government. A bitter foreign policy fight about Canada's role in the fight against ISIL, driven by the domestic imperatives of all three parties, would play out in the House of Commons in the final months of the Conservative government.

In early August 2015, when Canadians witnessed the start of the longest federal election campaign in modern history, the divisions between the three federal parties on that question became obvious. During seventy-eight days of marathon politicking, the Harper government made the security of Canadians a core issue. It resonated, in part, because of the tragic events on and near Parliament Hill on 22 October 2014 and Saint-Jean-sur-Richelieu, Quebec, two days earlier. In Ottawa, a lone gunman, influenced by ISIL's online recruitment outreach, shot and killed a Canadian Forces officer standing guard at the National War Memorial and then stormed across the capital's main boulevard into the Centre Block where he was shot dead by security. The attack came two days after a similarly inspired lone wolf fatally struck a soldier with his car in Quebec. The horrors of the outside world had come home to Canada.

*   *   *

The spectre of the United Nations hung over the House of Commons debates of March 2015. The Conservatives, New Democrats, and Liberals were sparring over the upcoming Canadian Forces mandate to join a one-year mission – along with Saudi Arabia, Jordan, Qatar, the United Arab Emirates, and Bahrain – to crush the onslaught of ISIL. Canada had already been participating in bombing northern Iraq, but this U.S.-led mission would take the aerial combat mission deeper into Syria.

Like the rest of the world, Canada had done nothing to stop the atrocities unfolding in Syria for the previous four years. The UN Security Council was deadlocked, blocked by the veto of its permanent member Russia, an ally of Syria. At the time of the March debate, the civilian death toll stood at 220,000, and more than eleven million Syrians had been forced to flee their homes, either as refugees to neighbouring countries or as internally displaced people within their country's borders.

The carnage started in March 2011 when a popular uprising, inspired by the Arab Spring, was brutally crushed by President Bashar Assad, who turned his armed forces' weaponry on his own people.

Militant groups began battling the government, and eventually, each other. These included well-intentioned democrats, who were eventually crushed, as well as offshoots of al-Qaida, and then ISIL, which seized large tracts of land inside Syria and northern Iraq. ISIL enslaved the local populations, killed non-Muslims, and forced everyone to adhere to their medieval interpretation of Islam under the umbrella of their new "Caliphate." Though Canada's parliamentarians paid lip service to the tragedy, debate on the issue centred more on which party could use the events to their best advantage with the federal election only six months away.

The bitter exchange between NDP leader Tom Mulcair, leader of the official opposition, and Prime Minister Stephen Harper during Question Period on 25 March 2015 was a clear illustration of how domestic considerations had infected foreign policy. Mulcair wanted to know something perfectly reasonable: how, under international law, Canada was justifying the military action within another country's borders. Syria hadn't invited the other countries to bomb ISIL on its territory and there was no United Nations Security Council Resolution authorizing the use of force. Mulcair wanted to know if Canada had notified the United Nations secretary-general, as the American ambassador to the UN had done in September 2014, that it was invoking Article 51 of the UN Charter, the self-defence provision, as the legal basis for its decision.

Harper repeatedly dismissed the question and refused to answer. "The government is pursuing this action on exactly the same legal basis as its allies," the prime minister told the House of Commons, without offering any further explanation. "I am not sure what point the leader of the NDP is ultimately making. If he is suggesting that there is any significant legal risk of lawyers from ISIL taking the Government of Canada to court and winning, the Government of Canada's view is that the chances of that are negligible."

Mulcair was livid. "Mr Speaker, extraordinary. Living in Canada where that sort of idiocy passes for argument in the House of Parliament ..." Andrew Scheer, the Speaker of the House, admonished Mulcair over his choice of language and the NDP leader moved on to another topic of questioning.

But Harper wouldn't let it go. Twice, he brought the argument back to Mulcair's point, even though the topic had shifted. Harper wanted the last word at all costs, but that did not include answering the question. "I would be remiss if I did not return to the previous exchange," Harper said. "While I will obviously not repeat the terminology used by the leader of the NDP, if his idea of protecting Canada's national interest is that we do not do everything in our power, legally, militarily, and in terms of co-operation with allies, to defend the interest of this country against the terrorist caliphate, he and I obviously have very different ideas of what are the national interests of this country."

Mulcair responded by asking another question about the imprisoned blogger Raif Badawi, who faced a severe flogging in Saudi Arabia, but not before taking his own shot back. "The prime minister of Canada thinks he is above international law also; he is not and Canada is not. This is all we have."

Harper returned to the original fight. But he still didn't answer the question, though he vaguely invoked the UN and lunged for the moral high ground, suggesting that political parties in other countries had managed to leave their differences out of the war debate. "Once again, I do want to return to the previous exchange. If the leader of the NDP is suggesting for a moment that there is any case of the international legal community that stands behind ISIL, he is not only wrong, but the international community has united in opposition to this group," Harper said. "Five-dozen members of the United Nations have united to confront this international terrorist organization. Canada is working with them. Canada is working, not only with people from our own political family, but liberals and social democrats across the world in taking a strong stand to stay this ruthlessness."

As Canada was poised to plunge deeper into a new Middle East war, the tension between its traditional adherence to multilateralism and the tendency for the Harper Conservatives to join coalitions outside the UN framework was on full display. So, too, was the bitter partisanship that reared its head in the 2003 Iraq debate. This time it was the NDP that was in the fray with Mulcair and the party's foreign affairs critic, Paul Dewar, tangling with the government. "The new motion extends Canadian air strikes into Syria without a UN or NATO mandate and without the permission of the Syrian government ... First, the action may well be illegal. Second, the government has done nothing to show that it takes international law seriously at all," said Dewar.

Dewar also accused the government of moving quickly to cover up the fact that it had not informed the United Nations Security Council, in writing as required, of its intention to take part in the bombing.[1] The United States had done so on 23 September 2014, when its UN ambassador, Samantha Power, stated in a letter to the UN secretary-general, Ban Ki-moon, that her country had initiated "necessary and proportionate military actions" in Syria to combat the threat posed by ISIL and an al-Qaida affiliate.[2] Power's letter invoked Article 51 of the UN Charter, which affirms the right of all countries to an "inherent right of individual or collective self-defence" – as long as the UN was notified in writing.[3] Shortly after the Mulcair-Harper scuffle, Bernard Trottier, parliamentary secretary to the foreign affairs minister, told the CBC that Canada wouldn't be sending the UN any such letter, nor was one required.[4] Two and a half hours later, Trottier informed the public – in a Twitter message – that the government would, in fact, be notifying the UN "on same basis as Obama administration … as req'd by Art. 51."[5]

In all, the incident embodied the government's flagrant disregard for international norms in the face of a bitter partisan struggle. But the NDP didn't look a whole lot better. Mulcair boldly declared that his party would bring home the troops after it formed a government – a repeat of his party's strategy on the Afghanistan mission. Mulcair was playing to his core constituency: the left-leaning, anti-war voters who form a key part of the NDP's voting base. Meanwhile, the Liberals were spinning their wheels, evoking their party's foreign policy in the vaguest of terms, and voicing no concrete solutions. "These calamities are in urgent need of a constructed, coordinated international effort, both through the United Nations and beyond it. It is the kind of effort that ought to be Canada's calling card in the global community," Justin Trudeau said.

Trudeau's argument for not supporting a combat mission and advocating instead for a humanitarian response was, on the surface, not unreasonable. He had argued the government had not been forthcoming about the role of its special forces advisers in northern Iraq after the revelation that they had exchanged gunfire with ISIL fighters. But that was clouded by the juvenile joke Trudeau made the previous October about the deployment of Canadian fighter jets to Iraq in the first stages of the ISIL mission: "Why aren't we talking more about the kind of humanitarian aid that Canada can and must be engaged in, rather than trying to whip out our CF-18s and show them how big they are?"

On all sides there seemed to be a paucity of constructive ideas about the nation's place in the world, and no mature, rational discussion of how to improve the fractured system of global governance.

*   *   *

As it turned out, Trudeau was holding his foreign policy cards close to his chest. In December 2014, he assembled an impressive roster of advisers drawn from academia, diplomacy, and the military to help him craft a new foreign policy for Canada. He gave it the lofty title of "International Affairs Council of Advisors." It was co-chaired by Garneau, his foreign affairs critic, and retired lieutenant general Andrew Leslie. It included a handful of MPs and candidate hopefuls, and two notable retired ambassadors: Michael Bell, who served more than a decade and a half in the Middle East with postings to Israel, Egypt, and Jordan; and Jeremy Kinsman, who served in Russia, Britain, and the European Union. Over time, they would craft an approach to international affairs that amounted to this: returning Canada to its multilateral roots. They would strive to make Canada a constructive player on the world stage once more. Under Harper, Canada may have become the odd man out. The Liberals wanted Canada back in.

When they released their election platform in the final weeks of the campaign eleven months later, they made that goal crystal clear. It said Canada had a "proud tradition" of international leadership, including helping to create the United Nations after the Second World War, the Progressive Conservative–led campaign to end apartheid in South Africa in the 1980s, and the Liberal-led campaign to ban landmines in the 1990s. And it accused Harper of diminishing Canada's presence on the world stage. "Instead of working with other countries constructively at the United Nations, the Harper Conservatives have turned their backs on the UN and other multilateral institutions, while also weakening Canada's military, our diplomatic service, and our development programs," the platform said.

During the campaign, Trudeau put more meat on those bones. He promised that Canada would sign the UN Arms Trade Treaty. Trudeau also pushed for more active participation in multilateral forums dealing with Vladimir Putin's aggressive stance in Ukraine and Crimea. "Mr Harper has made a big deal out of talking loudly and strongly at Mr Putin, but the reality is Canada has such a diminished voice on the world stage that Mr Harper hasn't noticed that Vladimir Putin didn't listen to him when he told him to get out of Ukraine," Trudeau charged during the 28 September foreign-policy debate in Toronto, the first of its kind in a federal election campaign. "That is, unfortunately, a reflection of where we are, where we don't have the impact we used to have in multilateral organizations to push back effectively against bullies like Vladimir Putin."

Nine days later in London, Ontario, Trudeau was asked what he'd do to make Canada's voice on the issue louder. "We'd certainly make sure we don't lose an election to join the Security Council at the United Nations. Canada needs to be, once again, a constructive actor in the world stage focusing on our national interest, which includes security and stability in places like the Middle East," Trudeau replied. He referred to Russia's support of Syria on the Security Council.

The Conservative government regularly criticized Russia for continuing to shield Syrian president Bashar Assad. But the Conservatives never went much further than that, after having ruled out running for a seat on the council after Canada lost in 2010. Trudeau believed Canada could do more. "We need to make sure we are working with international partners to stop the Syrian civil war, to stop the barrel-bombing of Bashar al-Assad, to look towards a transition out of the government that Vladimir Putin still supports of al-Assad who continues to attack his own citizens. This is something that Canada has a credible voice and a capacity to help on."

Eight days later – and just four days before the 19 October Canadian election – the UN Security Council met in New York City and elected five new non-permanent members. Ukraine was one of them. This victory, said Ukrainian Foreign Minister Pavlo Klimkin, was important because his country was "fighting against Russian aggression."[6] For the next two years, the Ukrainian government would have a seat at the world's most important international security body, as hobbled as it was. It would allow the Ukrainians to speak directly to their Russian antagonist.

*   *   *

After one month of arguing over the economy, and whether the Prime Minister's Office behaved ethically during the Senate spending scandal, the Canadian federal election suddenly focused on events outside the country's borders. On the morning of 3 September 2015, the world woke up to the now iconic image of three-year-old Alan Kurdi lying face down on a Turkish beach. The young Kurdish refugee died along with his five-year-old brother Ghalib and their mother, Rehanna. Their father, Abdullah, survived.

Adullah had a sister in Canada who had been trying to help the family from afar.

That connection personalized the Syrian tragedy – which had been unfolding on an epic scale for more than four and a half years – for the Canadian public. Canadians flooded international aid agencies with massive amounts of money, organized meetings, and pushed their politicians to do more to help refugees. Municipal mayors and provincial premiers announced they would try to do more.

This popular concern forced all three party leaders to answer a core foreign policy question: when should the country go to war? Predictably, Harper and Mulcair were at opposite ends of the spectrum on this. Harper staunchly defended Canada's participation in the U.S.-led coalition to attack those responsible for the misery being inflicted on innocent civilians, in tandem with helping displaced people. "And part of the way we need to help them is to stop the awful violence that is being directed at them, displacing them and killing them." Mulcair's position was to end all military involvement in the region by bringing home the fighter jets as well as the dozens of special-forces trainers helping the Peshmerga in Iraq. As for Trudeau, he opted for the middle ground. "We have a federal government right now that thinks military action is the only solution to the humanitarian crisis in the Middle East," Trudeau said. He accused the NDP of taking "the opposite extreme position that there is never a military role to play in solving challenges like the crisis in the Middle East." Trudeau said he'd bring home the fighter jets, but leave the trainers on the ground in Iraq. And he said he would bring more refugees to Canada.

It was on refugees that Trudeau began to put forth this narrative: that somehow Canada, in the last decade under Harper, had become a meaner country. Again, it fit Trudeau's theme of returning Canada to its multilateral foreign policy roots, a view that Mulcair also adopted, in part, as the campaign progressed. The Liberals upped the ante on the Conservatives and the NDP, promising to admit 25,000 Syrian refugees compared with the 10,000 that each of the other parties was promising.

Trudeau and Harper went toe to toe on refugees during the 28 September 2015 debate on foreign policy in Toronto. The debate at Roy Thomson Hall in Toronto provided a rare opportunity for Canadians to see how Trudeau and Mulcair stacked up against Harper as potential international statesmen. There had never been a leaders' debate focused solely on foreign policy during a federal election campaign. One of its most telling moments was the clash between Trudeau and Harper over whether the country had become a meaner place in the eyes of the world during the past decade.

Both leaders were exceptionally strong in arguing the point. Trudeau went for the jugular, while Harper played the calm statesman. "Mr Harper," Trudeau intoned, "we stand here tonight just a few blocks from Ireland Park. Ireland Park was where, in 1847, 38,000 Irish men, women, and children fleeing the famine arrived on the shores of Toronto. There were 20,000 citizens of Toronto at that time, and they accepted 38,000 refugees, who proceeded to build and contribute to this country, to this city, and to who we are today." So, in Trudeau's view, it was time to open Canada's borders and do more because, as he put it, "Canada has always done more." This was not about politics, the Liberal leader continued. "It's about being the country that we have always been."

Then came Trudeau's final thrust; this shift in Canada's worldview came down to one man: Harper. "The entire world is looking at Canada and saying what is going on? 'You used to be a country that welcomed human beings, that appreciated diversity, people in crisis, people in distress who want to build a better future and a brighter future for their children,'" Trudeau said. "And yet now Mr

Harper talks about nothing but security and how we have to do the bare minimum."

Harper stood his ground, and faced down the dramatic attack by mustering all the gravitas that his nine-plus years as a statesman had allowed him to claim. "We're living in an era where people are fleeing a terrorist war zone, and we obviously must have security screening," Projecting the image of an experienced traveller, personally steeped in the *realpolitik* of a truly convulsive world, he insisted that "We have to do things responsibly. I have visited refugee camps in Jordan of Syrian refugees. I have visited refugees in northern Iraq. I have visited with families we have accepted from these regions. I have met with leaders from those communities, not just in Canada, but from the region itself, and I can certainly tell you from my visits to the refugee camps in Jordan and debriefings there, we cannot pretend there are no security risks."

Harper defended the need to screen refugees at source, and referenced some of the security problems taking place in the European Union after Middle East refugees arrived there. Canada, he suggested, would get it right, up front, and not have to suffer the consequences later. "Those countries in the world that responded to these headlines, as these others would have, by just opening the doors and doing no checking have rapidly regretted that and are now trying to put in place the very kind of system that Canada has been pursuing all along," he said. "It's a generous response. It's a responsible response. It is not based on the headlines."

Harper had one more point to make. In another twenty-one days, he would go down to defeat. But on this night, Harper would encapsulate, in one simple phrase, the reasoning that likely lay at the core of his worldview, and why he, in the end, made decisions that sometimes offended sensibilities and left some people thinking he was unravelling the fabric of the country. "It is based on the right thing to do."

And with that, many of the 3,000 paid spectators in Roy Thomson Hall burst into applause.

CHAPTER ELEVEN

Trudeau's First Hundred Days in the World

13 NOVEMBER 2015. OTTAWA

A grim-faced Justin Trudeau strides purposefully towards the microphone hastily assembled for him in the media's waiting room of the Canada Reception Centre. It has been only nine days since he was sworn in as Canada's twenty-third prime minister. Trudeau stops in front of four Maple Leaf flags. His government Airbus sits parked on the illuminated, rain-soaked tarmac beyond the dark windows to his immediate left. The blue and gray Royal Canadian Air Force passenger jet sits ready to take Trudeau on this first international trip as prime minister.

Trudeau is to make his debut at the G20 summit in Antalya, Turkey, and the Philippine capital of Manila for the Asia Pacific Economic Co-operation leaders' summit. He is keen to shed the austerity polices of the Conservative era and introduce the world to a new Canadian agenda, one that's largely in synch with most of the leaders he is about to meet. A big part of it endorses deficit-funded spending to kickstart economic growth, green-friendly infrastructure projects, and getting tough on climate change. For Trudeau, this trip was supposed to be about telling the world that Canada was somehow "back" after almost a decade of Harper Conservative rule. But the world is delivering its own message to Trudeau; one that is forcing him dramatically off-script.

Trudeau's dramatic departure is reminiscent of Prime Minister Stephen Harper's nine and a half years earlier, when Israeli warplanes began their bombardment of Lebanon just as he was headed to his first international summit. This time, Paris is under siege. The

City of Light is smouldering in the immediate aftermath of the worst act of violence on French soil since the Second World War. A few hours earlier, a coordinated terror attack by Islamic militants struck multiple locations across the French capital – a restaurant, a soccer stadium, and a nightclub full of concertgoers. The current death toll is in the dozens but it will soon balloon to 130, with hundreds more injured.

The prime minister appears hesitant and shaken, and speaks in a slow, methodical hush in French, then English. "Obviously, our hearts and thoughts and prayers go out to our French cousins in this dark and terrible time," Trudeau says. "These terrorist attacks are deeply worrying and obviously unsettling to people around the world. We have offered all of our help and support to the government of France, to the people of France at this time. And we'll continue to engage with our allies around the world in ensuring the safety of Canadians and others both here at home and around the world."

Trudeau says little more, except, "we will keep people apprised as more unfolds but I've been speaking with our national security team to ensure that everything is being done to keep people safe, and we will have more to say as we learn more about this terrible tragedy." Those of us travelling with Trudeau will be told by one of his officials during a refueling stop in Frankfurt eight hours later that those consultations included discussions with the RCMP and the Canadian Security Intelligence Service.

Trudeau takes one question before shutting down the unplanned, pre-trip media opportunity. Crafted in a huddle by a dozen or so of us, it boils down to this: are the Paris attacks making you reconsider your decision to withdraw Canadian fighters jets from the U.S.-led coalition that is bombing Islamic militants in Syria and Iraq, or your plans to amend Canada's anti-terror legislation, Bill C-51?

"Obviously," Trudeau replies, "it is still very early moments in figuring out what is indeed happening as we speak right now on the ground in France. It's too soon to jump to any conclusions. But obviously governments have a responsibility to keep their citizens safe while defending our rights and freedoms and that balance is something that the Canadian government and indeed all governments around the world will be focusing on. At this time, we have no information that any Canadians were even targeted or involved as victims in this, in these events. But obviously, there's still a lot to learn about what's happening in France as we speak."

And with that, Trudeau was bound for the G20, where terrorism and the plight of Syrian refugees had muscled their way onto the formal agenda. The G20 was officially charged with dealing with the world's economy. But because Turkey was at the forefront of the Syrian crisis – it has absorbed more than two million refugees – the G20's agenda had been expanded for the first time beyond purely economic matters. In his first hundred days, Trudeau came face to face with the hard realities of international affairs. He campaigned on a specific set of international policies: withdrawing Canada's fighter jets from the anti-ISIL coalition and retooling the mission while taking in 25,000 Syrian refugees; re-engaging diplomatically with Iran and Russia, two countries Canada hadn't been talking to lately; and generally bringing Canada back to multilateral commitments, with the UN in particular. But some unforeseen circumstances would test the new Canadian prime minister who, like his predecessor, was being forced to respond to unforgiving foreign policy issues, literally on the fly.

*　　*　　*

On 4 November 2015, the day he was sworn in as prime minister, Trudeau reached out to Canada's corps of discouraged diplomats, releasing them from the communication shackles that Harper's government had imposed. Trudeau sent a letter to Canada's ambassadors and high commissioners around the world, telling them that "Today begins a new era in Canadian international engagement."

The letter did not appear meant for public consumption, but I managed to get a copy. This document ended the communications control to which the Conservatives had subjected Canada's most seasoned diplomats, including having their speaking notes for public engagements vetted and approved in Ottawa. In his letter, Trudeau said he would follow through on his campaign promise to make Canada "an active and constructive member of the United Nations and other multilateral organizations." And he said he wanted them to be a part of "sharing a positive Canadian vision" with the world. "I expect that you will be engaged energetically in public diplomacy with other diplomats, host government officials, civil society, and the media – in all manner of ways – through direct contact, the media, and social media," the prime minister told them. "My cabinet colleagues and I will be relying on your judgment, insights, discretion, and work ethic in advancing our interests. I have every confidence that your reporting and our interactions when I am abroad will provide a critical, factual basis for our policies."

The vote of confidence provided an instant morale boost at Canada's foreign missions around the world. "It's a breath of fresh air and a completely new style – an inspiring expression of trust and confidence in us," one ambassador told me. Two days later, Trudeau was received with what appeared to be a spontaneous outburst of affection in the lobby of the Lester B. Pearson Building on Sussex Drive – the headquarters of Canada's foreign affairs department, which Trudeau had rebranded "Global Affairs Canada." Foreign affairs staffers also cheered Stephane Dion, their new minister, when his press conference got underway.

On the other hand, they groaned loudly when one journalist asked whether Trudeau had actually demoted five female cabinet-members because order-in-council documents listed them as having the lower rank of "parliamentary secretaries." That outburst was entirely unprofessional. It was an echo of the booing some reporters had endured from partisan Conservatives who stacked Harper's question-and-answer sessions during the election campaign, but this time it was indicative of the festering resentment of the Conservatives among public servants and diplomats within Foreign Affairs. This attitude amazed one senior U.S. State Department official. "I was a little astonished at how openly the career folks at the foreign and assistance ministries disliked their new political masters," Tom Adams, the senior U.S. State Department official, told Secretary of State Hillary Clinton in a 2012 email. "In my many years here I have never seen such open disloyalty with a change of administrations."[1]

When Trudeau arrived in the lobby of the Pearson building that day, the mood turned euphoric. Emerging from the throng of hundreds of cheering public servants, Trudeau decided it was time to say a few words himself, in both French and English. "I'm truly touched by the enthusiasm, by the support, because we're going to have an awful lot of really hard work to do in the coming months, in the coming years, and we're going to need every single one of you to give us – as you always do – your absolute best," Trudeau told them.[2] The crowd applauded even more. Trudeau had grown used to this sort of rockstar treatment during the election campaign. But this was something new: normally staid and reserved federal public servants were behaving like teenagers at a Backstreet Boys concert.

The adulation didn't stop at the water's edge.

A week later he found himself in Turkey after a long journey – preceded by an already growing reputation.

* * *

Justin Trudeau's international debut as prime minister came at the November G20 leaders' summit in Antalya, Turkey. There was an overwhelming sense of anticipation as he walked into the room to meet nearly two-dozen world leaders. "Everybody was very curious," UN secretary-general Ban Ki-moon recalled on his visit to Ottawa three months later. When it was Trudeau's turn to speak, Ban recalled, "the first words he said, 'Mr President, thank you for your hospitality and inviting me ... this summit is, by far, the best summit I have ever attended.'" As far as Ban was concerned, the little joke was a hit.

Trudeau was invited to speak publicly at the G20's business and labour forum. His audience in a small auditorium included the heads of some of the world's largest financial institutions including Mark Carney, Canada's former central bank governor, now transplanted to the Bank of England, as well as labour and business leaders and members of the world's chambers of commerce. Trudeau gave a well-received speech about his new infrastructure spending plans, which were in lockstep with the G20's philosophy.

Trudeau had no control over the packed international agenda that awaited him in his first month as prime minister. In the space of one week, his plane spent thirty-six hours in the air, flying 33,321 kilometres to Turkey and the Philippines.[3] Four days after returning from that trip he was airborne again, bound for London to meet Queen Elizabeth and his British counterpart, David Cameron, before moving on to the Commonwealth leaders' summit in Malta and then to Paris for the United Nations summit on climate change, known as COP 21.

In some ways, he had been groomed for this role since childhood, given his privileged upbringing as the son of Prime Minister Pierre Elliott Trudeau. Trudeau grew up in a house that often had famous visitors – from presidents to princesses – and he also accompanied his father on travels across the globe. When he was nine, Trudeau met his first U.S. president, Ronald Reagan, who paid a visit to 24 Sussex. The younger Trudeau recalled relaxing in the sunroom with the president and his father prior to a working lunch. "Reagan smiled warmly at me as we sat down and asked if I'd like to hear a poem, which made my father cock his head with interest," Trudeau wrote in his autobiography. "He loved poetry and often assigned us verses to memorize from works such as Racine's *Phedre* and Shakespeare's *The Tempest*. But Reagan had different tastes. Instead of classical verse he launched into Robert Service's 'The Shooting of Dan McGrew'..." Trudeau said it had an impact and led him to memorize poems that his father never would have taught him such as "The Cremation of Sam McGee."[4] On another occasion, Trudeau was playing in the driveway of 24 Sussex with a friend when Diana, Princess of Wales, and Prince Charles showed up unannounced, taking a break from their tour of Canada. He had been told the princess "was discreetly coming over to swim some laps" in the property's pool.[5]

On travels overseas, the young Trudeau was privy to foreign policy briefings from the likes of career diplomat Robert Fowler, who would go on to become Canada's ambassador to the United Nations, and would later be kidnapped by an al-Qaida affiliate in North Africa and held for 130 days before his release in 2009. And he would sometimes accompany his father to formal events, meeting British prime minister Margaret Thatcher, German chancellor Helmut Schmidt, and Swedish prime minister Olof Palme.[6]

"Sometimes I had a front-row seat at events of major importance, such as the time I was with him on a tour of Canadian military bases in western Europe in 1982 and a bulletin announced that Soviet leader Leonid Brezhnev had died. The next day we were on our way to Moscow for the funeral," Trudeau recalled. They were met at the airport by ambassador Geoffrey Pearson and the discussion on the drive to the hotel centred on who would succeed Brezhnev.

"Passing through Moscow, I watched evening fall over the dark, sullen city while my father carried on a long and detailed discussion of internal Soviet politics in which he easily matched a diplomat who was stationed in Moscow."[7]

These experiences taught Trudeau an important lesson: "in foreign relations, relationships are vitally important. I was struck by how my father's briefings were often as much about the personalities of his counterparts as about the issues."[8]

Justin Trudeau had always loved travelling. In 1994, after graduating from McGill with a bachelor's degree in English literature, he spent the summer touring Normandy before settling in Paris, "where I spent most of my days in museums and libraries." In contrast, the young Stephen Harper spent most of his twenties in Calgary, dating a young journalism student with whom he watched sports on television while ordering take-out food.[9] In fact, before becoming prime minister, Harper's only travel outside Canada was to the United States. "He is incurious about museums and vistas. Since he doesn't easily engage with people in the first place, the thought of seeking out and connecting with new and strange situations and people leaves him cold," wrote Harper biographer John Ibbitson. "He'd rather look down at a book than up at the Eiffel Tower."[10]

Trudeau, meanwhile, crossed the globe after completing his undergrad degree, seeking out and revelling in new experiences. He travelled with friends in a motorcade of Brits, Aussies, and a Finn from London to Africa, overland through France and Spain, over Gibraltar and by ferry to Morocco. They crossed North Africa and headed for Mali, Burkina Faso, Ghana, Togo, and Benin. The saw the forts used by slavers to warehouse Africans bound for bondage across the Atlantic. They flew from Nigeria to Malta, then to Helsinki, and finally Moscow, where they boarded the Trans-Siberian Express for a nine-thousand-kilometre train trip to Beijing. They saw Shanghai, Hong Kong, Hanoi, and Bangkok.

"Wherever I went, there were locals. A clear majority. A mainstream. And any minorities be they North Africans in Paris, European expats in Burkina Faso, Lebanese supermarket owners in Ivory Coast, Chinese students in Russia, Australians in Thailand or even tribal or cultural minorities that made up a significant chunk of the country's population, were always 'others,' an exception to the rule, to the national identity," Trudeau wrote. He says it gave him a true appreciation of Canadian cultural diversity, its "shared national identity" based on compassion, justice, equality, and opportunity.[11]

"And while many of the almost one hundred countries I've travelled through in my life aspire to those values, Canada is pretty much the only place that defines itself through them. Which is why we're the only place on earth that is strong not in spite of our differences but because of them."[12]

Speaking to the world for the first time as Canada's prime minister, Trudeau was unwavering in delivering a very firm message to the G20 about respecting and embracing ethnic diversity. He also stated his plan to stimulate growth through investment in infrastructure, while running modest deficits, and sustainable "green" infrastructure built to last for future generations. But because of the Paris attacks, these incentives didn't receive as much attention as two of Trudeau's main foreign-policy platforms from the election: withdrawing Canada's six CF-18 fighter jets from the U.S.-led coalition bombing ISIL and accepting 25,000 Syrian refugees. During a question-and-answer session after his speech, Trudeau was asked about his plans to admit all those Syrian refugees. He used the question as a platform to make a strong argument for multiculturalism as a unifying source of strength.

"Canada has always known that drawing people in and giving them paths to integrate and to succeed is truly a way to create economic growth and a pluralistic diverse society. Canada figured out a long time ago that differences should be a source of strength, not a source of weakness," Trudeau said. "And indeed, to define a country not based on national identity or ethnicity or language or background, but on values, shared by all people in our country, values of openness, respect, compassion, a willingness to work hard and be there for each other, is truly how countries in this globalized world where migrations and immigration is going to be norm rather than the exception, this is a lesson we all need to learn."

Trudeau's message was confident and it was deeply held, but it was nearly overshadowed by what happened after he walked into that G20 meeting and took his seat in the front row. For several minutes, enthusiastic participants in this tony, high-level business and political crowd mobbed Trudeau – the new kid on the block – for photos, including a few selfies. I watched from the top row as the scene unfolded and then walked down to the crowd. It was clear that he did nothing to encourage the attention. It started innocently with a trickle of attendees who approached Trudeau to congratulate him, before it mushroomed into a desire to be photographed with a celebrity. Though more than a few men were curious, there was no shortage of women angling to pose with the new Canadian prime minister. Some held their cameras for selfies, while Trudeau patiently posed for group shots. Through it all, he listened attentively and offered polite words of encouragement. It was obvious that if he had ignored the attention or tried to brush it off, headlines depicting an aloof and rude Canadian prime minister would have been far more embarrassing to him than the ones showing his warmth and popular appeal.

Perrin Beatty, a former Progressive Conservative cabinet minister who became the head of the Canadian Chamber of Commerce, watched the scene with a smile. "It's tremendous," he told me. "There's an enormous amount of interest both here in Turkey and right around the world in the new prime minister and having a chance to meet him. It's exciting for all Canadians." The scene quieted down in a few minutes, as a firm voice over the loudspeaker commanded: "We need to take our seats immediately."

* * *

Justin Trudeau's first foreign trip had echoes of the Trudeaumania that enveloped his father, as well as the Beatlemania of a few years earlier. As I watched his departure from the Asia Pacific Economic Co-operation leaders' summit in Manila, I couldn't help but think of the opening scene of the film *A Hard Day's Night*, in which a screaming gaggle of young women chases a sprinting John, Paul, George, and Ringo. Trudeau's exit was preceded by a final press conference in the summit's media centre, four long, jetlagged days after his maiden speech in Turkey. It was, without a doubt, the hottest ticket at APEC's international media centre. Several dozen local journalists lined up outside the entry of the prefabricated conference

. room and tried to push their way through to occupy a limited number of seats. Many were disappointed. Canadian embassy staff had to seal the door to prevent a stampede.

From inside our temporary and roofless room, we could hear the shriek and drone of young voices swirling above us in the cavernous conference centre. Trudeau walked towards the podium. He carried no notes. Smiling, he began to speak. Camera phones popped up on cue on one side of the room where a couple of dozen young Filipinos, mostly women, occupied chairs. Trudeau's opening remarks were almost inaudible because of the dull roar. It wasn't quite as bad as trying to hear what the Beatles were playing at Shea Stadium in 1965, but it was in that ballpark.

Trudeau was greeted as a full-on sex symbol when he arrived at APEC. Photos of him and Mexican president Enrique Peña Nieto were plastered across the top half of the front page of the *Philippine Daily Inquirer* broadsheet. The two leaders were branded "APEC hotties" and the caption asked: "LADIES CHOICE Are you with Team Nieto or Team Trudeau?" After his closing press conference two days later, as he made his way through hundreds of young journalists and volunteers, he was mobbed. The shrieking continued, as the young people strained for a glimpse, or better yet a touch, of the young Canadian prime minister. In contrast, the RCMP officers assigned to Trudeau's security detail were stone-faced and steely-eyed as they guided the prime minister through the conference centre towards an exit.

At his closing press conference, I asked the prime minister how his celebrity was affecting the serious foreign policy that he was trying to put forward. Trudeau had clearly given that topic some thought. "I'm pleased that Canada's getting a little more attention right now because it gives us an opportunity to highlight the issues that are important to us," he replied. "The big challenges we're facing in the world don't get solved unless individual citizens feel like they have a way to engage, they have a way to make themselves heard, to their leaders, to their representatives. Anything that can highlight that perspective, that positive engagement Canada wants to have on the world stage, at a time where quite frankly we need Canada to engage positively on the world stage, I take as a positive."

Trudeau had something else going for him: the legacy of his father. Earlier in Turkey, Trudeau had his first meeting with Chinese president Xi Jinping. After shaking hands, the Chinese leader rocked back slightly and seemed to be sizing Trudeau up. The two leaders took seats facing each other in the middle of parallel tables, flanked by two dozen officials, in a high-ceilinged hotel ballroom. Speaking in Mandarin, Xi praised Trudeau's father for his decision to establish diplomatic relations with his country forty-five years earlier. "That was an extraordinary political vision," the Chinese leader told Pierre Elliott Trudeau's son. "China will always remember that."

Canada's new prime minister replied that he was celebrating "forty-five years of strong relations between Canada and China." Trudeau went on to say that he was "well aware we have an opportunity to set a fresh approach in our relationship right now. I know that there are many opportunities for us to work together on economic, political, and cultural ties and I look forward to a very productive engagement in the coming years." (Privately, Trudeau raised human rights concerns with Xi.) Trudeau closed his public remarks by renewing the invitation he'd extended to Xi the previous day to visit Canada and "continue to build on our tremendous friendship" and open "an era of greater cooperation and mutual benefit for both Canada and China in the coming years."

It was a profoundly different meeting than in 2009 in Beijing, when Stephen Harper received a less than friendly greeting from Premier Wen Jiabao. "This is your first visit to China and this is the first meeting between the Chinese premier and a Canadian prime minister in almost five years," Wen told a stone-faced Harper through an interpreter.[13] "Five years is too long a time for China-Canada relations and that's why there are comments in the media that your visit is one that should have taken place earlier."

South Korean president Park Geun-hye was equally nostalgic and upbeat with Trudeau at their meeting later at APEC. Park said she hoped Trudeau had succeeded in "achieving real change" in Canada. "Your father, the late Pierre Trudeau, really shaped Canada's modern trajectory during his term in office as prime minister. In the foreign policy realm, he was also integral to raising Canada's international stature in the world," Park told Trudeau. "In particular, he spent a great deal of energy strengthening and enhancing Canada's relationship with Asian countries and likewise I do trust that you will serve the cause of peace and prosperity in the Asia Pacific as well."

Trudeau had clearly risen above the white noise caused by his celebrity to make some progress in relations with China and its Asian neighbours after the shortcomings of previous governments, both Liberal and Conservative. David Mulroney, Harper's first foreign policy adviser, said Canada had been asleep at the wheel in Asia, and was playing a desperate game of catch-up to break into new markets, especially in China. During his time as ambassador to China, from 2009 to 2012, Mulroney also worked on making inroads for Canada with ASEAN, the ten-country Asian alliance that does not include the People's Republic. But it has been an uphill struggle, because a lot of ground has been lost in the decades since the last right-of-centre government held power in Canada. "Everybody talks about Joe Clark," Mulroney told me, noting that the external affairs minister scored points by inviting his Asian counterparts to visit his home province of Alberta. "The point I make to ministers is: it isn't a huge investment, you've got to find the time, they like being invited, they like coming to Canada." Wendy Dobson, co-director of the Rotman School of Management, said Trudeau's unique upbringing as the son of a prime minister who engaged with China could be invaluable to Canada moving forward. "We were ahead of the U.S. in recognizing the Chinese communist regime. And the Chinese remember that."

* * *

A week later, Canada's young prime minister was raising a glass to a formidable woman more than twice his age, and perhaps funnier. Trudeau was in Malta at the Commonwealth leaders' summit: his second major trip in less than a week. He was tasked with toasting the head of the Commonwealth, Queen Elizabeth, two days after his private audience with her at Buckingham Palace in London. Trudeau praised the eighty-nine-year-old monarch for her devotion to "selfless service" and for championing "respect, inclusiveness, and dignity." He then recalled seeing the Queen seated next to his father, Pierre, when she signed the Constitution Act on Parliament Hill in April 1982, bringing the Charter of Rights and Freedoms into force. "Pierre Elliott Trudeau was your fourth Canadian prime minister," he said. "I am your twelfth."

The Queen replied with some very short remarks of her own. She said it was a pleasure to welcome everyone, and she delivered a killer punch line of her own: "Thank you, Mr Prime Minister of Canada, for making me feel so old!"

Perhaps the Queen was repaying Trudeau for the famous image of his father pirouetting behind her back at Buckingham Palace in May 1977, during the G7 summit. The Canadian Press photo, by photographer Doug Ball, was picked up by the Associated Press and distributed worldwide, and caused an international sensation. Pierre Trudeau later revealed that what appeared to have been a spontaneous moment was not: he planned it in advance to protest the palace protocol that separated heads of state from heads of government.[14] At any rate, Trudeau took her witticism in stride, taking to Twitter later to say: "On the contrary, you are forever young. I was honoured to toast your lifetime of service tonight."

It was a light moment in an otherwise whirlwind trip for Trudeau, one packed with extreme emotion. Malta was the opening act for the climate-change talks two days later, when world leaders would converge on Paris just two weeks after the deadly terrorist attacks on the city. The U.S. is not a member of the Commonwealth, so Trudeau was seen to be twisting a few arms on behalf of the Americans. He announced that Canada would contribute $2.65 billion over five years to the UN climate fund, topping up a $1.5 billion contribution by the Harper government. India, one of the world's biggest pollution-emitters, took a pass on the Commonwealth meeting. Trudeau said he had a meeting planned with Indian prime minister Narendra Modi when he touched down a day ahead of the leaders' summit to push for his country's participation. But after Trudeau let that be known, the Modi meeting was off. India's own rockstar of a prime minister was not in the mood for a lecture from his telegenic counterpart.

Before the Paris attacks, French president François Hollande had been invited to the Commonwealth leaders' meeting as a special guest, so he was given a podium to address the organization ahead of the UN summit. Hollande thanked Canada and other countries for their climate-funding announcements. He used his podium to passionately connect the fight against terrorism to the one against climate change. "Man is the worst enemy of man," the French president declared. "We can say it with terrorism but we can say the same when it comes to climate. Human beings are betraying nature, damaging the environment. It is therefore up to human beings to face up to their responsibilities."

When Trudeau arrived at the Paris conference, known as COP 21, he declared once more: "Canada is back, my friends. We're here to help." In an unprecedented show of solidarity, the premiers of Alberta, British Columbia, Ontario, Quebec, and Saskatchewan and opposition leaders including the NDP's Tom Mulcair, Elizabeth May of the Greens, and Conservative MP Ed Fast joined Trudeau. International observers noted the change from the Harper era. "Canada was just hated," May told CBC News. "It's just night and day. People are happy to see Canadian delegates … I'm going to get emotional about this, I'm sorry. It was just amazing. Negotiators from other countries were coming up and hugging me."[15]

There was hope among Canada's allies that something might change on the environment file. Werner Wnendt, the German ambassador, told me four days after the October election that his country was hoping for a "significant, positive signal" from the new government on climate change because "this is the future of our planet and Canada is an important country." Francisco Suárez, Mexico's outspoken ambassador to Canada, told me that Trudeau would be a true "amigo" to his country and the United States in the fight against climate change. "I'm sure one issue we'll be working very, very closely with the prime minister is on the COP meeting. Obama, Trudeau – the three amigos – will be acting as three amigos on climate change in Paris," said Suárez. Another diplomat offered a far more unvarnished assessment when I spoke to them on the condition of anonymity, calling Harper simply "unhelpful" on the climate file. The diplomat said no one was getting "starry-eyed" over what Trudeau could deliver. And no one was expecting him to show up in Paris with a concrete new position so early in his government. But as the diplomat said: "The fact that it's someone else, it will be helpful."[16]

But the emotional high of joining the world in the fight against greenhouse gases was almost eclipsed by the profound grief that awaited Trudeau and his fellow leaders in the City of Light.

*   *   *

Trudeau stepped tentatively up to the wall of flowers, flags, candles, and notes that was piled up the plastic sheeting covering the Bataclan Concert Hall. It was sixteen days after the massacre that left ninety concertgoers dead, the scene of the worst carnage in the series of attacks by Islamic militants on Paris. Trudeau paused, holding a single white rose in two hands, allowing his wife, Sophie Grégoire-Trudeau, and a large entourage that included the French prime minister Manuel Valls, Montreal mayor Denis Coderre, Quebec premier Philippe Couillard, and Canadian ambassador Lawrence Cannon to go ahead. Then he moved forward, knelt down, and placed his rose on the pile. He remained there for about ten seconds before rejoining the group listening to a choir from Quebec sing a solemn rendition of "Quand les hommes vivront d'amour" ("When men will live for love, there will be peace on earth").

Trudeau had come face to face with the destruction inflicted on innocent people by Islamic militants in their war against the West. Nonetheless, he held to the promise he made during the campaign that brought him to power: the six CF-18 fighter jets that the Harper government had committed to the U.S.-led bombing campaign against ISIL in Iraq and Syria were to be brought home. Trudeau faced much criticism for not reconsidering his position in the wake of Paris. The new interim Conservative leader, Rona Ambrose, said the official opposition would support Trudeau if he kept the jets in theatre. "It's important that we remain resolute and support our allies."

Some of Canada's allies enhanced their military contributions to the anti-ISIL coalition in response to the Paris attacks. That trend created the perception that Canada was once again the odd man out in a major international effort. Britain decided to join the bombing of Syria after Prime Minister David Cameron won the approval of his parliament after a ten-hour debate that extended late into the night. The British parliament voted 397–223 to allow air strikes on ISIL targets in Syria, reversing its 2013 decision – by a slim 285–272 margin – to stay out of the air war. Germany's lower house of parliament approved a substantial new military contribution to the cause – 1,200 troops, a frigate to sail with the French aircraft carrier

Charles de Gaulle, and six Tornado reconnaissance jets – by a wide margin of 445–146.

Still, the Prime Minister's Office insisted that Canada's allies were not pushing Trudeau to change his mind and that they accepted his explanation that Canada could do more on the ground – though there were few details about what that contribution would be. Finally, on Trudeau's ninety-sixth day after being sworn in, the Liberals released their ISIL plan. The fighter jets were to be withdrawn within two weeks, but Canada's CC-150 Polaris refueller and two CP-140 Aurora surveillance planes were staying. In addition, Canada planned to triple its contingent of sixty-nine special forces trainers currently on the ground with Peshmerga fighters in northern Iraq. And it also earmarked $1.6 billion over the next three years for security, stabilization, humanitarian, and development assistance in the region.

The two main opposition parties criticized the plan from seemingly contradictory points of view. Ambrose said it was "shameful" that Trudeau was pulling Canada out of a fight alongside of its allies. "Mr Trudeau likes to say 'Canada is back,' when in fact we are stepping back," Ambrose said in Moncton, New Brunswick, the day the reconfigured mission was unveiled. "Every ally in the fight against ISIS has stepped up their military efforts in the bombing mission, and Canada is now, today, ending our combat role against what is the most heinous terrorist organization we've seen in my generation," she added. "If he doesn't think that we should use our military against this group, I don't know when he thinks we would ever use our military." The New Democrats were concerned that Canada was still very much in the fight, and that the extra special-forces trainers were simply a backdoor to putting boots on the ground to take the fight directly to ISIL. "We are concerned that the Liberal government has chosen to place Canadian Forces personnel deeper into an open-ended combat military mission in Iraq," said the party's foreign affairs critic, Hélène Laverdière. "The Liberals are tripling the size of so-called advisers to the Iraqi military, with some forces working in a 'battlefield context' and others working to 'enhance in-theatre tactical transport.'" She said there needed to be "a clearer line between combat and non-combat. Today's announcement actually blurs these lines even more."

The NDP was likely closer to the truth of what Trudeau was trying to accomplish. During the election campaign, Trudeau staked out a position that was quite different from those of his political opponents. He was clearly an adherent of soft power, and had established himself as a critic of the aerial bombardment from the moment he made his crude joke about "whipping out" the CF-18s. But the attack on Paris called for a hard power response. Boosting the special forces capability did that. A former commander of Canada's JTF2 elite commando unit gave Trudeau's decision his seal of approval because "for the long-term win, you need to build that indigenous capacity and capability. Tripling the training mission is a great call."[17] The JTF2 had already proven their mettle on the ground when the Defence Department confirmed in January 2015 that their snipers shot, in self-defence, at ISIL militants, taking out one of their mortar positions.

The fact that a bolstered force of elite commandos was headed to the northern Iraqi battlefield raised the question: was Canada actually undertaking a combat operation? The short answer, according to Gen. Jonathan Vance, the chief of the defence staff, was no, even if it meant taking on the militants from time to time. "I want Canadians to know that we will be involved in engagements as we defend ourselves or those partners who we are working with," Vance said, adding that Canadian troops would also "mark" targets for future strikes by coalition fighter jets or artillery. Foreign affairs minister Stephane Dion told me in an interview that it was Iraqis "who have to free their country" and although Canadians would not be involved in front-line combat, "if their life is in danger in different circumstances, then they may have to fight."

For Vance, none of this met the definition of combat, even though some thought that it strained credulity that any scenario that involved exchanging gunfire was something other than combat. "The prime minister has clearly described it as non-combat" and even though there's a "penchant ... for people to try and parse the words," Vance concluded: "In my view, it's a non-combat mission in that we are not the principal combatants here." Ten days later, Vance defended that position once more in a speech to military symposium in Ottawa, stating again that this was not a combat mission, as he declared: "I'm the expert on what is combat."

Yet others in Trudeau's inner circle had a different view. Trudeau's senior foreign policy advisor was Roland Paris, the founding director of the University of Ottawa's Centre for International Policy Studies. A year earlier, in his old life as an academic, Paris weighed into the debate on whether that firefight between the JTF2 and ISIL fit the definition of combat. On a blog posting, Paris said it most certainly did:

> There is no universally-accepted, bright-line definition of "combat," but common sense suggests the following: (1) If you send armed troops to front-line positions where combat can be realistically expected, and (2) if these troops are calling in airstrikes from the front lines in order to destroy enemy positions, and (3) if they are returning fire, even in self-defence, in order to kill enemy forces who are firing on them, then by any reasonable standard they are engaged in combat.[18]

But for Trudeau, it was simply anathema to publicly acknowledge the possibility that Canadian soldiers could get drawn into a combat on Iraqi soil. "What I've said I'm concerned about, from the very beginning, is anything that leads towards active engagement by the West and boots on the ground," Trudeau said during a seventy-five-minute question-and-answer session before the full Ottawa bureau of the Canadian Press in December 2015. "And I think that's something – whether it's Libya, whether it's the previous Iraq conflicts – we know doesn't necessarily lead to the kind of long-term, positive outcomes that people would hope for and would justify the human cost of engaging in that way."[19] The "military and the use of force needs to be a part" of the long-term solution, he added, but the mix also had to include "diplomatic, political and governance structures."[20]

Trudeau signalled his preference for soft power during the federal election campaign, when he resurrected a piece of foreign policy from the golden age of Pearson: he called for Canada to make a return to peacekeeping. It was especially timely for Trudeau that the foreign policy debate fell on the same day U.S. president Barack Obama was addressing the UN General Assembly in New York. During his speech, Obama made a plea for an increased international contribution to peacekeeping missions. He asked for 30,000 troops; within a day pledges totalling 40,000 had rolled in.[21]

The Liberal platform was also guilty of indulging in some domestic mudslinging. "Under Stephen Harper, Canada has dramatically scaled back its involvement in peace operations – a decision that could not come at a worse time. As the number of violent conflicts in the world escalates, demand for international peace operations has never been greater," it stated. The core assertion – that the Harper government had gutted peacekeeping – ignored the decline that previous Liberal governments had presided over. Yes, the Conservatives were in power when the Pearson Peacekeeping Centre closed its doors in 2013, its government funding gone, effectively ending Canada's role in international operations. But Canada's commitment to peacekeeping had been in decline a decade before Harper won power, during the Liberal government of Jean Chrétien. In April 1993, Canada had 3,300 military personnel on peacekeeping missions, in the Balkans, Cyprus, the Golan Heights, and Cambodia.[22] But Canada's contribution dropped sharply in 1995 and 1996, dipping to below one thousand troops. "In 1997, Canada began a long relative decline: slipping from a top-ten position to 30th–35th position in the 2000s," wrote Walter Dorn, the Royal Military College of Canada professor, in his 2007 study titled *Canadian Peacekeeping: No Myth – But Not What It Once Was.*

Dorn told me in an interview that the Conservatives deserve most of the blame for gutting peacekeeping. "The real decade of darkness for peacekeeping was the last decade." Yet it can't be ignored that by the time the Conservatives had arrived in power, a lot of the damage had already been done. When the Liberals were sworn in, there were thirty-one peacekeepers deployed on five UN missions. The burden of peacekeeping now falls on developing countries, which receive a financial stipend from the UN. The top five countries that contribute peacekeeping troops are Bangladesh, Ethiopia, India, Pakistan, and Rwanda.[23]

The world changed after 11 September 2001. The military focus of Western countries shifted to combat and counter-terrorism. The new military reality after 9-11 for Western countries became fighting terrorists such as al-Qaida in Afghanistan or their Taliban remnants. Retired colonel Pat Stogran led the six-month mission of the 3rd Battalion, Princess Patricia's Canadian Light Infantry, to Kandahar in 2002. He offered an unvarnished assessment of the state of play during a 2004 interview when I asked him about Canada's traditional "peacekeeping role." "We have a bunch of mandarins, an elite upper crust that shove this peacekeeping down the throats of Canadians, and say we're not a militaristic society," Stogran told me. "I can't stand the word 'peacekeeping.' It's thrown around by this elite upper crust in Canada. And we sort of latched onto it as professional soldiers. But in actual fact we're either doing combat operations, security operations, stability operations. Peacekeeping is a nebulous, redundant empty term."

Even if Canada wanted to change gears and get back into the peacekeeping business, some believed its military lacked the skills to do so. Dorn's 2016 report concluded that the 2006 to 2011 period the Canadian Forces had spent fighting a counterinsurgency in Kandahar had all but eclipsed their ability to contribute to peacekeeping missions. "While there are similarities between these types of missions and international peace operations, there are also fundamental differences in the training, preparation and practice of peacekeeping deployments," Dorn wrote. "A major change in mentality and approach, as well as knowledge, would be needed to properly prepare Canadian Forces for future peace operations. Special skills, separate from those learned in Afghanistan and warfare training, would need to be (re)learned, including skills in negotiation, conflict management and resolution, as well as an understanding of UN procedures and past peacekeeping missions."[24]

As well, Canada's military resources had been severely strained since the late 1980s and the mid 1990s, when the successive Progressive Conservative and Liberal governments started making cuts to the defence budget and the number of full-time personnel in the Canadian Forces.

On 29 January 2016, the government held a one-day strategy session on peacekeeping at Global Affairs Canada, the renamed foreign affairs department. The agenda covered the full spectrum: assessment of the military's capabilities, the types of missions Canada should commit to, and how the country could play a role in conflict prevention, mediation, and post-conflict reconstruction. "The purpose of this session is to examine which are the most relevant frameworks and foreign policy interests that may underpin Canada's re-engagement in UN peace operations," said the agenda. "This exercise will serve to lay the ground for establishing the criteria for engagement in specific missions or initiatives."

Clearly, there was a lot of work ahead.

As Trudeau moved forward with his foreign policy agenda, strong and credible voices were warning him against a nostalgic return to the good old days. Times are changing, they argued, and the rules don't apply the way they used to. In their book, *Brave New Canada*, authors Derek Burney and Fen Hampson argued that the "painful reality" is that the UN and other international institutions that brought stability to the world at the end of the Second World War are becoming less effective and less relevant.[25] That also goes for the International Monetary Fund, the World Bank, the World Trade Organization, and NATO, they argued. "The declining effectiveness of these multilateral institutions has profound implications for middle powers like Canada as they search for traction in a rapidly changing world."[26] This has led to an increasing need for "coalitions of the willing" to fill the void "only to prove that military muscle in itself is not an adequate response."[27] But these coalitions have hardly produced positive results – witness the continuing instability in Iraq and Libya, and elsewhere.[28]

Trudeau was more interested in other views, ones that hearkened back to Canada's past as a player in the world's multilateral institutions. One of his preferred voices belonged to Roland Paris at the University of Ottawa. In March 2015, Paris penned a lengthy open letter addressed to the next prime minister, titled "Time to Make Ourselves Useful." "Rather than maintaining the virtuous circle of effective bilateral and multilateral diplomacy, Canada has been marginalizing itself. It is one thing to excoriate our adversaries, as we have recently taken to doing, but carelessly alienating our friends and disconnecting ourselves from international discussions is simply self-defeating," Paris wrote. "Canada is not powerful enough to dictate to others, even if we wished to do so. We have succeeded in international affairs by building bridges, not burning them."[29]

This paper provided a template for the theme that Trudeau would develop over the course of his election campaign. That included making Canada a more proactive player in the fight against climate change, and reclaiming the country's multilateral foreign policy roots. Eight months later, Paris was working in the PMO.

* * *

When Trudeau arrived at the World Economic Forum in Davos for its 20–23 January 2016 annual meeting, he was determined to burnish his financial credentials. In his keynote speech, the new prime minister deliberately distanced himself from Harper, who had performed well at this summit in the past. "My predecessor wanted you to know Canada for its resources," Trudeau told the gathering. "I want you to know Canadians for our resourcefulness." He pointed to innovative work that came out of the University of Waterloo, and bragged about a diverse and creative population. In addition to downplaying the resource sector, which Harper was found of bragging about, Trudeau stressed the need to spend to stimulate growth, not implement austerity measures, which Harper favoured. "We have social stability, financial stability and a government willing to invest in the future."[30]

Trudeau's dig at the resource sector didn't go over well with some Canadians at Davos. "We are a resource economy," Calgary mayor Naheed Nenshi said. "Our biggest export is still energy and I do not see a path where that does not continue to be the case." The future of Canada's economy, he said, could be best defined as "resource-plus."

Similarly, Brian Tobin, the vice-chairman of BMO Capital Markets, who as a Liberal cabinet minister in the mid 1990s fought the Turbot wars against Spanish fishing-trawlers encroaching on the east coast, said Canada should not "run away" from the resource sector.[31]

Before he left Davos, Trudeau found himself riding gallantly to the defence of Canada's resource sector, which was being battered by the free-fall in oil prices. Two days later, Trudeau confronted

Hollywood actor Leonardo DiCaprio, a climate activist, who used
Davos to criticize the "corporate greed" of the energy sector. Di-
Caprio had travelled to northern Alberta to see the oilsands, made
a documentary on the subject, and departed unimpressed. Trudeau
pulled him aside for a chat. "I pointed out that both Alberta and
Canada have new governments over the past year that are committed to action on climate change," Trudeau told reporters in
Davos, "and that there are families suffering, out of work, who need
to be supported and inflamed rhetoric doesn't necessarily help either the families or help Canada achieve its significant carbon reduction targets."

*   *   *

On his ninety-ninth day, Trudeau welcomed UN secretary-general
Ban Ki-moon to Ottawa. As Trudeau embarked on his new mandate
to govern, there was no shortage of work to be done on foreign affairs. For starters, there was some serious business with the United
Nations. He had promised during the campaign to join the UN Arms
Trade Treaty, but it was an open question whether he would recommit to the Convention to Combat Desertification or amend any of
the controversial clauses in the Convention on Cluster Munitions
on interoperability that had sparked so much criticism. In June
2016, Trudeau announced Canada's intention to rejoin the desertification convention, saying the government recognized its "important work." It was widely assumed that Canada would again run for
the United Nations Security Council. His transition briefings were
telling him that the earliest Canada could reasonably run for a seat
would be some time after 2020. Five weeks after Ban's visit to Ottawa, Trudeau announced that Canada would run in the 2020 elections for a two-year term beginning in 2021.

That meant Trudeau would have to win a second federal election.
It also meant there would be almost a quarter of a century between
Canadian stints on the council, an unprecedented absence. The im-
plication of that was straightforward: during the Harper years, countries such as Luxembourg, Rwanda, Angola, Lithuania, and, yes,
mighty Portugal had been at that table for much of the post-9-11 era.

As Harper departed office, Japan, New Zealand, and Ukraine were excitedly preparing to join the Security Council for the next two years. Egypt and Senegal were also joining them.

As Trudeau and Ban stood in the foyer of the House of Commons, Canada's desire to recommit to the UN was music to the secretary-general's ears. "I am here to declare that the United Nations enthusiastically welcomes this commitment." Before their day was out, Ban would heap more praise on Trudeau, not only in front of journalists on Parliament Hill, but with high school students in a boisterous auditorium at Glebe Collegiate, and at a gala dinner at the Canadian Museum of Nature in Gatineau, Quebec, that was attended by Chrétien, former Liberal cabinet ministers, and other diplomats and dignitaries. Throughout the day, Ban praised Trudeau for deciding to take in 25,000 Syrian refugees and for making what he described as a major contribution to the success of the Paris climate talks. And he also singled out Trudeau for appointing himself as his own minister of youth, something he said no other leader had done.

Ban said how impressed he was with Trudeau's father when he first heard him speak at the United Nations in 1982. "All countries, the powerful and weak, the rich and the poor, have an obligation to use the language of peace," Ban said, quoting Pierre Trudeau. "Having met you already several times, in multilateral forums such as the G20 summit and the Commonwealth summit and the climate summit in Paris last month, I have felt that you are even more popular than your father."

All of this left a bitter taste in the mouths of some Conservatives. Roy Rempel, Harper's former defence adviser, told me in an email that the "last I checked, our mission in New York was still there and we were still one of the top ten contributors to the UN budget. That was the case under the Harper government and I presume it will remain so under the new government." As far as Rempel was concerned, Ban had deliberately invoked Trudeau's "Canada is back" slogan so he would be in a position to ask more from Canada in the future. "We shouldn't fool ourselves into believing that the UN organization is only about altruism." Rempel, who had become a fellow at the Canadian Global Affairs Institute, predicted that increasing Canada's profile at the UN would "not be free." Canada, he said, would have to "meet the expectations, and the varied demands, of those countries/groups/individuals that might be prepared to support us" in an eventual bid for the Security Council.

For the moment, though, Ban's visit to Canada was more about symbolism and providing a smattering of substance to Trudeau's election-night declaration to the world that Canada was somehow "back." Ban was more than happy to provide Trudeau with the validation he was seeking. If he had plans to hit Trudeau up for favours in the future, Ban was keeping that to himself. He certainly didn't want to spoil the party.

CHAPTER TWELVE

Trudeau and Obama:
The Elephant Twitches

10 MARCH 2016. THE WHITE HOUSE

It was a day like no other for Canada in the United States. There were speeches, glowing tributes, affirmations of friendship and solidarity, too many jokes about hockey, and swooning – a lot of swooning. Prime ministers had visited Washington before, but it was never like this. Americans were excited about Canada's new celebrity, with the help of hype from some major U.S. news outlets. The week before his arrival, the *Washington Post* called Justin Trudeau the "anti-Trump," his "inclusive message" countering the bellicose Republican's outrageous pronouncements on Mexicans, Muslims, and women during the presidential primary season.[1] The CBS news program *60 Minutes* kicked off their last broadcast before the visit with a fourteen-minute profile of Trudeau. "Justin Fever Hits Washington," said the headline in *Politico*, one of DC's leading online news outlets; it quoted a "senior Obama administration official" describing Trudeau as "dreamy" and "my new political crush" because of "his looks, heart and mind."[2]

Obama did not hold back either. Moments after their arrival at the White House on an unseasonably balmy spring morning, the president offered Trudeau, his wife, Sophie Grégoire-Trudeau, their three children, and half a dozen Liberal cabinet ministers – "the quite good-looking Canadian delegation" – a red carpet welcome, complete with marching bands, an enthusiastic crowd, big-gun salutes, and glowing words. "We have a common outlook on the world, and I have to say, I have never seen so many Americans so excited about the visit of a Canadian prime minister," Obama told the Trudeau party on the South Lawn.

The two leaders had hit it off four months earlier at their first formal meeting in the Philippine capital of Manila. That's where Obama invited Trudeau to the White House. Obama reprised the story of his congratulatory telephone call to Trudeau on 20 October, the day after he won the election, and how he advised him to start dying his hair because being in power would turn it gray. At fifty-four, Obama was a decade older than Trudeau and, as they would joke repeatedly, he was definitely grayer. But he saw in Trudeau a leader who would carry on the work he believed needed to be done in the world. "Justin's talent and concern for the Canadian people and his appreciation of the vital role that Canada can play in the larger world is self-apparent. He is, I think, going to do a great job."

A few weeks after their initial Philippine meeting, the president's invitation to Washington had morphed into the red-carpet welcome that would include a formal dinner – the first such invitation since Bill Clinton's for Jean Chrétien in 1997. Pierre Elliott Trudeau attended two state dinners, the last one in 1977 when he brought his wife, Margaret, who faced public criticism for the style of her dress. Obama predicted Trudeau's wife and his First Lady would hit it off. He was right; Michelle Obama introduced Grégoire-Trudeau as "my soul mate" on this March 2016 visit.

It was apparent that Obama saw more than a little of himself in Trudeau. "He campaigned on a message of hope and of change. His positive and optimistic vision is inspiring young people at home. He's governing with a commitment to inclusivity and equality." Obama went further during his 29 June 2016 return visit to Ottawa to address Parliament and attend the North American leaders' summit with Mexico. During his joint press conference with Trudeau and Mexico's Enrique Peña Nieto, Obama attacked Donald Trump. "Somebody who has never shown any regard for workers, has never fought on behalf of social-justice issues or making sure that poor kids are getting a decent shot at life or have healthcare ... they don't suddenly become a populist because they say something controversial in order to win votes," the president said. "That's not the measure of populism. That's nativism or xenophobia or worse. Or it's just cynicism."

On Trudeau's visit to Washington, the U.S. media eagerly encouraged him to criticize Trump, but he declined.

Later that evening at the White House, as he rose to toast Trudeau at the star-studded gala dinner, Obama again recalled how in their first telephone call, they spoke not only as political leaders but as fathers as well. "We're not here for power. We're not here for fame or fortune, but we are here for our kids. We're here for everybody's kids, to give our sons and our daughters a better world. To pass to them a world that's a little safer and little more equal, and a little more just, a little more prosperous."

Obama praised Trudeau's parents, including his departed father, Pierre, and he paid an elegant tribute to his mother Margaret, one of his guests, who had made public her struggle with bipolar disorder. The president praised her "brave advocacy for mental healthcare," which sparked a standing ovation. Trudeau returned the favour, imparting some advice on being the child of a world leader to Obama's two teenaged daughters, Malia and Sasha, who were attending their first state dinner.

It was their shared views on the urgent need to fight climate change that cemented the Obama-Trudeau bond. Obama wanted to be remembered as someone who fought to preserve the planet for future generations long after he left the White House. Obama's legacy issue fit the core theme of Trudeau's own foreign policy like a glove; fighting climate change was a key instruction that Trudeau had given to cabinet ministers, including foreign affairs minister Stephane Dion and international trade minister Chrystia Freeland, in their mandate letters.

They emerged from their two-hour meeting in the Oval Office with a range of policy announcements, much of it a continuation of work that had begun under the Harper Conservative government. Measures on speeding travellers across the Canada-U.S. border might not see the light of day for years, but there also was a plan to reduce harmful methane emissions and do more to protect the Arctic.

"I'm especially pleased to say that the United States and Canada are fully united in combating climate change," Obama told their joint Rose Garden press conference. And he saw him as someone who could carry the fight forward when he was no longer in power. "I'm grateful that I have him as a partner. We've got a common outlook on what our nations can achieve together," Obama said. "On the world stage, his country is leading on climate change and cares deeply about development. So from my perspective, what's not to like?

* * *

19 FEBRUARY 2014. TOLUCA, MEXICO
Barack Obama and Stephen Harper stand at opposite ends of a large stage in one of the grand inner courtyards of the sixteenth-century Spanish colonial building. Between them is their host, President Enrique Peña Nieto, but the message being delivered by the American president is aimed at the Canadian prime minister, as hundreds watch the closing press conference of the "Three Amigos" summit. The one question that Canadian journalists get to ask is about the big, unresolved irritant in the Canada-U.S. relationship: the construction of the Keystone XL pipeline from Alberta to the U.S. Gulf Coast, which, were it to be approved and built, would fulfill Harper's dream of transforming Canada into an "energy superpower." Three years earlier, Harper called the project "a complete no-brainer," which didn't go over well in Washington. On this day, the White House has yet to approve Keystone.

Obama's answer amounts to a lecture aimed directly at Harper: the urgent need to reduce greenhouse gas emissions in order to fight climate change. "Stephen and I, during a break after lunch, discussed a shared interest in working together around dealing with greenhouse gas emissions. And this is something that we have to deal with," Obama reveals. Earlier, Harper's office provided a read-out of his thirty-minute meeting with Obama but it failed to mention that topic of discussion.

"I said previously that how Keystone impacted greenhouse gas emissions would affect our decision. But frankly, it has to affect all of our decisions at this stage because the science is irrefutable," Obama continues. "It has the potential of displacing people in ways that we cannot currently fully anticipate and will be extraordinarily costly. So I welcome the work that we can do together with Canada."

It is as if Obama is giving a remedial tutorial to a student who just doesn't get it. He says that increasing "severe weather patterns" have "consequences for our businesses, for our jobs, for our families, for safety and security." He believes in economic growth, but it has to be balanced against the need to wean the world off fossil fuel use. "We only have one planet," the president concludes.

None of this is new, but the fact that this is his response to a question about Canada's oilsands is significant. The two leaders started out on a good footing in February 2009, when the president paid his inaugural foreign visit to Ottawa and declared: "I love this country." But since then, there has been no love lost between them, due to their disagreement about climate change.

Harper originally aspired to bring the U.S. and Canada closer together after several years of anti-U.S. sentiment. In the 1960s, John Diefenbaker labelled John F. Kennedy a "boastful son of a bitch." In the 1970s, Richard Nixon called Pierre Trudeau "an asshole"; the latter quipped: "I've been called worse things by better people." On the flip side, Brian Mulroney and Ronald Reagan had a warm relationship. The two leaders sang "When Irish Eyes Are Smiling" at what became known as the Shamrock Summit in Quebec City in 1985. Mulroney was equally close with Reagan's Republican successor, George H.W. Bush.[3]

But in the waning years of the Chrétien era, the Liberal government seemed to go out of its way to antagonize the Americans. During the 2000 U.S. presidential campaign that pitted Democratic vice-president Al Gore against George W. Bush, Canada's ambassador to Washington, Raymond Chrétien – the prime minister's nephew – made public remarks that were widely interpreted to mean that Canada would be more comfortable with Gore in the White House than Bush.[4] Jean Chrétien, his staff, and some of the caucus made matters worse after Bush narrowly defeated Gore. In 2002, his communications director Françoise Ducros was overheard calling Bush a "moron." Ducros was eventually forced to resign. A year later, as Chrétien presided over a divided Liberal caucus in the months leading up to the invasion of Iraq, MP Carolyn Parrish referred to Americans as "bastards" while cabinet minister Herb Dhaliwal called Bush a "failed statesman." Both kept their jobs.[5]

Chrétien insisted that he always got along well with Bush. He recalled using healthy doses of humour with his Democrat and Republican counterparts during a December 2015 dinner speech in Ottawa on Canada-U.S. relations to an audience of hundreds of politicians, business people, lobbyists, and journalists. Chrétien recalled telling Bill Clinton, "I don't want to be too close to you." He also told Clinton he would never go fishing with an American president the way Mulroney did with Bush Senior, "because I will look like the fish." As Chrétien explained it, "I didn't want to look like we were the fifty-first state of America. That was the development of a very good relationship between Bill Clinton and I." Chrétien said he liked to talk baseball with Bush because he was the former owner of the Texas Rangers. He kidded the president for signing Alex Rodriguez to a massive, multimillion-dollar contract "just to pick up the ball to throw it to first base. I said you will have to be president of the United States 400 years to make the same amount of money." Jokes around baseball had serious economic overtones because the two countries were embroiled in their softwood lumber dispute. "I told him, George, all the best baseball bats are made near Ottawa here." Chrétien said he told Bush that if he didn't allow imports of Canadian softwood, he'd cut off the supply of bats. Chrétien went further. "I told him, if you don't buy my softwood lumber, I will stop selling you oil, selling you natural gas, selling you electricity, and you will need a hell of a lot of softwood lumber to heat your homes down there."

When Paul Martin succeeded Chrétien in 2003, he made it clear that the U.S. was important to Canada. He said Canada would have to carefully consider participating in the Pentagon's ballistic missile defence-shield program for North America. The shield – a system of sensors and rockets that would detect and shoot down incoming missiles in midair during an attack on North America – would be run out of the joint Canada-U.S. continental air-defence command, known as NORAD, inside Cheyenne Mountain, Colorado. But there was domestic opposition to Canada taking part, including concerns that the plan would lead to the "weaponization" of space. With a federal election on the horizon, the Liberals needed the support of Quebec voters and of the NDP, who were against the plan. In February 2005, during a sparsely attended lunch-hour session of the House of Commons, foreign affairs minister Pierre Pettigrew stood up and announced that Canada was taking a pass on ballistic missile defence. The Americans didn't take it well, especially since Martin, Pettigrew, and Bush had all been in Brussels together days earlier at a NATO summit. They were particularly infuriated that Pettigrew said the decision was based on "Canadian values."

The *Wall Street Journal* castigated the Martin government for the decision. "Of course, the reason Canadians can indulge their moral afflatus against 'weaponizing space,' and in favour of maintaining 'Canadian values,' is because they know their proximity means the Americans will always come to their rescue. It's a classic example of what economists call the 'free-rider' problem."[6] The decision was seen as particularly weak in comparison to Pierre Trudeau's thirty-two years earlier accepting cruise missile tests over Canadian airspace during the Cold War. In an open letter to Canadians in May 1983, Trudeau explained his rationale – it was all about Canada *not* being seen as a free rider: "It is hardly fair to rely on the Americans to protect the West, but refuse to lend them a hand when the going gets rough. In that sense, the anti-Americanism of some Canadians verges on hypocrisy. They're eager to take refuge under the American umbrella, but don't want to help hold it."[7]

After defeating Martin in 2006, Harper was determined to do away with anti-Americanism and make a fresh start with the White House. This didn't look like a very big challenge given the aligning of the political stars between the Bush Republicans and the reconfigured Canadian Conservatives. But Harper's first statement on Canada-U.S. relations surprised many. It came just days after his election victory, before he was sworn in as prime minister.

Harper was asked what he thought about U.S. ambassador David Wilkins's comment that his country doesn't recognize Canada's sovereignty over the Northwest Passage. Wilkins said Canada and the U.S. had "agreed to disagree," and called it "a problem that doesn't exist." The veteran South Carolina Republican questioned why Harper had promised during the campaign to strengthen Canada's military footprint in the Arctic. Harper didn't let the remark stand. After he'd answered a series of questions on Parliament Hill, an aide called an end to the availability with journalists. But the prime minister–designate paused and returned to the microphone.

"It is the Canadian people we get our mandate from," Harper said, "not the ambassador of the United States. I was very clear about this in the election campaign: The United States defends its sovereignty; the Canadian government will defend our sovereignty." Harper had what was described as an amicable sixteen-minute telephone conversation with Bush.[8] But he was clearly adhering to the old adage about how Canadian prime ministers should get along with U.S. presidents: stay close, but not too close.

At first, Harper got along well with Obama. The two men looked like they genuinely liked each other when Obama made a whirlwind visit to Ottawa in February 2009, his first foreign excursion after his inauguration a month earlier. Obama declared his love for Canada. Harper returned the sentiment, making it clear that Canada wasn't soft on security, and would always be there to support its friend and ally. "There is no such thing as a threat to the national security of the United States which does not represent a direct threat to this country," Harper said. Just months into the Great Recession, they spoke about their respective stimulus packages, and they said positive things about free trade, despite the protectionist "Buy American" legislation south of the border. Behind closed doors, Harper and Obama had a lot to say to each other. They were supposed to have a ten-minute one-on-one chat, alone, with no officials present to take notes. It stretched to thirty-three minutes.[9]

But they sowed the seed of their future discontent with the only new measure they would announce that day: a Clean Energy Dialogue requiring officials from both countries to pool their research to find new sources of clean energy. It went nowhere, as did bilateral cooperation on clean energy projects or jointly reducing greenhouse gas emissions. Eventually, their differences over the Keystone XL pipeline exposed a wide chasm between the two leaders. Harper was infuriated when Obama called him in November 2011 to say that he couldn't approve Keystone as it stood.[10] Their relationship never recovered.[11] After all, a key tenet of Harper's international agenda was transforming Canada into what he called "an energy superpower."

Harper used that label in his first major speech to an international audience, at the Canada-U.K. Chamber of Commerce in London in July 2006. The invited audience of several hundred in the posh London hotel room that day was not unlike the one to which Justin Trudeau would make his maiden speech as prime minister at the G20 nine years later. But there were stark differences in those speeches. Trudeau positioned Canada as a leader in the fight against cli-

mate change; Harper saw his country as possessing a mighty bounty of natural resources waiting to be liberated from the earth. Harper said Canada was the world's fifth-largest energy producer, ranking
third in gas, seventh in oil, and top in both hydroelectric power and
uranium. "And let's be clear," Harper added, "We are a stable, reliable
producer in a volatile unpredictable world."

When Harper and Obama arrived in Mexico in 2014, the U.S.
president was unmoved by those ambitions. He left Harper holding
very few cards after his passionate arguments on fighting climate
change. Harper replied that Canada had a "shared concern" and reminded the president that a recent State Department report gave
the Alberta oilsands good marks on environmental impact. Ultimately, none of that would prove to be persuasive. In November
2015, a few weeks after Harper lost power to Trudeau, Obama rejected the pipeline. (The timing was likely the American president's
way of not interfering in the Canadian election.) Obama concluded that a pipeline that shipped Canadian crude, over American soil,
to an American port in the Gulf of Mexico for export elsewhere was
of no use to his country. "Shipping dirtier crude oil into our country would not increase America's energy security. America is now a
global leader when it comes to taking serious action to fight climate
change and, frankly, approving this project would have undercut
that global leadership."

The Liberals expressed disappointment, but said they were ready
to move on. Two weeks later, Obama and Trudeau were all smiles
seated next to each other in Manila. They had been chatting informally throughout the week, since meeting in person for the first
time in Turkey at the G20 summit. But on this day, at the APEC summit, they had just finished their first bilateral meeting – twenty-three
minutes of closed-door talks covering a wide range of issues, including the fight against terrorism, the unfolding global refugee crisis, trade, and climate change. With the Paris climate summit just
weeks away, Obama told Trudeau he was "glad we've got such a
strong partner in Canada." Being on the same page with the United
States is always in Canada's interest, and in this case it was on an
issue that mattered to an American president keen to establish his
legacy during his final year in office. So Canada was making itself
useful to its American neighbour as well.

The importance of Canada's relationship with the United States simply cannot be overstated. The long, undefended border, the massive trade relationship, our military alliance, the fact we are actually good friends. All of this is true in spite of that other important dynamic in the relationship – America is ten times Canada's size and a true superpower, while we, quite simply, are not. As the current prime minister's father said in 1969, having the United States as our neighbour is like "sleeping with an elephant."[12] Forty-six years later, the whiplash realignment that repositioned Canada and the United States as allies on the environment marked the most profound shift in Canadian foreign policy during the months that marked the end of the Harper era and the start of the Trudeau one.

Before he won power, one of Trudeau's earliest and most substantive foreign-policy pronouncements came in June 2015. Like his predecessors, it was all about re-establishing what he saw as a broken relationship with the United States. In a luncheon speech to the Canada 2020 think tank in Ottawa, Trudeau accused Harper of undermining Canada's most important international relationship because he couldn't get his way with Keystone. He took Harper to task for his "no-brainer" remark about the pipeline, and accused him of being blinded by political ideology. "Does anyone doubt that Harper would have taken a different approach with a Republican in the White House?"[13]

There had been reports that U.S. ambassador Bruce Heyman had been placed on a blacklist by the Harper government over Keystone[14] after his arrival in Ottawa in 2014.[15] In public, Heyman played down the growing tension between Ottawa and Washington. He sparked applause from the same business crowd that Chrétien had regaled in Ottawa in December 2015 when he pointed out the bilateral relationship was chugging along on many levels, deeply intertwined on trade and security. "When you say Canada is back, for the United States Canada has always been there," Heyman said. "In the past, in the present, in the future, our strongest ally, our best friend, our largest trading partner."

At their Manila meeting, Trudeau delivered a jab at Harper, but not by name, telling Obama that "Canada hasn't been doing enough on the environmental front." The new prime minister used the setting to once again repudiate one of the Harper's key messages on climate and the economy: "There is no longer a choice to be made between what's good for the environment or what's good for the economy. They go together in the twenty-first century and one of the first tasks I have on energy and climate issues is to reassure Canadians and others that we are serious about meeting reduction targets, about being positive actors in the fight against climate change and demonstrating a future in renewable and smart investments around energy."

Obama's tone on energy and the environment was noticeably more amicable than the one he adopted with Harper in Mexico. The president easily sidestepped the single question from the Canadian media to restate his characterization that Alberta oil was "dirty." Instead, he provided a thoughtful analysis of the need for both oil-producing countries to move forward in the necessary transition from carbon-based energy to renewable sources. "Both of us are large oil and gas producers and that's an important part of our economy. We make no apologies for that," Obama said, as Trudeau nodded in agreement. "But I also think we have to recognize if we want to preserve this planet for our kids and grandkids, we're going to have to shift increasingly away from carbon-emitting energy sources," Obama added. "This is going to be a messy, bumpy process world-wide but I am confident that we can get it done and the fact that we now have a very strong partner in Canada to help set up some global rules around how we approach this I think will be extraordinarily helpful."

In the week that followed, Trudeau and his new government did its best to be helpful on climate change. They offered some specific support to the American position going into the climate talks – one that had become surprisingly controversial. In an 11 November interview with the *Financial Times*, Secretary of State John Kerry said he didn't think the Paris talks would yield a legally binding agreement to cut carbon emissions.[16] He said whatever agreement was reached was "definitively not going to be a treaty." Kerry was giving voice to a view that was being heard in European corridors: that even though the Obama administration wanted a strong agreement, it did not favour legally binding targets because that would bring the issue before the hostile, and Republican-dominated, U.S. Congress.[17] Two weeks later, and just a few days ahead of Trudeau's arrival in Paris for the leaders' portion of the climate talks, Catherine

McKenna, Canada's minister of the environment and climate change, backed up the U.S. position in a conference call with reporters in Ottawa. "Everyone," McKenna said, "wants to see the United States be part of this treaty." But there are "political realities in the United States," and she spelled out the implications of that: "they cannot have legally binding targets. We don't expect that the targets will be internationally binding."

During that first sit-down meeting with Trudeau in the Philippines, Obama didn't make a fuss over the decision to withdraw Canada's fighter jets from the anti-ISIL air combat mission. "We talked about terrorism and security issues off the top and how Canada is committed to continuing to engage as a strong member of the coalition against ISIL in ways that will continue to support international efforts, including through military engagement around training to ensure that Canada continues to be a strong player doing its part – and more than its part – to defend against ISIL," Trudeau said, as Obama watched him from his chair.

The president did not contradict Trudeau. In fact, Obama noted in his opening remarks he and Trudeau had just held "excellent conversations about how our defence teams can co-ordinate and work not only on military operations there, but also how do we work on being able to stabilize the situation in Syria." Two and a half months later, when Trudeau finally announced the reconfigured Canadian contribution to the ISIL mission, minus the fighter jets but with three times as many JTF2 trainers on the ground in Iraq, he and Obama spoke again on the telephone. As the White House said afterwards, the president "welcomed Canada's current and new contributions to coalition efforts and highlighted Canada's leadership in the coalition."

As for the question of allowing Syrian refugees into their countries, there wasn't a shred of daylight between Trudeau and Obama. They were both resolute in the face of domestic opponents who accused them of being too soft, and not doing enough to keep terrorists posing as asylum-seekers out of North America. "The overwhelming numbers who have been applying are children, women, families themselves victims of terrorism. We already have in place the most vigorous vetting process for anybody that is admitted and

in fact if you look at how our process currently works, with the involvement of the National Counterterrorism Centre, the FBI, the
Defense Department, our intelligence organizations, we subject
them to a process that takes anywhere from eighteen to twenty-four
months before they are admitted," Obama said in Manila. "The idea
that they pose somehow a more significant threat than all the
tourists who pour into the United States every single day, just does-
n't jibe with reality."

*   *   *

For all the good will between Trudeau and Obama, they would only
overlap for a year in office. But before he left the White House,
Obama was determined to make a difference on a pair of key issues:
climate change and ratification of the twelve-country Trans-Pacific
Partnership deal. Trudeau seemed ready to to work constructively
with him on these projects. "One of the things I pointed out in our
very first conversation on the phone was his focus on getting big
things done in his final year. Looking at legacy dovetails nicely with
my desire to get big things done off the bat, in my first year, to set
the tone for the coming years, and to a certain extent to make up
for some years in which we weren't quite as active as we could have
been," Trudeau told us on his airplane as it was bound for the Philippines. "So I think there's a nice dovetailing of a desire to get things
done and not put things off. That means we're going to have a lot to
agree on."

Obama knew he could count on Trudeau to be in agreement on
climate change. Trudeau couldn't possibly have sent any clearer signals about that. But on the question of the Trans-Pacific Partnership
– the world's largest trade deal, encompassing 40 per cent of the
global economy – the president wanted to see far more enthusiasm.
Trudeau maintained that he and his party were pro-trade and recognized the importance of connecting Canada to the Pacific Rim.
But the TPP was controversial. The Harper Conservatives, who
announced the deal just two weeks before the federal election, had
negotiated it. Trudeau promised to consult with Canadians, to give
the various critics of the deal – which included the very vocal

automakers union – space to air their views. He planned to put it to a vote in Parliament, one that his majority government would have no trouble winning. But that didn't look like it was going to happen anytime soon. Later on, the Liberals would refer the TPP for study by the House of Commons trade committee, a move that took up much of 2016.

Obama wasn't in the mood to wait – on anybody. The day before their bilateral in the Philippines, Obama hosted a luncheon for the leaders and trade ministers of the twelve TPP countries. Trudeau was there, along with Chrystia Freeland, his international trade minister. "TPP is at the heart of our shared vision for the future of this dynamic region," Obama told the room. "Today, we're going to discuss the road ahead to ensure that TPP is enacted in each of our countries as swiftly as possible. Obviously, execution is critical after we have arrived at the text." Obama went on to explain why it was so important to get the deal done. He said it was the most progressive one ever struck, with the highest standards. He said it offered strong and enforceable protections for workers, it prohibited child and forced labour, and it ensured environmental protection.

Obama displayed a sliver of empathy to anyone in the room who might be having second thoughts. "The politics of any trade agreement are difficult." But he quickly added: "The fact that everyone here stepped up and made some hard decisions that are going to pay off for decades to come, I think is testimony of the vision that was reflected."

The next day, as he sat next to Trudeau after their bilateral, the president all but announced that Canada would be signing on to the TPP. "We are both soon to be signatories of the TPP agreement. That's another area we can continue to have important discussions," Obama said. "I know Justin has to agree with what's happened but we think that after that process has taken place Canada, the United States and the other countries that are here can establish the high standards agreement that protects labour, protects the environment, protects the kind of high value-added goods and services that we both excel in." Overall, Obama said, he'd just had a "wonderful meeting" with Trudeau as he dangled his invitation to the White House.

Justin Trudeau had embraced the sleeping American elephant that his father had talked about before he was born. Now, it was snoring quite loudly. The situation called to mind the second sentence of his father's famous quotation: "No matter how friendly or temperate the beast, one is affected by every twitch and grunt."[18]

* * *

11 MARCH 2016
Justin Trudeau is almost finished in Washington. The former schoolteacher is very much in his element with his shirt sleeves rolled up and his jacket doffed as he prowls the stage before a large gathering of students at American University. There's a different elephant in the room today: Donald Trump. More than one pundit has pointed out that Obama's bromance with Trudeau is as much about sending a message to Trump as it is about Canada-U.S. relations. The bellicose billionaire has been getting much closer to the presidency than anyone would have predicted. Among his many controversial utterances, Trump has said he wanted to build a wall between Mexico and United States and make the Mexicans pay for it. He also suggests temporarily banning Muslims from coming to the U.S.

Trudeau was first asked about the possibility of a Trump presidency during a televised town-hall meeting hosted by *Maclean's* magazine back in December 2015. Trudeau replied that it is important for Canadian jobs and prosperity "to be able to have a positive relationship with whoever Americans choose as their president." Without mentioning Trump, he added an important qualifier. "I don't think it comes as a surprise to anyone that I stand firmly against the politics of division, the politics of fear, the politics of intolerance or hateful rhetoric," he said. "If we allow politicians to succeed by scaring people, we don't actually end up any safer. Fear doesn't make us safer. It makes us weaker."

During this Washington trip, many people have been trying to get Trudeau to weigh in on Trump, but so far he has resisted. Instead, he uses the opportunity to attack the Harper Conservatives. For example, when one student asks Trudeau how to prevent the rise of a Donald Trump in Canada, Trudeau replies that Canada used to have a Conservative government "that was talking about fear and division as a way of moving forward," that had proposed a snitch lines to inform on your neighbours. "They could never quite explain why

911 wasn't an effective line when you see mistreatment or such,"
Trudeau says. "There was also real division around headscarves, a
sort of tone of negativity that was very compelling and certainly
gained a certain amount of traction. But I found that Canadians in
any case find it hard to sustain anger and fear for very long." He notes
that Canada's last election featured a "number of different narratives
that are repeating themselves around the world," including in Europe and in the U.S. at the moment. But "the things that unite us are
always far greater than the things that divide us," Trudeau concludes.

Another student asks Trudeau how he handles "angry, hateful"
people.

"It's easy to stoke anger and it's easy to feel angry if you're worried
about your next pay cheque, you're worried about being able to pay
your rent, you're worried that your kids are not going to have the
kind of future that you would want for them," he replies. He goes on
to describe the controversy in Quebec in 2013 when the Parti
Québécois introduced a bill to ban religious symbols in public
places. He says it may not have seemed a bad idea at first, but it
became problematic when it became apparent that it meant, for
example, a young woman who chooses to wear a hijab could lose
her job. He calls for a "public discourse that goes beyond knee-jerk
reactions."

He goes on to recount how he fought against the Conservative
government's law that would strip dual citizens of their citizenship
if they were convicted of a terrorist offence. His government has
since introduced a bill that would eventually strike that down, because it was essentially unfair. "That means someone convicted of
terrorism with a dual citizenship could have a different consequence
under the law than a Canadian homegrown terrorist who has Canadian citizenship and is a sixth-generation Canadian and therefore
can't have their citizenship removed at all," he explains.

Trudeau has made his point, but he keeps on going. It's time to
vanquish the Conservatives once more, this time before an American audience. He recalls going toe to toe with Harper during the
federal election's foreign policy debate on the issue. "So I found myself in the situation on stage against the former prime minister arguing that yes, a man who he had just stripped the citizenship of, for
being convicted of a terrorist act, should have his Canadian citizen-

ship restored even though he had literally and figuratively, but perhaps even literally, ripped up his Canadian passport," he says.

"And yet I stand here as prime minister of Canada."

Applause follows.

The anecdote could have easily been saved for a domestic audience. It was a blatant injection of partisan politics into international affairs, even though everything he said was interpreted as a veiled reference to the Trump camp's emphasis on the politics of "fear and division."

Trudeau had talked a lot about returning Canada to its foreign policy traditions. On more than one occasion he evoked the 1947 Gray Lecture by Louis St Laurent, the one in which he made a plea for bipartisan unity in foreign affairs like that embodied by the cooperation in the United States between Harry Truman, its Democrat president, and Arthur Vandenberg, a Republican senator who headed the foreign relations committee. Vandenberg invented the "water's edge" axiom about the imperative of keeping domestic politics out of foreign policy. With many Americans questioning the role of their country in the world and "lamenting the pettiness of our political dialogue," some argued that the "landmark partnership of Truman and Vandenberg offers a timely, inspiring, and instructive history lesson."[19]

After he left American University, Trudeau addressed a luncheon at the Center for American Progress, which had strong links to the Obama administration. There he once again hauled out his greatest hits of the federal election campaign – criticizing the Conservatives over the niqab issue, the barbaric cultural practices tip-line, and the citizenship law aimed at terrorists. It had been almost five months since the night of Trudeau's decisive election victory, when he evoked Abraham Lincoln and told Canadians, "you can appeal to the better angels of our nature, and you can win while doing it." The ghosts of Arthur Vandenberg, Harry Truman, or perhaps even Louis St Laurent might not have been impressed by Trudeau's punchline. But it got a round of applause from his lunch crowd.

"That's the reason I am here," said Trudeau, "and not Stephen Harper."

Epilogue

29 MARCH 2016
The glass-walled meeting room on the fourth floor of the University of Ottawa's social sciences building is filled to capacity. About two hundred people have come to hear Canada's new foreign affairs minister, Stephane Dion, offer his vision for the country's international engagement. The venue is smaller than the one Louis St Laurent addressed in 1947 when he gave a similar speech. Canada had emerged confidently from the Second World War then. Today, many in this room are revelling in the outcome of another recent battle: the defeat of the Harper Conservatives by the Trudeau Liberals. Allan Rock, a former Liberal cabinet minister, introduces Dion as an old friend. Rock is now the president of this university, which has already supplied some policy advisers to the new prime minister, including his top foreign policy aide. Former foreign minister Lloyd Axworthy is also here. Any vestiges of the last decade of Conservative rule or its philosophical underpinnings are being erased. Dion is seeing to that today.

It has been two weeks since Dion accompanied Prime Minister Justin Trudeau to the United Nations headquarters in New York to formally announce Canada's candidacy for the 2020 Security Council election for a two-year term beginning in 2021. "It's time. It is time for Canada to step up once again," Trudeau said, repurposing his "Canada is back" slogan for the occasion. On this day, though, Dion is looking for something more than a slogan. A former university professor, he has gone back a century to the writing of German sociologist Max Weber to come up with his own motto for Canada's foreign policy. He calls it "responsible conviction."

With professorial earnestness, Dion explains how this framework embodies the notion that one's values and convictions should be tempered by a sense of responsibility. As a battle-scarred politician, Dion also says: "Certain policy shifts made over the past few months reflect the different convictions of the Liberal and Conservative parties." Dion says he is setting out to correct Canada's "disengagement" with the world under the former Conservative government. "Our government shares the same conviction as the previous government, but it assesses the consequences of its chosen method of promoting this conviction differently." Dion gives the Conservatives credit for doing a few things right: the Liberals will carry on promoting maternal, newborn, and child health in developing countries but will reverse the Conservative ban on funding abortion and family-planning, and will fight for religious freedom but close the office the Conservatives dedicated exclusively to that purpose. On a series of other issues, Dion uses the speech to tie together many of the new policy strands he has been defending in the House of Commons in recent months.

"It is out of a deep concern for the consequences of our actions that we are re-engaging with the UN and with some countries with which the Harper government had cut ties," Dion says. "We take no more joy than our Conservative friends in keeping open channels with authoritarian regimes. Of course, we would like it if the world were made up of nothing but exemplary democracies. But our world is highly imperfect, and to improve it we must engage in it with our eyes open, not withdraw from it."

Dion also resurrects the "honest broker" label for Canada, which the Conservatives scorned and branded as a policy of weakness. "Since the classic concept of the honest broker is now too often confused with moral relativism or the lack of strong convictions, I prefer to say that Canada must be a fair-minded and determined peace-builder." Dion says Canada is determined to work with its friends and allies moving forward on "a quest for peace, security, sustainable development, respect for diversity and human rights, peaceful pluralism, and justice for all."

In their first months in power, there was much evidence that the self-proclaimed "sunny ways" of the Trudeau Liberal government had indeed been shining beyond the country's borders. Canada had its first celebrity prime minister. This was in part due to the ability of social media to magnify his behaviour, as images of him doing one-armed push-ups and strenuous yoga poses burned up the Internet. He was featured in magazines such as *GQ*, *Vanity Fair*, *Paris Match*, *Marie Claire*, and *Time*, sometimes in glamour photo-shoots with his wife. He even staged a boxing photo-op at Brooklyn's storied Gleason's Gym, once a haunt of Muhammad Ali's, while on a trip to UN headquarters in April 2016 to sign the Paris climate-change deal.

Harper had tried to rebrand Canada with the new conservative stamp, but within months of assuming power, Trudeau was erasing it through his savvy use of social media. He was drawing attention to Canada in novel ways. Public relations firm Edelman said the "Trudeau effect" was the reason Canada had suddenly parachuted into the top five of its annual "Trust Barometer" measuring international trust in a country's government, business, media, and non-governmental agencies.[1] Michael Bloomberg, former New York mayor and billionaire business-leader, called Trudeau "energetic and pragmatic" and endorsed his commitments to fight climate change and to spend money to improve infrastructure.[2]

But did Trudeau's popularity mean that people would be more interested in him than his foreign policy? Trudeau addressed that question a couple of times early on in his mandate, first in the Philippines when I raised it at the APEC press conference and again in December 2015 when he spent seventy-five minutes answering questions in the Canadian Press boardroom in Ottawa. On both occasions, he maintained that his personal appeal was to Canada's benefit because it would draw attention to "the issues that are important to us." He also believed that posing in a magazine like *Vogue* could pay dividends. "People get their news through a variety of sources. And for a lot of people, certainly in the United States, reading that *Vogue* article will have been the only thing they see about Canada or Canadian politics all year."[3]

But Trudeau's rebranded government faced a long, hard road in moving its international policies forward in a world full of com-

peting and contradictory interests. The cornerstone of this engagement was greater cooperation with the UN, but the new government
faced an uphill fight for a seat on the Security Council. By mid-2016,
the reality at the heart of two strategically important bilateral relationships, those with Saudi Arabia and with China, was clear: Canada's national interest dictated engagement with both G20 partners
despite their dismal human-rights records. Saudi Arabia was an ally
in the Middle East, particularly in the war against ISIL. China was,
well, China, and Canada continued to make strengthening business,
trade, and investment a major priority.

Louise Arbour, the former justice of the Supreme Court of Canada and an ex-chief prosecutor with the International Criminal Court
in The Hague, was critical of Dion's justification for moving ahead
with the multi-year, $15 billion contract to sell light armoured ve-
hicles to Saudi Arabia. Groups such as Amnesty International and
Project Ploughshares were calling on Canada to cancel the deal because of Saudi Arabia's record, one that included mass executions,
subjugating women, and imprisoning and flogging anyone who
disagreed with how the desert kingdom was run. The Conservatives
had approved the deal, and the Liberals made it clear, both during
the election campaign and afterwards, that they were not going
to cancel it. In his speech, Dion framed the government's rationale
for this decision under his "responsible conviction" rubric. "We are
honouring a contract concluded under the previous government,
as breaking it would lead to damaging consequences." These consequences would involve massive, unspecified financial penalties,
damage to Canada's future credibility during other negotiations, the
loss of at least 2,000 jobs at the London, Ontario, plant building the
armoured military vehicles, as a well as a "ripple effect in an industry on which 70,000 jobs in Canada directly depend, including
many veterans."

Dion also said he would take a closer a look at future export permits to Saudi Arabia, and would consider the implications for
human rights and international law. But in the end, Dion approved
a series of permits in early April 2016 that approved the export of 70
per cent of the contract, about eleven billion dollars' worth. Dion
eventually released his department's latest human-rights assessment
on Saudi Arabia, which spelled out the details of country's abysmal

situation, including how it institutionalized women as inferior to men. It pointed out that Saudi Arabia was an ally of Canada, one that was fighting the same terrorist threat, and therefore needed the vehicles for that purpose. The assessment did not provide Dion with a legal basis to halt the deal. It concluded that while Saudi Arabia's rights record was poor, there was no evidence the armoured vehicles would be used on its own citizens, including its female population. The decision sparked fresh criticism from Amnesty, Ploughshares, and others who would later release an open letter to Trudeau, Dion, and Freeland calling the deal "immoral and unethical," and saying it breached Canada's own export law. Sunny ways had crashed head-on into *realpolitik.*

Dion explained that if the Saudis didn't buy these armed vehicles from Canada, another country would sell to them anyway. "Of course, I would like to live in a world without weapons. But my peaceful conviction must take the real world into account if I want to be a responsible decision-maker," Dion concluded. "That is what responsible conviction demands." Arbour was less than impressed. "I think this export permit system might be the ultimate guarantor of at least some comfort that this will not be misused," she said, "but this argument that if we don't do it somebody else will do it, I find frankly the least convincing." Overall, Arbour said Dion's speech was "very encouraging" but she urged the government to do something in the spirit of Louis St Laurent: She urged the government to move forward in a smart way, and to expand its tent to include its political opponents. She suggested that not everyone had "bought in" to the new Liberal foreign policy.

"I am not repudiating my allegiance to democratic liberal values that I think have been the hallmark of Canada's foreign policy," Arbour said. "The danger is nostalgia, cheerleading, speaking only to the like-minded. This is not the way to go. We need to reengage. We need to talk to people who disagree. I think it's a kind of principled pragmatism that's going to allow us again to punch above our weight."

Others agreed with Arbour's warning about avoiding the temptation of nostalgia. "There's an African proverb that you cannot dip your hand into the same river twice ... by the second time, it's not the same river," said former Nigerian foreign minister Ibrahim Gambari, co-chair of the Commission on Global Security, Justice and Governance. "Canada is coming back, hopefully, to the Security Council. But it's a different Security Council. It's a different world. It's a different United Nations."

Ian Martin, a UN careerist who led missions in several countries before becoming the executive director of the UN Security Council Report, had nothing good to say about what lay ahead if Canada was lucky enough to win a seat in 2020. He made it clear that if the government had any aspirations for a repeat of the activist term it pursued in 1999–2000 during Lloyd Axworthy's "human security" era, it was wearing rose-coloured glasses. Martin said there was now "diminished space for elected members to be effective and take initiatives within the council. And unless things have changed significantly by the time Canada becomes a member of the council, that too will be Canada's experience."

The council's business also lacked much actual talk about solving problems, Martin said. "What we have seen instead are set piece statements, rigid positioning, and attempts to publicly embarrass and undermine other council members even within our so-called informal consultations." The permanent five – the United States, Britain, France, Russia, and China – were the worst offenders, and the rotating ten countries, who were elected, weren't much better behaved, Martin said. "Canada needs to begin thinking about its future membership of the Security Council by recognizing just how bad is the current shape of the Security Council."

Then there was another more fundamental question: was Canada facing another defeat at the Security Council in 2020? Canada's opponents in the 2020 election were formidable: Norway and Ireland. Both those countries won seats in the 2000 race for the council, but it was a hard-fought contest. Ireland won handily on the first ballot, but Norway was forced into four rounds of voting before getting just enough votes to win, even though the country had stellar credentials and was one of the few to consistently reach the UN's 0.7 per cent of GNI development-spending target. Canada once again faced the possibility of Europe circling the wagons in support of one of its own, as it was assumed to have done in 2010 when Canada lost to Portugal. "There is this issue, or not, of the solidarity of the European Union. We were able to split the Europeans in 1999,

but it's not obvious to me that you can do that again," Paul Heinbecker, Canada's ambassador to the UN during its last stint on the
council in 1999–2000, told me.

Yves Fortier, the ambassador for Canada's previous council stint
in 1989–90, told me that Canada had "a steep hill to climb before
it can confidently look at an election to the Security Council in
2020." Fortier said he approved of the "tone and the message" that
Trudeau had delivered to the UN early in his mandate, but winning
a seat would not happen overnight. Brian Mulroney's former
envoy to the UN said the Liberals would have to mount a sustained
effort for support not only in New York but also at the UN institutions in Geneva and Vienna. Fortier also called for greater engagement with Russia. And he made this clear: "We have to
become more neutral in the Middle East in order to attract votes
from Arab nations."

Canada's ambassador to the UN, Marc-André Blanchard, told me
in June 2016 that Canada's eventual campaign for the Security
Council would likely focus on peacekeeping and foreign aid. He
didn't give specifics, but he made it clear that's why the government
had begun foreign policy reviews of its military and its international
development strategy; they were going to be at the "core" of the eventual bid. Blanchard, who had been appointed a few months earlier,
was already making his rounds at the UN and had met fifty of his
counterparts. He was reminding them Canada was running, but he
was also in listening mode, hearing what others were saying about
his country. "We think it's important that before we come out with
our platform that we listen to countries, to be responsive." Blanchard
acknowledged the tough fight that lay ahead against Ireland and
Norway, but he said the campaign wouldn't be about attacking them
but highlighting something that was uniquely Canadian, something
Trudeau himself had trumpeted in his first speech to the world in
Turkey eight months earlier: "Our experience with peaceful pluralism is an experience that is relevant to the challenges we're facing
with migration at the moment." He was talking about the millions
of refugees on the move from Syria and elsewhere into Europe, and
the backlash against them. Blanchard, like his prime minister, saw
Canada's multiculturalism as a source of strength, not division: "The
rise of xenophobia, the rise of division, the rise of mistrust, we think

that the Canadian experience is very valuable to bring a very positive, inclusive solution to these challenges."

Dion did some early politicking of his own in June 2016, when he was invited by France to join a discussion in the Security Council on the protection of civilians in peacekeeping operations. Dion said Canada was committed to increasing its support of UN peacekeeping missions, including supporting its mediation efforts and conflict prevention. The following month, when Dion was in Washington, he was forced to confront the more immediate threat posed by ISIL at a major international conference that was trying to raise money to help Iraq rebuild. The battle to retake the Iraqi city of Mosul from ISIL was on everyone's minds, including Dion's. He said that even if the "Daesh," as he called them, were defeated, the fight against terrorism would be a long one. "Once it's done, terrorism is still there. Daesh as an organization is likely to survive that … So we'll need to continue to work very hard, all together, with our police, intelligence services and deradicalization efforts, and we'll continue to fight."

The government's economic priorities, boosting trade with Asia and Europe, faced some pressing problems. When China's foreign minister, Wang Yi, visited Ottawa on 1 June 2016 things seemed to be going smoothly at first. Wang paid a visit to Trudeau's Parliament Hill office, which was unusual because visiting foreign ministers usually stuck to meeting their counterparts. He and Dion met later in the day, and when Wang emerged from a press conference at Global Affairs Canada, he waxed optimistic about how the two countries might be headed into "a new golden age" in relations, recalling the historic 1970 breakthrough with Pierre Trudeau and the gains made by Liberal prime ministers Jean Chrétien and Paul Martin.

Then a reporter from the web outlet *iPolitics* posed a tough question endorsed by all the journalists in attendance, and Wang lost his cool, waving his finger and accusing the reporter – and by extension all Canadian media – of "arrogance," being "full of prejudice" and downright irresponsible. The crime? The reporter made note of China's less-than-stellar human rights record, which included jailing a Canadian man, Kevin Garratt, for espionage.

After the event, outside the glare of the press conference, Dion and department officials took the matter up with Wang and the Chinese ambassador to Canada. Trudeau said they had expressed "our

dissatisfaction with the way our journalists were treated." Trudeau affirmed the role of the media to ask tough questions, and he made it
clear that he wouldn't be backing down on human rights in future
dealings with the Chinese. "We will continue to bring up human
rights concerns every chance we get, while at the same time we work
to create economic opportunities both for Canadian and for Chinese citizens."

Luo Zhaohui, the Chinese ambassador to Canada, replied two
days later with a column in the *Globe and Mail* that essentially
warned the Liberals to back off. "Microphone diplomacy does no
good to the control and solution of disputes or differences, it will
only serve to mislead the public, adversely affect co-operation and
harm both sides' interests," the ambassador wrote. "China stands for
a constructive approach and mutual understanding of each other's
concerns. It is important that the two sides work together to properly manage disputes and differences and focus on co-operation."4

A shadow was cast over potential trade deals after the unexpect-
ed 23 June 2016 referendum result committing Britain to leave the
European Union. The British decision to leave the EU drove down
global financial markets, cost British prime minister David Cameron
his job, and triggered what was expected to be a two-year round of
unprecedented departure negotiations. Many, including Canada's
high commissioner to the United Kingdom, predicted a Brexit had
the potential to distract the EU from bringing the CETA agreement
into force by early 2017. As High Commissioner Gordon Campbell
told me days before the vote: "If Europe is engaged in what would
be a very challenging negotiation about the United Kingdom leaving, they're certainly not going to be nearly as focused on engaging
in ratifying the Comprehensive Economic and Trade Agreement."

The day after the referendum, international trade minister Chrystia Freeland was on the phone with EU trade commissioner Cecilia
Malmström to reinforce Canada's commitment to a free-trade deal
with the twenty-eight-country bloc. But that wasn't the problem;
what mattered was what the EU was thinking. Eventually EU officials started affirming their support for the deal. Trudeau said Canada's economy was strong, diversified, and resilient. But he had little
to offer beyond a general reassurance: "Canadians can be reassured
that we are monitoring the situation closely and that we will work

with our partners across the world to maintain stability and create economic growth."

Months earlier, the government had been told what a crowded place the world had become, and how difficult that might make it for Canada's voice to be heard. The federal public service delivered that message shortly after the October 2015 election. Buried in the briefing book prepared for Freeland was a memo titled "Evolving Global Governance and Challenges in International Organizations." It described trends in international institutions and the many multilateral forums that Canada held to be important. This included not only the UN but also other influential bodies such as the International Monetary Fund and the World Bank. It described how "emerging powers" wanted more of a voice in these organizations, including "UN Security Council membership," and more influence in the IMF.

"As new powers grow their economies and contribute more to the multilateral system, Canada's assessed financial share, and its influence in governance discussions, will fall in relative terms." Canada remained committed to making the international system work, "but exercising influence and promoting innovative approaches across a wider range of institutions, in a more crowded political context, may prove more challenging."

Sixty-nine years earlier, when Louis St Laurent offered his foreign policy vision, Canada was near the head of the pack because it had survived the Second World War in better shape than most of its allies. But Canada's relative standing fell as other countries rebuilt. Now, despite the sunny optimism of the Trudeau Liberals and the indisputable appeal of the country's young new leader, the government was being quietly told to digest another reality: that Canada's voice in the world was destined to become that much harder to hear.

* * *

10 DECEMBER 2015. PARLIAMENT HILL
They are back at it, but not for long. The House of Commons is a day away from rising after its one-week session following the Liberal election victory. Justin Trudeau wants to get a big piece of legislation passed before Christmas – the tax cut for middle-class Canadians

that was at the heart of his campaign promises. All week, he has projected an aura of confidence and satisfaction in this place, fending off opposition attacks before sliding confidently into his chair and leaning back to survey the political theatre unfolding before him.

Across the aisle, the diminished ranks of the Conservative Party have trained their sights on another big Liberal campaign promise: the withdrawal of fighter jets from the U.S.-led air combat mission against ISIL in Syria and Iraq. This is top of the agenda for the party that made this commitment to the international anti-terror coalition in their final days of power. So the Conservatives have introduced a motion calling on the government to keep Canada's six CF-18 jet fighters deployed as part of the combat mission.

The Conservatives have no prospect of succeeding because they are a minority. Former prime minister Stephen Harper, now an MP for Calgary, will drop by to cast his vote, but has been reduced to a ghostly presence as he slips silently in and out of the chamber, saying nothing. Behind the scenes, he is making plans to leave politics. Six months from now, Canada's twenty-second prime minister will give his farewell address to Conservative party faithful in Edmonton, as word emerges that he will resign his seat in Parliament. But on this day, Harper's hobbled party carries on, determined to score domestic points on a major international issue.

"Canada must always stand shoulder to shoulder with our allies. We believe that the government needs to maintain our commitment to the air combat mission against ISIS and to leave our CF-18s in the fight. While our coalition partners are stepping up their efforts to degrade and defeat ISIS, the Liberal government is stepping back," says Tony Clement, the Conservative foreign affairs critic. Clement is met with a firm rebuttal from Harjit Sajjan, Canada's new defence minister, a highly decorated Canadian Forces combat veteran who has been cited for his bravery in helping kill Taliban enemies in Afghanistan. He reminds the House that Canada's battle-hardened troops trained more than one hundred Afghanistan battalions over three years, and will bring those lessons to the Iraqi fighters. "As career warriors molded by training, exercises, and deployments, our military members are adept in helping other nations build capacity and enabling them to defend themselves. Having spoken with many of our key allies on this matter, it is this strength that is most needed right now. Therefore, this fight continues, and we will continue to take on a different burden."

The debate turns ugly when Conservative MP Kellie Leitch stands to speak. Leitch was centre stage for one of the pivotal moments of the past election campaign, one that many pundits say helped her party lose the election. Along with ex-immigration minister Chris Alexander, she promised that the government would establish a snitch line so that Canadians could inform on "the barbaric cultural practices" of their neighbours. "Leaving the battlefield mid-fight is cowardly and tells our allies that we cannot be depended on when we are actually needed the most," says Leitch, who would later become the first to enter the Conservative leadership race to replace Harper.

The suggestion of cowardice leaves foreign affairs minister Stephane Dion cold. "Of course our forces are courageous. Nobody has any doubt about that in this House. It is outrageous for the member to have mentioned it as a possibility that we think otherwise. It is an insult, and it is why they are in the opposition. It is this kind of dogmatism and this kind of pretending that they alone support our forces that Canadians rejected."

As the Harper years faded into the new Trudeau era, the political discussion of Canada's role in the world still remained polarized and driven by domestic partisan interests. It is perhaps too much to expect Canada's elected representatives to look to the past for wisdom on how to guide debates on their country's future international endeavors. But if they did, they could benefit from the writing of John Holmes, one of Canada's foremost postwar diplomats. Some argue that the world is changing with unprecedented speed, and that this makes the reliance on old assumptions misguided and dangerous. This may be true. But reading what Holmes wrote in 1970, as he reflected on his foreign service career in the 1940s and 1950s, it is hard not find his words relevant – and instructive.

Holmes quoted Shakespeare's Falstaff, who said, "The better part of valour is discretion."[5] He was making an argument that subtlety and nuance – getting along with others and, perhaps, not engaging in self-interested grandstanding – were a more productive way to conduct international relations. "Above all it lies in the recognition of contradiction and the acceptance of paradox," Holmes wrote.[6] "This is a wisdom which Canadians might well ponder when they contemplate the foreign policies of their country. A sound foreign policy must be based on an acceptance of paradox. This is true for great powers, but it is especially true for a middle power whose reach ought not to exceed its grasp."[7]

Stephen Harper wasn't one for paradoxes. There was little valour in Harper's use of foreign policy to advance the domestic interests of his party. He was by no means the first Canadian leader to do this, but he was a pioneer in situating international policy in the realm of domestic political necessity. At the very least, it cast a shadow over his efforts, some of them successful, and his global leadership on helping reduce the needless deaths of mothers, newborns, and young children in the developing world. There was also little valour in Justin Trudeau taking a victory lap at Harper's expense at American University in Washington, or blaming him for killing the Canadian peacekeeping tradition when his own Liberal party also played a role.

The Liberals were more willing to allow paradoxical thinking into their foreign policy; Stephane Dion appeared to be taking a stab at that with his "responsible conviction" label. But some Canadians had a hard time swallowing Dion's worldview, saying it was a licence to "say what sounds good, do what's easy, and deny any apparent contradiction."[8]

Such were the spasms as Canada tried, once more, to find its way in the world. At this moment, the new Liberal government seemed intent on finding inspiration from their country's past. Trudeau's "Canada is back" slogan may have been right for the moment it was uttered. But it wasn't enough to move the country forward, into his mandate, and into the second decade of the twenty-first century. Yes, there were traditions and institutions, flawed as they may have been, to rely upon, but reversing the clock to some pre-Harper utopia was never a viable option.

Canada's success in the world is dependent on something else: its politicians learning to get along with each other when debating foreign policy. The water's edge seems to be eroding like a coastline, yet it is more imperative than ever that they find a way to temper their own short-term interests to attempt to reclaim at least some part of it.

This has never been, and will never be, easy.

Occasionally, there are signs that they have tried. On 10 December 2015, the plane carrying the first 163 Syrian refugees touched down at Pearson International Airport. Trudeau, three of his cabinet ministers, and the Liberal premier of Ontario were among those on hand to greet them. So too was a pair of opposition MPs, Conservative Michelle Rempel and New Democrat Jenny Kwan. "This is a wonderful night where we get to show not just a planeload of new Canadians what Canada is all about, we get to show the world how to open our hearts and welcome in people who are fleeing extraordinarily difficult situations," Trudeau said.

The world took notice. The new prime minister was already making headlines with a splashy story and photo shoot in the American fashion magazine *Vogue* that featured him and Grégoire-Trudeau, clad in an expensive designer dress, in a seductive clutch. Another American magazine, *GQ*, said Trudeau's trip to the airport was a lesson for some vitriol-spewing U.S. politicians because it showed "just how far leadership traits like compassion and open-mindedness can go toward endearing" a politician towards their voters. MTV.com also heaped praise on the prime minister, posting video of him interacting with some of the first Syrian children to arrive. "Just in case your heart isn't bursting out of your chest, also peep Trudeau talking sweetly to a baby wearing a flower crown and helping a young girl into her new winter coat to have your faith in humanity restored." The story also led the websites of the *New York Times*, *Paris Match*, the BBC, and several British newspapers.[9]

Pop culture may have awarded Trudeau a political victory. But the next day an event that was hardly noticed but was far more significant took place. The House of Commons showed these newly arrived Canadians something that has been in short supply in the country's domestic politics. Kwan introduced a motion to "warmly welcome our new Syrian and Iraqi neighbours and indeed all refugees who have escaped conflict around the world and arrived safely in Canada, a country with an unwavering commitment to pluralism, human rights, and the rule of law."

The House of Commons voted unanimously to support it. The politicians had decided this might not be a bad time to try to get along.

Notes

PROLOGUE

1 Louise Frechette, "Canada and the United Nations: A Shadow of Its Former Self," in *Canada among Nations, 2009–2010: As Others See Us*, ed. Fen Osler Hampson and Paul Heinbecker (Montreal and Kingston: McGill-Queen's University Press, 2009), 273.

2 Ian Brodie, "Canada Disengaging from NATO, the UN and Multilateralism? Not a Chance," OpenCanada.org, 25 September 2014.

3 Ibid.

4 David Black and Greg Donaghy, "Manifestations of Canadian Multilateralism," *Canadian Foreign Policy*, Spring 2010, http://www3.carleton.ca/cfpj/Without%20subscription/16-2_1_BlackDonaghy.pdf.

5 Tom Keating, *Canada and World Order: The Multilateralist Tradition in Canadian Foreign Policy* (Toronto: Oxford University Press, 2002), 118.

6 Brodie, "Canada Disengaging from NATO, the UN and Multilateralism?"

CHAPTER ONE

1 Adam Chapnick, "The Gray Lecture in Canadian Citizenship and History," *The American Review of Canadian Studies* (Washington: Taylor and Francis, 2007), http://www.tandfonline.com/doi/abs/10.1080/02722010709481811.

2 Ibid.

3 Ibid.

4 David B. Dewitt and John Kirton, *Canada as a Principled Power: A Study in Foreign Policy and International Relations* (Toronto: John Wiley and Sons, 1983), 49.

5 Ibid.

6 Robert J. Lieber, "Politics Stops at the Water's Edge? Not Recently," *Washington Post*, 10 February 2014, https://www.washingtonpost.com /news/monkey-cage/wp/2014/02/10/politics-stops-at-the-waters-edge-not-recently/.

7 Tom Keating, *Canada and World Order: The Multilateralist Tradition in Canadian Foreign Policy* (Toronto: Oxford University Press, 2002), 17.

8 John Holmes, *The Better Part of Valour* (Toronto: McClelland and Stewart, 1970), 2.

9 Keating, *Canada and World Order*, 26.

10 Elizabeth Riddell-Dixon, "Canada at the United Nations 1945–1989," *International Journal* 62, no. 1 (Winter 2006–07), https://www.questia .com/library/journal/1P3-1262406861/canada-at-the-united-nations-1945-1989.

11 Adam Chapnick, "UN Security Council Reform and Canadian Foreign Policy: Then and Now," *Canadian Foreign Policy Journal*, 2006, http://www.tandfonline.com/doi/abs/10.1080/11926422.2006.9673420 ?journalCode=rcfp20.

12 Keating, *Canada and World Order*, 26.

13 DeWitt and Kirton, *Canada as a Principled Power*, 21.

14 Keating, *Canada and World Order*, 27.

15 Ibid.

16 Ibid., 28.

17 Ibid., 20.

18 Beth Tomalin, "Canada at the Opening Session of UNO," *International Journal*, 1946, https://www.jstor.org/stable/40194085?seq=1#page _scan_tab_contents.

19 Holmes, *The Better Part of Valour*, 19.

20 Keating, *Canada and World Order*, 103.

21 Riddell-Dixon, "Canada at the United Nations 1945–1989."

22 Keating, *Canada and World Order*, 103.

23 Holmes, *The Better Part of Valour*, 62.

24 Canada. Foreign Affairs and International Trade Canada (DFATD), *Documents on Canadian External Relations* (Vol. 12, Chapter VIII, Part 2, 1946), Ottawa, Ontario.

25 Ibid.

26 Tomalin, "Canada at the Opening Session."

27 *Documents on Canadian External Relations.*

28 Tomalin, "Canada at the Opening Session."

29 *Documents on Canadian External Relations.*

30 John Hilliker and Donald Barry, *Canada's Department of External Affairs, Volume 2: Coming of Age, 1946–68* (Montreal and Kingston: McGill-Queen's University Press, 1995), 32.

31 Ibid.

32 Ibid.

33 Ibid.

34 Ibid.

35 Ibid.

36 "Canada Gets Seat on Security Council: Given Votes to Spare on First Ballot," *Globe and Mail*/Canadian Press, 1 October 1947, 1.

37 Ibid.

38 Robert A. Spencer, *Canada in World Affairs: From UN to NATO 1946–49* (Toronto: Oxford University Press, 1959), 118.

39 Ibid., 119.

40 Ibid., 120.

41 Ibid., 122.

42 Norman Hillmer and J.L. Granatstein, *Empire to Umpire* (Toronto: Nelson, 2007), 194.

43 Ibid., 195.

44 Ibid.

45 James Eayrs, *The Art of the Possible: Government and Foreign Policy in Canada* (Toronto: University of Toronto Press, 1961), 26.

46 Chapnick, "The Gray Lecture in Canadian Citizenship and History."

47 John G. Diefenbaker, *One Canada: Memories of the Right Honourable John G. Diefenbaker, the Crusading Years 1895–1956* (Toronto: Macmillan, 1975), 280.

48 Ibid.

49 Ibid.

50 Keating, *Canada and World Order*, 41.

51 Trevor Lloyd, *Canada in World Affairs: Volume X. 1957–59* (Toronto: Oxford University Press, 1968), 132.

52 CBC Newsmagazine. Guests: Howard Green, interviewed by Charles Lynch, 22 November 1959, CBC archives,

http://www.cbc.ca/archives/entry/canada-elected-to-un-security-council-in-1959.

53 Derek H. Burney and Fen Osler Hampson, *Brave New Canada: Meeting the Challenge of a Changing World* (Montreal and Kingston: McGill-Queen's University Press, 2014), 20.

54 Ibid.

55 Ibid.

56 Keating, *Canada and World Order*, 117.

57 DeWitt and Kirton, *Canada as a Principled Power*, 39.

58 Hillmer and Granatstein, *Empire to Umpire*, 250.

59 Ibid., 253.

60 Ibid.

61 Keating, *Canada and World Order*, 106.

62 Ibid.

63 Ibid., 107.

64 John English, *Just Watch Me: The Life of Pierre Elliott Trudeau 1968–2000* (Toronto: Vintage Canada, 2009), 377.

65 Ibid.

66 Lloyd Axworthy, *Navigating a New World: Canada's Global Future* (Toronto: Vintage Canada, 2003), 38.

67 Ibid.

68 Ibid., 39.

69 English, *Just Watch Me*, 597–8.

70 Ibid., 599.

71 Ibid., 604.

72 Keating, *Canada and World Order*, 113.

73 Ibid.

74 Brian W. Tomlin, Norman Hillmer, and Fen Osler Hampson, eds, *Canada's International Policies: Agendas, Alternatives, and Politics* (Toronto: Oxford University Press, 2008), 242.

75 Ibid., 235.

76 Ibid., 243.

77 Ibid., 249.

78 Ibid.

79 Ibid., 254.

80 Fen Osler Hampson, "The Axworthy Years: An Assessment" (presentation prepared for the National Press Club, October 2000),

http://group78.org.previewdns.com/wp-content/uploads/2013/12
/Hampson_Axworthy-Years_2000-10-31.pdf.

81 Ibid.

82 Ibid.

83 Mike Blanchfield, "Canada's Torturous Path to a New Foreign Policy,"
    Ottawa Citizen, 12 March 2005, A1.

CHAPTER TWO

1 Tom Flanagan, *Harper's Team: Behind the Scenes in the Conservative
   Rise to Power* (Montreal and Kingston: McGill-Queen's University
   Press, 2007), 3.

2 Stephen Harper and Tom Flanagan, "Our Benign Dictatorship," *Next
   City Magazine*, 1996, https://www.scribd.com/doc/51938443/Stephen-
   Harper-and-Tom-Flanagan-Our-Benign-Dictatorship-Next-City-
   Winter-1996-97.

3 Ibid.

4 Ibid.

5 Ibid.

6 William Johnson, *Stephen Harper and the Future of Canada* (Toronto:
   McClelland and Stewart, 2005), 259.

7 Ibid.

8 Ibid.

9 Ibid., 315.

10 Ibid., 316.

11 Ibid.

12 Lloyd Mackey, *Stephen Harper: The Case for Collaborative Governance*
   (Toronto: ECW Press, 2005), 173.

13 Ibid.

14 Ibid., 174.

15 Ibid.

16 Kim Richard Nossal, "The Liberal Past in the Conservative Present:
   Internationalism in the Harper Era," *Canada in the World: Internation-
   alism in Canadian Foreign Policy*, ed. Heather A. Smith and Claire
   Turenne Sjolander (Oxford: Oxford University Press, 2013), 24.

17 Johnson, *Stephen Harper and the Future of Canada*, 45.

18 Ibid.

19 Ibid., 46.

20 Ibid., 47.

21 Ibid., 49.

22 Stephen Harper, "Rediscovering the Right Agenda: The Alliance Must Commit to Ideals and Ideas, Not Vague Decision-Making Processes: The Canadian Alliance Leader Outlines How Social and Economic Conservatism Must Unite," *Citizens Centre Report*, October 2014, http://post.queensu.ca/~nossalk/Harper_2003.pdf.

23 Ibid.

24 Johnson, *Stephen Harper and the Future of Canada*, 51.

25 Ibid., 52.

26 Ibid., 53.

27 Harper, "Rediscovering the Right Agenda."

28 Johnson, *Stephen Harper and the Future of Canada*, 49.

29 Flanagan, *Harper's Team*, 209.

30 Ibid., 89.

31 Ibid.

32 Stephen Harper, "A Departure from Neutrality," *National Post*, 23 May 2003, A18.

33 Stephen Harper and Stockwell Day, "Canadians Stand with You," *Wall Street Journal*, 28 March 2003, http://www.wsj.com/articles/SB104881540524220000.

34 War Resisters Support Campaign – Canada, "Reason #1 to Let War Resisters Stay – Stephen Harper Admits the Iraq War Was 'Absolutely an Error,'" YouTube video, 1 March 2009, https://www.youtube.com/watch?v=JYTTbmCL4RQ.

CHAPTER THREE

1 Louise Frechette, "Canada and the United Nations: A Shadow of Its Former Self," in *Canada among Nations, 2009–2010: As Others See Us*, ed. Fen Osler Hampson and Paul Heinbecker (Montreal and Kingston: McGill-Queen's University Press, 2009), 269.

2 Richard Nimijean, "Domestic Brand Politics and the Modern Publicity State," in *Publicity and the Canadian State: Critical Communications Perspectives*, ed. Kirsten Kozolanka (Toronto: University of Toronto Press, 2014), 176.

3 Derek Burney, Fen Osler Hampson, and Simon Palamar, "The Call of

Duty," in *Canada among Nations 2015: Elusive Pursuits*, ed. Fen Osler Hampson and Stephen M. Saideman (Waterloo, Ontario: The Centre for International Governance Innovation and Carleton University, 2015), 200.

4 Ibid., 201.

5 Ibid., 219.

6 Ibid., 202.

7 "Quebec's Van Doos Head to Afghanistan," *CBC News*, 15 July 2007, http://www.cbc.ca/news/canada/quebec-s-van-doos-head-to-afghanistan-1.650530.

8 Paul Wells, *The Longer I'm Prime Minister: Stephen Harper and Canada, 2006–* (Toronto: Random House, 2013), 263.

9 Confidential source.

10 Bashir Ahmad Naadim, "Azizi Officially Requests Probe in Dahla Dam Corruption," *Pajhwok Afghan News*, 14 January 2016, http://www.pajhwok.com/dr/node/443632.

11 Tim Hume, "Migrant Drownings Rise by a Third This Year on Mediterranean, UN Says," *CNN*, 31 May 2016, http://www.cnn.com/2016/05/31/world/migrant-deaths-rise-mediterranean/index.html.

12 Yaroslav Trofimov, "Libya Will Need American Help to Defeat Islamic State, General Says," *Wall Street Journal*, 29 February 2016, http://www.wsj.com/articles/libya-will-need-american-help-to-defeat-islamic-state-general-says-1456776041.

13 Eric Reguly, "Canada Won't Act in Libya until Single Government in Place, Dion Says," *Globe and Mail*, 2 February 2016, http://www.theglobeandmail.com/news/world/canada-wont-act-in-libya-until-single-government-in-place-dion-says/article28507720/.

14 Arshad Mohammed and Crispian Balmer, "ISIS Pushed Back in Iraq, Syria, But a Threat in Libya: Kerry," Reuters, 2 February 2016, http://www.reuters.com/article/us-mideast-crisis-coalition-idUSKCN0VA3RE.

15 Micah Zenko, "The Big Lie about the Libyan War," *Foreign Policy*, 22 March 2016, http://foreignpolicy.com/2016/03/22/libya-and-the-myth-of-humanitarian-intervention/.

16 Ibid.

17 "NATO and Libya – Arms Embargo: Boarding a Suspicious Vessel," YouTube video, 24 May 2011, https://www.youtube.com/watch?v=oKh6Kzqc428.

18 Bruce Cheadle, "Flypasts, Medals: Military Mission in Libya Gets Lavish Thank-You from Harper," Canadian Press, 24 November 2011, http://globalnews.ca/news/181526/flypasts-medals-military-mission-in-libya-gets-lavish-thank-you-from-harper/.

19 Christopher K. Penney, "Mandating Responsibility," in *Canada among Nations 2015: Elusive Pursuits*, ed. Fen Osler Hampson and Stephen M. Saideman (Waterloo, Ontario: The Centre for International Governance Innovation and Carleton University, 2015), 23.

20 Alan J. Kuperman, "Obama's Libya Debacle," *Foreign Affairs*, March/April 2015, https://www.foreignaffairs.com/articles/libya/obamas-libya-debacle.

CHAPTER FOUR

1 Steven Edwards, "Ottawa Learns the Real Value of UN Promises," *National Post*, 12 October 2010. http://news.nationalpost.com/full-comment/stephen-edwards-ottawa-learns-the-real-value-of-un-promises.

2 Denis Stairs, "Being Rejected in the United Nations: The Causes and Implications of Canada's Failure to Win a Seat in the UN Security Council," *Canadian Defence and Foreign Affairs Institute*, 2011, https://d3n8a8pro7vhmx.cloudfront.net/cdfai/pages/43/attachments/original/1413677044/Being_Rejected_in_the_United_Nations.pdf?1413677044.

3 Bruce Carson, *14 Days: Making the Conservative Movement in Canada* (Montreal and Kingston: McGill-Queen's University Press, 2014), 285–6.

4 "The UN's Oil for Food Scandal: Rolling Up the Culprits," *The Economist*, 15 March 2008, http://www.economist.com/node/10853611.

5 Stairs, "Being Rejected in the United Nations."

6 Ian Brodie, "Canada Disengaging from NATO, the UN and Multilateralism? Not a Chance," OpenCanada.org, 25 September 2014, https://www.opencanada.org/features/canada-disengaging-from-nato-the-un-and-multilateralism-not-a-chance/.

7 Robert Fowler, "Why Canada Was Not Elected to the Security Council…," in *The United Nations and Canada: What Canada Has Done and Should Be Doing at the United Nations*, ed. John E. Trent (Ottawa: World Federalist Movement, 2013), https://www.worldfederalistscanada.org/documents/CanadaUNEng.pdf.

8 "Mulroney on Harper's Supreme Court Spat: 'You Don't Do That,'"
    Canadian Press, 9 September 2014, http://www.huffingtonpost.ca
    /2014/09/04/brian-mulroney- stephen-harper-supreme-court_n
    _5769568.html.

9 Derek Burney and Fen Hampson, "No More Mr. Fixit at the UN,"
    iPolitics, 1 October 2012, http://ipolitics.ca/2012/10/01/burney-
    hampson-no-more-mr-fixit-at-the-un/.

10 Ibid.

11 Derek Burney and Fen Hampson, "Stephen Harper Is Right to Snub
    the UN," *iPolitics*, 23 September 2013, http://ipolitics.ca/2013/09/23
    /stephen-harper-is-right-to-snub-the-un/.

12 Burney and Hampson, "No More Mr. Fixit at the UN."

13 Ibid.

14 Derek H. Burney and Fen Osler Hampson, *Brave New Canada: Meet-
    ing the Challenge of a Changing World* (Montreal and Kingston:
    McGill-Queen's University Press, 2014), 73.

15 Ibid.

16 Ibid., 80.

17 Ibid., 82.

18 Ibid.

19 Roy Rempel, *Dreamland: How Canada's Pretend Foreign Policy Has
    Undermined Sovereignty* (Kingston: Breakout Educational Network,
    2006), 2.

20 Ibid., 71.

21 Ibid., 73.

22 Ibid., 78.

23 "Canada, Fire This Diplomat," *Toronto Sun*, 4 July 2011, http://www
    .torontosun.com/2011/07/04/canada-fire-this-diplomat.

24 Kim Richard Nossal, "The Liberal Past in the Conservative Present:
    Internationalism in the Harper Era," in *Canada in the World: Interna-
    tionalism in Canadian Foreign Policy*, ed. Heather A. Smith and Claire
    Turenne Sjolander (Oxford: Oxford University Press, 2013), 22.

25 Louise Frechette, "Canada and the United Nations: A Shadow of Its
    Former Self," in *Canada among Nations, 2009–2010: As Others See Us*,
    ed. Fen Osler Hampson and Paul Heinbecker (Montreal and
    Kingston: McGill-Queen's University Press, 2009), 269.

26 Ibid.

27 Kim Richard Nossal, "Primat der Wahlurne: Explaining Stephen

Harper's Foreign Policy," *International Studies Association*, 29 March 2014, http://post.queensu.ca/~nossalk/papers/Nossal_2014_Harper.pdf.

28 Confidential source.

29 Norman Smith, "Security Council Membership: A Challenge to Canada," *International Journal* 2, no. 3 (Sage Publications Ltd, 1948), http://www.jstor.org/stable/40197781?seq=1#page_scan_tab_contents.

30 Robert A. Spencer, *Canada in World Affairs: From UN to NATO 1946–49* (Toronto: Oxford University Press, 1959), 120.

31 Ibid., 122.

32 Smith, "Security Council Membership."

33 Alexander Panetta, "Canada's Big Announcement at UN Climate Summit: Follow the U.S.," Canadian Press, 23 September 2014, http://www.macleans.ca/news/canada/canadas-big-announcement-at-un-climate- summit-follow-the-u-s/.

34 United Nations Security Council, 4251st meeting (S/PV.4251), 19 December 2000, http://www.un.org/en/ga/search/view_doc.asp?symbol=S/PV.4251.

CHAPTER FIVE

1 Confidential source.

2 Tony Czuczka, "Merkel Cites Canada as Debt-Deficit Model in Europe," *Bloomberg*, 16 August 2012, http://www.bloomberg.com/news/articles/2012-08-16/merkel-cites-canada-as-debt-deficit-model-in-europe-s-crisis.

3 Aaron Wherry, "Justin Trudeau's Davos Trip 1 More Star Turn before Promises Meet Reality," *CBC News*, 17 January 2016, http://www.cbc.ca/news/politics/justin-trudeau-s-davos-trip-1-more-star-turn-before-promises-meet-reality-1.3407348.

4 David Black and Greg Donaghy, "Manifestations of Canadian Multilateralism," *Canadian Foreign Policy*, Spring 2010, http://www3.carleton.ca/cfpj/Without%20subscription/16-2_1_BlackDonaghy.pdf.

5 John Kirton, "Stephen Harper: World Statesman," *OpenCanada.org*, 27 September 2012, https://www.opencanada.org/features/stephen-harper-world-statesman/.

6 Ian Brodie, "Canada Disengaging from NATO, the UN and Multilateralism? Not a Chance," *OpenCanada.org*, 25 September 2014,

https://www.opencanada.org/features/canada-disengaging-from-nato-the-un-and-multilateralism-not-a-chance/.

7 Bruce Cheadle, "Eurozone Crisis: Stephen Harper Says Canadian Government Won't Put Cash into Bailout," Canadian Press, 4 November 2011, http://www.huffingtonpost.ca/2011/11/04/canadian-government-wont-fund-eurozone-bailout-greece-euro_n_1076415.html.

8 Bruce Cheadle, "Eurozone Crisis: Canada Urges 'Extraordinary Actions,' but No One Sure What Those Should Be," Canadian Press, 3 November 2012, http://www.huffingtonpost.ca/2011/11/03/eurozone-crisis-canada-extraordinary-actions_n_1073255.html.

9 Cheadle, "Eurozone Crisis."

10 Ibid.

11 Jennifer Ditchburn, "G20 Summit: Harper Stakes Firm Position on Syria, Debt Reduction," Canadian Press, 5 September 2013, http://www.ctvnews.ca/politics/harper-stakes-firm-position-on-syria-debt-repayment-at-g20-summit-1.1441124.

12 Theophilos Argitis, "Harper Speaks on Canada, Economy, Election Choices Transcript," *Bloomberg*, 18 October 2015, http://www.bloomberg.com/news/articles/2015-10-18/harper-speaks-on-canada-economy-election-choices-transcript.

13 Ibid.

14 Ibid.

15 Stephen Brown, "Germany Wants Investment Clause Scrapped in EU-Canada Trade Deal," Reuters, 25 September 2014, http://www.reuters.com/article/us-trade-eu-canada-idUSKCN0HK1DM20140925.

16 "Chrystia Freeland Says Review of Canada-EU Deal Is Done," Canadian Press, 29 February 2016, http://www.macleans.ca/news/canada/chrystia-freeland-says-review-of-canada-eu-deal-is-done/.

17 Joschka Fischer, "Angela Merkel Must Accept That Her Austerity Policy Is Now in Tatters," *Guardian*, 31 January 2015, http://www.theguardian.com/commentisfree/2015/jan/31/growth-decide-eurozones-future-greek.

CHAPTER SIX

1 Andrew Cohen, *While Canada Slept: How We Lost Our Place in the World* (Toronto: McClelland and Stewart, 2003), 80.

2 Ibid.

3 Brian W. Tomlin, Norman Hillmer, and Fen Osler Hampson, eds, *Canada's International Policies: Agendas, Alternatives, and Politics* (Toronto: Oxford University Press, 2008), 173.

4 Ibid., 168.

5 Richard Horton, "Offline: Canada's Big Promise," *The Lancet*, 7 June 2014, http://www.thelancet.com/journals/lancet/article/PIIS0140-6736(14)60927-2/abstract.

6 Ibid.

7 Lee Berthiaume, "Hundreds of Millions in Foreign Aid Go Unspent, New Figures Show," *Ottawa Citizen*, 12 July 2013, http://o.canada.com /news/hundreds-of-millions-in-foreign-aid-go-unspent-new-figures-show.

8 Mike Harris and Preston Manning, *International Leadership by a Canada Strong and Free* (Montreal: Montreal Economic Institute, 2007), 69.

9 Ibid., 71.

10 Ibid., 79.

11 Ibid., 112.

12 *Canada's International Policies*, 156.

13 Ibid., 157.

14 Ibid., 158.

15 Elizabeth Riddell-Dixon, "Canada at the United Nations 1945–1989," *International Journal* 62, no. 1 (Winter 2006–07), https://www.questia .com/library/journal/1P3-1262406861/canada-at-the-united-nations-1945-1989.

16 Ibid.

17 *Canada's International Policies*, 183.

18 Ibid., 160.

19 Ibid., 161.

20 Norman Hillmer and J.L. Granatstein, *Empire to Umpire* (Toronto: Nelson, 2007), 315.

21 Ibid., 197.

22 Ibid., 198.

23 "Canada's G8 Health Leadership," *The Lancet*, 8 May 2010, http://the-lancet.com/journals/lancet/article/PIIS0140-6736(10)60685-X /fulltext.

24 Ibid.

25 Marie Vastel and Fannie Olivier, "Ottawa Ignored Its Own Advice on Abortion, Documents Show," Canadian Press, 24 May 2010,

https://www.thestar.com/news/canada/2010/05/24/ottawa_ignored
_its_own_advice_on_abortion_documents_show.html.

26 Tonda MacCharles, "Trudeau Calls UN Goal to Boost Aid Spending
'Too Ambitious,'" *Toronto Star*, 10 May 2016, https://www.thestar.com
/news/canada/2016/05/10/justin-trudeau-un-goal-to-boost-spending-
on-aid-too-ambitious-for-canada-right-now.html.

CHAPTER SEVEN

1 "Use of Cluster Bombs," *Cluster Munition Coalition (CMC)*, 26 December 2014, http://www.stopclustermunitions.org/en-gb/cluster-bombs
/use-of-cluster-bombs/a-timeline-of-cluster-bomb-use.aspx.

2 Brian W. Tomlin, Norman Hillmer, and Fen Osler Hampson, eds,
Canada's International Policies: Agendas, Alternatives, and Politics
(Toronto: Oxford University Press, 2008), 209.

3 Ibid.

4 Ibid., 210.

5 Ibid., 222.

6 Ibid.

7 Mark Tran, "US Studies Israel's Cluster Bomb Use in Lebanon,"
Guardian, 29 January 2007, http://www.theguardian.com/world/2007
/jan/29/israelandthepalestinians.usa.

8 *Canada's International Policies*, 231.

9 Ibid.

10 Canada. Library of Parliament, (2012) *Bill S-10: An Act to Implement
the Convention on Cluster Munitions* (Publication No. 41-1-S10-E), 11
July 2012.

CHAPTER EIGHT

1 Adam Day, "One Martyr Down: The Untold Story of a Canadian
Peacekeeper Killed at War," *Legion Magazine*, 2 January 2013,
https://legionmagazine.com/en/2013/01/one-martyr-down-the-
untold-story-of-a-canadian-peacekeeper-killed-at-war/.

2 Ibid.

3 Canada. National Defence (DND), (2006) *Board of Inquiry: Death of
Major P. Hess-Von Kruedener* (CF 285 (10-84)), 1 November 2006,
https://legionmagazine.com/inquiry.pdf.

4 Ibid.
5 Ibid.
6 Ibid.
7 Ibid.
8 Day, "One Martyr Down."
9 DND.
10 Ibid.
11 Sue Bailey, "Canadian Described Bombing in the Days before Deadly Strike," *Whitehorse Star*/Canadian Press, 27 July 2006, 8.
12 Norma Greenaway, Matthew Fisher, and Aileen McCabe, "Terrible Tragedy," *Regina Leader Post*, 27 July 2006, A1.
13 David Pugliese, "DND Removes Report on Killing of Canadian Soldier by Israeli Forces," 25 December 2012, http://vigile.quebec/DND-removes-report-on-killing-of.
14 Joe Clark, *How We Lead: Canada in a Century of Change* (Toronto: Random House, 2013), 84.
15 Alexander Panetta, "Days of Easy 'Middle Path' for Canadian Foreign Policy Are Over," Canadian Press, 14 May 2014, http://www.macleans.ca/politics/ottawa/days-of-easy-middle-path-for-cdn-foreign-policy-over-baird/.
16 Ibid.
17 Rex Brynen, "Canada's Role in the Israeli-Palestine Peace Process," in *Canada and the Middle East in Theory and Practice*, ed. Paul Heinbecker and Bessma Momani (London: Wilfred Laurier University Press, 2007), 74.
18 Ibid.
19 Norman Hillmer and J.L. Granatstein, *Empire to Umpire* (Toronto: Nelson, 2007), 81.
20 Andrew Cohen, *Lester B. Pearson* (Toronto: Penguin Canada, 2008), 101.
21 Hillmer and Granatstein, *Empire to Umpire*, 81.
22 Brynen, "Canada's Role in the Israeli-Palestine Peace Process," 74.
23 "The Situation in the Middle East, Chapter IX," *The Yearbook of the United Nations 1967*, http://www.unmultimedia.org/searchers/yearbook/page.jsp?bookpage=158&volume=1967.
24 Brynen, "Canada's Role in the Israeli-Palestine Peace Process," 74.
25 Ibid., 75.

26 "Questions Relating to the Middle East, Chapter XI," *The Yearbook of the United Nations 1977*, http://www.unmultimedia.org/searchers /yearbook/page.jsp?volume=1977&bookpage=266.

27 Canada. External Affairs (DEA), (1977) *Message: Ministerial Level Security Council Meetings* (Orig. No.: UNO-1381), Ottawa, Ontario.

28 Ibid.

29 Lee-Anne Goodman, "Harper, Netanyahu Sign Broad Agreement at Jerusalem Meeting," Canadian Press, 21 January 2014, http://www .macleans.ca/news/canada/harper-netanyahu-sign-broad-agreement-in-jerusalem-meeting/.

30 Brynen, "Canada's Role in the Israeli-Palestine Peace Process," 77.

31 Ibid.

32 Mike Blanchfield, Anne Dawson, and Steven Edwards, "Liberals Fight over Mideast Policy: Rock Speaks of Pro-Israel Shift," *National Post*, 2 December 2004, A13.

33 Canada. Standing Senate Committee on Human Rights, (2008) *Canada and the United Nations Human Rights Council: A Time for Serious Re-Evaluation*, http://www.parl.gc.ca/Content/SEN/Committee/392 /huma/rep/rep13jun08-e.pdf.

34 Ibid.

35 Canada. Standing Senate Committee on Human Rights, (2010) *Canada and the United Nations Human Rights Council: Charting a New Course*, http://www.parl.gc.ca/Content/SEN/Committee/403/huma /rep/rep04jun10-e.pdf.

36 Ibid.

37 Mike Blanchfield, "Canada Rejects UN Rights Panel Call for Review of Violence on Aboriginal Women," Canadian Press, 19 September 2013, http://www.theglobeandmail.com/news/national/canada-to-reject-un-panels-call-for-review-of-violence-on-aboriginal-women /article14406434/.

38 Cathal J. Nolan, "The Human Rights Committee," in *Human Rights in Canadian Foreign Policy*, ed. Robert O. Matthews and Cranford Pratt (Montreal and Kingston: McGill-Queen's University Press, 1988), 109.

39 Kim Richard Nossal, Stephane Roussel, and Stephane Paquin, *International Policy and Politics in Canada* (Toronto: Pearson, 2011), 39.

40 Laura Payton, "UN Official Sparks Debate over Canadian Food Secu-

rity," *CBC News*, 16 May 2012, http://www.cbc.ca/news/politics/un-official-sparks-debate-over-canadian-food-security-1.1130281.

41 Gloria Galloway, "Canada Condemns UN 'Hatefest,'" *Globe and Mail*, 25 November 2010, http://www.theglobeandmail.com/news/politics /canada-condemns-un-hatefest/article1315601/.

42 Mike Blanchfield, "Baird Blasts UN Rapporteur on Palestinian Territories for Bias against Israel," Canadian Press, 26 October 2012, http://www.theglobeandmail.com/news/politics/baird-blasts-uns-richard-falk-for-bias-against-israel-in-call-for-boycott/article4688289/.

43 Patrick Martin, "Baird Sticks to Party Line – Israel's Likud Party," *Globe and Mail*, 3 February 2012, http://www.theglobeandmail.com/news/world/baird-sticks-to-party-line---israels-likud-party/article5547279/.

44 Murray Brewster, "John Baird Unfazed by Criticism after Meeting with Israelis in East Jerusalem," Canadian Press, 11 April 2013, http://news.nationalpost.com/news/canada/canadian-politics/john-baird-unfazed-by-criticism-after-meeting-with-israelis-in-east-jerusalem.

45 Ibid.

46 "Palestinians Summon Canadian Envoy over Baird's East Jerusalem Meeting," Canadian Press, 15 April 2013, http://news.nationalpost .com/news/world/israel-middle-east/a-deplorable-step-palestinians-summon-canadian-envoy-over-john-bairds-east-jerusalem-meeting.

47 Ibid.

48 John Ibbitson, *Stephen Harper* (Toronto: McClelland and Stewart, 2015, e-book).

49 Ibid.

50 "Mark Adler, Tory MP, Pleads to Get in 'Million Dollar Shot' of Harper at Holy Site," *Huffington Post*, 21 January 2014, http://www .huffingtonpost.ca/2014/01/21/mark-adler-stephen-harper-western-wall_n_4638965.html.

51 "Israel Invited to Join UN's Western Nations Group in Geneva," *Jerusalem Post*, 2 December 2013, http://www.jpost.com/Diplomacy-and-Politics/Israel-invited-to-join-UNs-Western-nations-group-in-Geneva-333577.

52 "Baird Maligns UN Human Rights Council on Gaza Resolution Defends Israel," Canadian Press, 23 July 2014, http://www.macleans.ca

/news/world/baird-maligns-un-human-rights-council-on-gaza-
resolution/.

53 Rashid Rasheed and Daniel Estrin, "UN Chief in Gaza Voices Shock
at Destruction from Summer War as Construction Material Arrives,"
Associated Press, 14 October 2014, http://www.elkharttruth.com
/news/national/2014/10/14/UN-chief-in-Gaza-as-reconstruction-
efforts-begin.html.

54 Confidential source.

CHAPTER NINE

1 Bill Curry, "Tory-Linked Charity behind Monument Declared It Was
Not Active Politically," *Globe and Mail*, 19 March 2015, http://www
.theglobeandmail.com/news/politics/tory-linked-charity-behind-
monument-declared-it-was-not-active-politically/article23533178/.

2 Kim MacKrael, "Bureaucrat with Finance Expertise Appointed to
Lead Foreign Aid Agency," *Globe and Mail*, 14 June 2013, http://www
.theglobeandmail.com/news/politics/bureaucrat-with-finance-
expertise-appointed-to-lead-foreign-aid-agency/article12573847/.

3 "Response to the Report by Director of the OSCE's Office for Democratic Institutions and Human Rights, Michael Link," United States
Mission to the Organization for Security and Cooperation in Europe,
12 March 2015, http://www.osce.org/pc/147411?download=true.

4 Joan Bryden, "Harper Government Ignores Advice on Ukraine Election Observation Missions," Canadian Press, 24 May 2014, http://o
.canada.com/news/harper-government-ignores-advice-on-ukraine-
election-observation-missions.

5 Confidential source.

6 Joan Bryden and Mike Blanchfield, "Tories under Fire for Staffing of
Canadian Monitor Mission to Ukraine," Canadian Press, 19 October
2012, http://www.theglobeandmail.com/news/politics/tories-under-
fire-for-staffing-of-election-monitor-mission-to-ukraine/article
4622918/?page=all.

7 Lee-Anne Goodman, "G20 Summit: Harper Tells Putin to 'Get Out
of Ukraine,'" Canadian Press, 15 November 2014, http://www
.huffingtonpost.ca/2014/11/14/g20-summit-harper-australia-russia_n
_6158268.html.

8 Confidential source.

CHAPTER TEN

1 Aaron Wherry, "Stephen Harper on the Legality of Bombing Syria:
   LOL," *Maclean's*, 26 March 2015, http://www.macleans.ca/politics
   /stephen-harper-on-the-legality-of-bombing-syria-lol/.
2 "Here's Obama's Legal Case for Bombing inside Syria," *Vox*, 23 September 2014, http://www.vox.com/2014/9/23/6836195/read-us-letter-
   to-un-security-council-claiming-self-defense-justifies.
3 Ibid.
4 Wherry, "Stephen Harper on the Legality of Bombing Syria."
5 Ibid.
6 Edith M. Lederer, "Ukraine to Sit alongside Russia on UN Security
   Council," Associated Press, 15 October 2015, http://www.ctvnews.ca
   /world/ukraine-to-sit-alongside-russia-on-un-security-council-
   1.2610662.

CHAPTER ELEVEN

1 Alexander Panetta, "Clinton Emails Reveal Deep Rift between Harper, Canada's Foreign Service," Canadian Press, 1 December 2015,
   https://www.thestar.com/news/canada/2015/12/01/clinton-emails-
   reveal-deep-rift-between-harper-canadas-foreign-service.html.
2 Bruce Cheadle, "Foreign Affairs Employees Give Trudeau Out of This
   World Reception," Canadian Press, 6 November 2015, http://www
   .macleans.ca/politics/ottawa/foreign-affairs-employees-give-trudeau-
   out-of-this-world-reception/.
3 Bruce Campion-Smith, "Analysis: Trudeau Makes an Impression on
   International Debut," *Toronto Star*, 20 November 2015, https://www
   .thestar.com/news/canada/2015/11/20/analysis-justin-trudeau-makes-
   an-impression-in-international-debut.html.
4 Justin Trudeau, *Common Ground* (Toronto: HarperCollins e-books,
   2014).
5 Ibid.
6 Ibid.
7 Ibid.
8 Ibid.

9 John Ibbitson, *Stephen Harper* (Toronto: McClelland and Stewart, 2015, e-book).

10 Ibid.

11 Trudeau, *Common Ground*.

12 Ibid.

13 John Ibbitson, "China Publicly Scolds Harper for Taking Too Long to Visit," *Globe and Mail*, 3 December 2009, http://www.theglobeandmail .com/news/politics/china-publicly-scolds-harper-for-taking-too-long-to-visit/article4312718/.

14 "Trudeau to Meet Queen Elizabeth 38 Years after Sensational 'Pierre Pirouette,'" Canadian Press, 12 November 2015, https://www.thestar.com/news/canada/2015/11/12/trudeau-to-meet-queen-elizabeth-38-years-after-sensational-pierre-pirouette.html.

15 Nahlah Ayed, "Canada's Youth Call Out Justin Trudeau before the World's Cameras at Paris Climate Talks," *CBC News*, 6 December 2015, http://www.cbc.ca/news/politics/cop21-paris-canada-youth-delegation-1.3352246.

16 Confidential source.

17 John Paul Tasker, "Rona Ambrose Brands Liberal Changes to ISIS Mission 'Shameful,'" *CBC News*, 8 February 2016, http://www.cbc.ca /news/politics/rona-ambrose-isis-trudeau-1.3439016.

18 Roland Paris, "Canadian Mission Creep in Iraq? A CIPS Debate – Part 1," *UOttawa: Centre for International Policy Studies*, 30 January 2015, http://www.cips-cepi.ca/2015/01/30/canadian-mission-creep-in-iraq-a-cips-debate-part-1/.

19 Murray Brewster, "Trudeau's ISIS Tightrope Act Gets More Tricky Following Iraq Offensive," Canadian Press, 18 December 2015, http://www.huffingtonpost.ca/2015/12/18/trudeau-isil-tightrope-act-gets-trickier-thanks-to-iraq-offensive_n_8840780.html.

20 Ibid.

21 Carole Landry, "Obama Draws Pledges of 40,000 Troops for UN Peacekeeping," *Agence France Press*, 29 September 2015, https://www .yahoo.com/news/nations-offer-30-000-troops-police-un-peacekeeping-193338715.html?ref=gs.

22 Walter Dorn, "Canadian Peacekeeping: No Myth – But Not What It Once Was," *Sitrep: A Publication of the Royal Canadian Military Institute* 67, no. 2 (April–May 2007), http://walterdorn.net/pdf/Canadian-Peacekeeping-NoMyth_Dorn_SitRep_April2007.pdf.

23 Ibid.

24 Walter Dorn and Joshua Libben, "Unprepared for Peace? The Decline of Canadian Peacekeeping Training (and What to Do about It)," *Canadian Centre for Policy Alternatives and Rideau Institute on International Affairs*, February 2016, https://www.policyalternatives.ca /publications/reports/unprepared-peace.

25 Derek H. Burney and Fen Osler Hampson, *Brave New Canada: Meeting the Challenge of a Changing World* (Montreal and Kingston: McGill-Queen's University Press, 2014), 9.

26 Ibid.

27 Ibid.

28 Ibid., 10.

29 Roland Paris, "Time to Make Ourselves Useful," *Literary Review of Canada*, March 2015, http://reviewcanada.ca/magazine/2015/03/time-to-make-ourselves-useful/.

30 "PM to Davos: 'Know Canadians for Our Resourcefulness,'" Canadian Press, 20 January 2016, http://www.macleans.ca/news/canada/what-justin-trudeau-plans-to-tell-davos/.

31 Ibid.

CHAPTER TWELVE

1 Ishaan Tharoor, "The Many Ways Canada's Trudeau Is the Anti-Trump," *Washington Post*, 29 February 2016, https://www.washingtonpost.com/news/worldviews/wp/2016/02/29/the-many-ways-canadas-trudeau-is-the-anti-trump/.

2 Nahal Toosi, "Justin Fever Hits Washington," *Politico*, 8 March 2016, http://www.politico.com/story/2016/03/justin-trudeau-visits-washington-220387.

3 Martin O'Malley and Justin Thompson, "Prime Ministers and Presidents," *CBC News Online*, 22 November 2003, http://www.cbc.ca /canadaus/pms_presidents1.html.

4 Mike Blanchfield, "U.S. Ties Top Martin's Foreign Agenda: Series: Social, Foreign and Economic Policy," *Edmonton Journal*, 5 November 2003, A2.

5 Ibid.

6 Mike Blanchfield, "Canada's Torturous Path to a New Foreign Policy," *Ottawa Citizen*, 12 March 2005, A1.

7 Ibid.

8 Mike Blanchfield, "Harper Draws Line in Ice: Arctic Sovereignty. PM-Designate Fires Back at U.S. Envoy for Challenging Canada's Claim," *Montreal Gazette*, 27 January 2006, A1.

9 Mike Blanchfield, "Sweeping Agenda Unveiled; Harper, Obama Look to Tackle Climate Change, Afghanistan," *National Post*, 20 February 2009, A2.

10 John Ibbitson, *Stephen Harper* (Toronto: McClelland and Stewart, 2015, e-book).

11 Ibid.

12 O'Malley and Thompson, "Prime Ministers and Presidents."

13 "Justin Trudeau Blames Stephen Harper for Fumbling Canada's Key Relationship with U.S.," Canadian Press, 22 June 2015, http://news .nationalpost.com/news/canada/canadian-politics/justin-trudeau-blames-stephen-harper-for-fumbling-canadas-key-relationship-with-u-s.

14 Lawrence Martin, "Trudeau Hits Reset on U.S. Relations," *Globe and Mail*, 8 March 2016, http://www.theglobeandmail.com/opinion /trudeau-hits-reset-on-us-relations/article29060638/.

15 Tom Clark, "Friend and Foe: The Twists and Turns of Canada-U.S. Relations," *Global News*, 2 March 2016, http://globalnews.ca/news /2554083/friend-and-foe-the-twists-and-turns-of-canada-u-s-relations/.

16 Demetri Sevastopulo and Pilita Clark, "Paris Climate Deal Will Not Be Legally Binding Treaty," *Financial Times*, 11 November 2015, https://next.ft.com/content/79daf872-8894-11e5-90de-f44762bf9896.

17 Ibid.

18 O'Malley and Thompson, "Prime Ministers and Presidents."

19 Lawrence J. Haas, *Harry & Arthur: Truman, Vandenburg, and the Partnership That Created the Free World* (Lincoln, Nebraska: Potomac Books, 2016), xix.

EPILOGUE

1 Daniel Tencer, "Canadian Businesses Are World's Most Trusted; 'Trudeau Effect' Sends Domestic Trust Soaring," *Huffington Post*, 3 February 2016, http://www.huffingtonpost.ca/2016/02/03/canadian-businesses-most-trusted_n_9143156.html.

2 Michael R. Bloomberg, "Canada's New Hope," *BloombergView*, 16

March 2016, https://www.bloomberg.com/view/articles/2016-03-16/canada-s-new-hope.

3 Bruce Cheadle, "Trudeau Says Image-Making Part of Governing, Not a Popularity Contest," Canadian Press, 17 December 2015, http://www.citynews.ca/2015/12/17/trudeau-says-image-making-part-of-governing-not-a-popularity-contest/.

4 Luo Zhaohui, "Canada Should Not Be 'Blinded' over Human Rights Differences with China," *Globe and Mail*, 5 June 2006, http://www.theglobeandmail.com/opinion/canada-should-not-be-blinded-over-human-rights-differences-with-china/article30282085/.

5 John Holmes, *The Better Part of Valour* (Toronto: McClelland and Stewart, 1970), vii.

6 Ibid.

7 Ibid.

8 John Robson, "Stephane Dion's Fog-Bound Foreign Policy Doctrine," *National Post*, 31 March 2016, http://news.nationalpost.com/full-comment/john-robson-stephane-dions-fog-bound-foreign-policy-doctrine.

9 Alexander Panetta, "PM Trudeau's Refugee Welcome Makes Headlines Worldwide," Canadian Press, 11 December 2015, http://www.ctvnews.ca/politics/pm-trudeau-s-refugee-welcome-makes-headlines-worldwide-1.2696820.

Index